THE BERNESE ALPS
SWITZERLAND

Engstligen Falls - A Swiss national monument

THE BERNESE ALPS
SWITZERLAND

BY

KEV REYNOLDS

CICERONE PRESS
MILNTHORPE, CUMBRIA

ACKNOWLEDGEMENTS

My thanks are due to a number of people who helped in one way or another in the planning and production of this guidebook, but especially to: Caroline Lawless at the Swiss National Tourist Office in London, Beat Anneler and Urs Kessler in Interlaken, Margrit Brawand in Grindelwald and the staff of various tourist offices throughout the Bernese Alps region. As always I am grateful to my publishers for their support and encouragement, and for giving me the excuse to spend long weeks wandering through some of Europe's most spectacular mountain scenery; to my brother Alan Reynolds who drew the maps and sketches; to my good friend Roland Hiss who knows the region much better than I do and who gave such good advice; and to Brian and Aileen Evans, Nigel Fry, Derek Roberts and my family, Linda, Claudia and Ilsa Reynolds who at various times shared some of the best days of all. This book is also theirs.

Kev Reynolds

Cicerone Press guidebooks by the same author:

Walks in the Engadine - Switzerland
The Valais - Switzerland
The Jura (with R Brian Evans)
Alpine Pass Route
Walks & Climbs in the Pyrenees
The Wealdway & The Vanguard Way
Walking in Kent
The South Downs Way & The Downs Link
The Cotswold Way
Chamonix to Zermatt - the Walker's Haute Route

Forthcoming:
Ticino - Switzerland

CONTENTS

INTRODUCTION

With the classic trio of Eiger, Mönch and Jungfrau their most potent symbol, the Bernese Alps are among the best-known mountains in all of Europe. Rising out of lush green meadows they tower above timber-built chalets bright with geraniums and petunias; a stark contrast of snow, ice and rock against a lively kaleidoscope of flower, shrub and pasture. A savage backdrop to an Alpine wonderland.

Flanking the northern slope of the Rhône valley the chain of the Bernese Alps is aligned roughly east to west, stretching from the Grimsel Pass above the Haslital in the east, to the Col du Pillon below Les Diablerets in the west, thus forming the longest continuous range of mountains in the Alps. Their more familiar title, the Bernese Oberland, in fact refers to the northern side of the range only - the highlands of canton Bern. But of the Bernese Alps proper, among their numerous summits almost forty reach above 3,600 metres, while the huge glacial basin on the south side of the Jungfrau gives birth to the Grosser Aletschgletscher, the largest icefield not only in Switzerland, but of all the Alpine regions. Elsewhere delicate but lofty waterfalls cascade into gorge-like valleys carved out of the mountains by the glaciers of long ago. Lakes fill the lower valleys like small inland seas (the Thunersee and Brienzersee), while more modest tarns lie trapped here and there in scoops of hillside to throw the mountains on their heads as a mirror-like bonus to those who wander by.

It's a paradise for walkers. Footpaths - thousands of kilometres of them - lead enticingly through the valleys, over hillsides and across high passes. Waymarked with the thoroughness and efficiency for which Switzerland is noted they offer sufficient scope and variety to satisfy the dreams of most mountain walkers for a decade and more of holidays, while the resorts of Grindelwald, Wengen, Lauterbrunnen, Mürren, Kandersteg and Adelboden - to name but a few - have their own unique atmosphere and appeal. They are, of course, among the most notable in all of Switzerland.

The heart of the Bernese Alps is an arctic wasteland. In that huge basin behind the notorious walls of rock that glower over

Grindelwald's bowl of luxury there lies a vast tract of snowfield and glacier jelled into a mass of permanent winter, like some displaced polar ice-cap. It's a monochrome landscape of stark, yet resounding beauty; a wonderland of white from which stiletto peaks and raw massifs emerge as islands of stone in a great ice sea.

Glaciers hang suspended on the north-facing slopes too, of course, but by comparison these are just modest streams, the last remaining vestiges of those tremendous icefields that long ago carved and fretted some of the loveliest valleys in all of Europe.

But by far the greater part of the Bernese Alps is covered with flower-rich grasslands; meadows and tilted pastures, broad crests neat and gentle from which you gaze with a sense of wonder at majestic, towering mountains, at their snowy crowns and at blue-tinged glaciers snaking between them.

Every corner of the range has its own touch of magic. There are the rock climbers' slabs of the Engelhörner above Rosenlaui, and the multi-summited Wetterhorn up-valley at the Grosse Scheidegg, which peers down on Grindelwald and stands as a cornerstone, not only of the Bernese Alps, but of mountaineering history. Grindelwald boasts so much of appeal; its glaciers, its tremendous scope for walkers, climbers and skiers, its magnetic views and, of course, the Eiger. But in truth the Eiger is only one of many stunning peaks here. More attractive still are the Schreckhorn, Finsteraarhorn and the Fiescherhorn, seen in astonishing detail from some of the walks outlined within these pages.

The Jungfraujoch railway is one of the engineering marvels of Switzerland and is accessible from either Grindelwald, Wengen or Lauterbrunnen. But since this volume is primarily intended for walkers, the railway lies outside the scope of this book. Wengen, of course, is not. Set on its perch high above the Lauterbrunnen valley, it has an exquisite outlook - especially to the cradled snows of the Jungfrau, one of the loveliest mountains to be seen anywhere. Among the more popular outings from this resort is the walk to the Wengernalp, from whose safe and gentle pastures one may gaze in delight at the avalanches pouring from the Jungfrau almost every day in summer.

Lauterbrunnen lies in its own deep-cut trench, an amazing place of huge walls and feathery cascades. At the head of its valley, in a more open level of grassland, is the little hamlet of Stechelberg which makes a superb base for a walking holiday, for it has numerous possibilities for exploratory outings to mountain huts, to 'lost' tarns, raw screes and hidden hillside terraces.

On its own privileged hillside terrace above the western wall of the Lauterbrunnen valley, Mürren has long been known and loved for its stunning mountain vista. Perhaps better-known these days as a skiing centre, it is no less lovely in summer when a splay of footpaths leads to scenes of enchantment. A little lower than Mürren, but a near-neighbour, Gimmelwald shares those scenes, and shares too a cableway to the summit of the Schilthorn, sometimes known as *Piz Gloria* since a James Bond movie was shot there.

To the west of Gimmelwald the high pass of the Sefinenfurke, approached in the shadow of the long ridge of the Gspaltenhorn, will take adventurous walkers over the mountains to the charming little hamlet of Griesalp at the head of the quiet backwater of the Kiental. This is a gentle pastoral valley of considerable charm; so different from the blockbuster tourism of Grindelwald or Lauterbrunnen, and with the sub-valley of Spiggengrund nearby it gives plenty of scope for those walkers who prefer to wander in solitude.

From the Kiental one peers up at the big snowy mass of the Blümlisalp whose several three-and-a-half-thousand metre summits overlook the ice-cap of the Petersgrat to the south, and the deep fjord-like bowl that contains the Öeschinensee to the north-west. This lake is pictured on so many calendars, chocolate boxes and jig-saw puzzles that it is a familiar sight to many long before they actually see it for themselves. It is probably the most visited feature of the mountains around Kandersteg. Kandersteg draws walkers and climbers alike with its wide variety of outings. No one who loves the mountains need fear boredom here. There is so much to explore, including the superb Gasterntal, a peaceful valley with stern walls from which waterfalls spray, and with meadows so rich in flowers that it is sometimes difficult to find the grass.

Running parallel to the Kandertal (the valley of Kandersteg) is the Engstligental, with Adelboden in its upper reaches. The village is set on the hillside, not in the valley bed, and it looks south to the handsome snowy face of the Wildstrubel, a mountain that Adelboden shares with its neighbour to the west, Lenk.

Lenk's valley is the Simmental, one of the most important of all in the Bernese Alps by virtue of its ease of communications with country to the west over a brace of passes. But Lenk lies near its head in a tranquil landscape, untroubled by through-traffic, unbothered by big mountains. It is a neat village set in a shallow plain, and with a fine western wall of rolling pastures pitted by limestone pots and with easy walkers' passes that lead to the next valley, the lovely Lauenental, with the Wildhorn at its head.

By comparison with Lauenen, Lenk is a bustling metropolis. For Lauenen is a secretive place that nevertheless deserves to be on the list of all who delight in mountain walking. It has much to commend it; not least a day's circuit that takes you to a green tarn, a nature reserve, a superb waterfall and a mountain hut in an idyllic setting. There are other outings of value, too, of course, and one that takes you over another gentle pass among woods and meadows and leads down to Gsteig, last of the villages tucked under the mountains on the northern side of the chain. Above Gsteig rises the big massif of Les Diablerets which marks the last of canton Bern and the first of canton Vaud. All to the west is French-speaking territory; some fine mountains and charming valleys, it is true, and which long distance walkers tackling the classic Alpine Pass Route explore on their way to Montreux. But for the purposes of this guidebook, Col du Pillon above Gsteig, which marks the canton border, is the extent of the countryside under review.

The Bernese Alps continue south, though, sloping down to the Rhône valley. Yet the border of canton Bern follows the crest of the main ridge. All to the south falls into canton Valais (Wallis to German-speaking Swiss), and it is this region that is treated to its own walkers' guidebook in the same series: *The Valais*.

MOUNTAINS OF THE BERNESE ALPS

In the public eye mountaineering in the Bernese Alps has been focussed on the Eiger through an avalanche of publicity matched only, perhaps, by that afforded the Matterhorn. The Eiger's north wall has been the scene of many epic dramas played out in full view of the telescopes of Kleine Scheidegg, but elsewhere along the chain there are other peaks, other faces, other ridges that offer sport of considerable charm yet without notoriety, and whose features make a colourful background for walkers wandering the magnificent network of footpaths nearby.

Meiringen is not a mountaineering centre as such, but it has some fine mountains almost on its doorstep - most of which are largely unsung. On the approach to the Grosse Scheidegg, by which Grindelwald is more conveniently reached, the slabs of the Engelhörner group are laced with routes, while to the south of these wild glaciers stream from several good-looking peaks, including the Wellhorn, Wetterhorn and the Hangendgletscherhorn, the last mentioned of which also looms over the little-known Urbachtal that flows out to Innertkirchen.

Grindelwald, with Alpiglen and Kleine Scheidegg on green slopes to the west, has long been the historical base for major climbs on the Eiger. But also accessible to Grindelwald are several mountain huts that lie on the approach to big mountains too far from any village base; huts that make ideal destinations for walkers, lying as they do amid wildly romantic surroundings. The Schreckhorn hut springs instantly to mind. The walk to it leads alongside glaciers, scrambles up rocks that wall an icefall, and gives the most incredible views of the Fiescherhörner, Agassizhorn and Finsteraarhorn (highest summit in the Bernese Alps at 4,274 metres), not to mention a curious peep at the 'back' of the Eiger.

Another hut approach that reveals the inner sanctum of the mountain world, is that which goes from Stechelberg to the Rottal hut on the south-west flanks of the Jungfrau. Here you virtually rub noses with the Gletscherhorn and Ebnefluh, and have a privileged view of the Breithorn seen in profile. All the mountains around rise in an unbelievable sweep of upthrusting rock and ice - the fabled Lauterbrunnen Wall that was so assiduously explored by the great München-based climber, Willo Welzenbach, in the thirties.

Next to the Breithorn stands the Tschingelhorn, with the saddle of Wetterlücke between them. On the far side of the Tschingelhorn

11

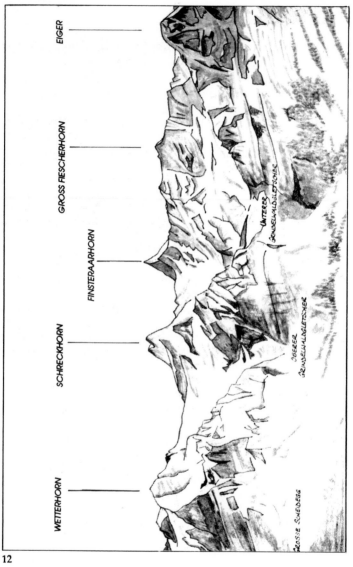

EIGER

GROSS FIESCHERHORN

FINSTERAARHORN

SCHRECKHORN

WETTERHORN

UNTERE GRINDELWALDGLETSCHER

OBERER GRINDELWALDGLETSCHER

GROSSE SCHEIDEGG

12

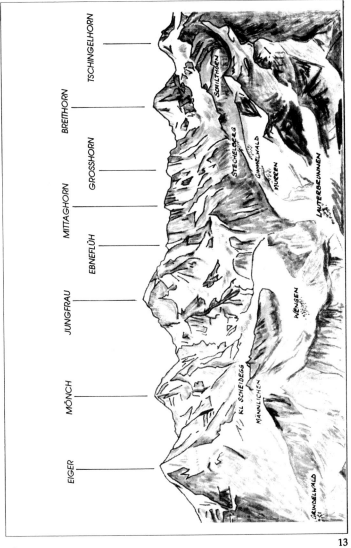

nestles the Mutthorn hut, almost entirely surrounded by ice. With several fine peaks made accessible from it, this hut proves popular with mountaineers in summer and is also visited on one of the walks described here, prior to making the crossing of the Petersgrat and a descent into the Lötschental in full view of the Bietschorn (one of the most difficult mountains in the Bernese Alps) and the glorious Gletscherstafel Wall.

After Grindelwald, Kandersteg is probably the main mountaineering centre of the chain. Again, several huts are accessible from the village, and climbs are to be had on the various Blümlisalp peaks as well as on the Balmhorn and Altels which rise to the south at the entrance to the Gasterntal.

Of the easier high summits of the Bernese Alps, both Wildstrubel and Wildhorn should be mentioned. The Wildstrubel has as one of its major features the large expanse of the snow-filled basin of the Plaine Morte Glacier, from which several tops rise. But the Wildstrubel itself consists of a number of regular summits barely rising above its southeastern glacier. It is climbed from either Kandersteg, Adelboden or Lenk.

West of the Wildhorn massif comes Les Diablerets, a great lump of mountain with summer skiing on its glaciers; a mountain that tops out at 3,210 metres and across whose main summit runs the invisible boundary separating canton Bern from canton Vaud. It dominates a large area of country and is seen to great effect from the softer, more luxurious hillsides to the north, where tarns gleam in the sunshine, where insects seethe among the flower-strewn meadows and birds warble in the forests. Walkers' country, this is, with views of the lofty mountain peaks. Far away in the west a glimpse is to be had of the Dents du Midi and the distant snows of Mont Blanc. Big mountains all.

Big mountains with snow and ice-caked summits indeed; but this book is concerned not with climbing mountains, not with reaching summits, but with wandering in their shadow; spending days of delight exploring valleys, ambling over hillsides clattering with cowbells and crossing remote passes in order to gain fresh valley systems. The Bernese Alps are not short of prospects.

APPROACH TO THE BERNESE ALPS

Travel to Switzerland is not difficult. There are international airports at Basle, Bern, Geneva and Zürich, and regular scheduled flights between the U.K. and Switzerland are operated by Swissair in conjunction with British Airways. Scheduled routes are from London (Heathrow and Gatwick) to Geneva, Basle or Zürich. Services also operate from Manchester, Birmingham and Dublin. Dan Air provides a service from London (Gatwick) to Bern and Zürich. Full information regarding flights may be obtained from the Swiss National Tourist Office whose address is given in the Appendix.

Air services from North America fly to Geneva and/or Zürich from Boston, Chicago, Los Angeles, Montreal and New York. Those airlines that maintain a routing across the Atlantic are Swissair, Trans World Airlines, Air Canada and Pan American.

Each of the main airports within Switzerland is served with reliable train or bus services to town terminals. Bern is the most convenient airport for visitors to the Bernese Alps, but with fast and frequent train services from Basle, Geneva and Zürich, all parts of the region covered by this book will be accessible without undue difficulty.

By rail the journey from Britain to the Bernese Alps is straightforward, key towns to make for being Thun and/or Interlaken. Either take the super-fast TGV *(Trains à Grande Vitesse)* from Paris *(Gare de Lyon)* to Lausanne where connections may be made to destinations farther east; or use the service Calais-Basle and from there to Interlaken or Thun. Local trains and/or Postbuses will continue your journey from either of these towns with admirable efficiency.

For those already in the Alps the Lötschberg rail tunnel between Goppenstein and Kandersteg makes an ideal link for those travelling from the south.

By road there is a first-class network of motorways through Switzerland which, upon payment of a special motorway tax at the point of entry into the country (or in advance from the Swiss National Tourist Office), enables a fast journey to be made to the Bernese Alps. Main road passes into the region are the Susten (open June-November), Grimsel (open June-October), Col du Pillon (open all year) and the

Jaun Pass, also open all year. (Dates when passes are open are of course approximate, and depend on the depth of snow lying.)

TRANSPORT IN THE BERNESE ALPS

Switzerland's public transport system is second to none. It is efficient, punctual, extensive, convenient and, for the walker, of enormous value. From a single valley base it is possible to travel to any one of a number of locations by Postbus or train to begin the day's walk. Or, when a walk begins from a valley base and aims in a single direction along the valley or across a pass into a neighbouring valley, there will invariably be a convenient means of returning to the hotel or campsite at the end of the day.

Railways serve many parts of the region covered by this book. From Thun or Interlaken trains run along the south side of the Thunersee and the north side of the Brienzersee. Trains go to Meiringen and Innertkirchen in the Haslital; to Grindelwald and Lauterbrunnen, and from both these places to Kleine Scheidegg and tunnelling through the Eiger to emerge on the Jungfraujoch - the highest railway in Europe. Wengen is also reached on the Lauterbrunnen-Kleine Scheidegg line, while on the other side of Lauterbrunnen's valley, Mürren is fed by funicular with a change of trains being made at Grütschalp. Down-valley another funicular climbs steeply from Wilderswil to Schynige Platte for the start of one of the finest walks in Switzerland.

Railways also serve Kandersteg via Spiez by way of a frequent and fast link on an international line that goes beyond Kandersteg through the Lötschberg Tunnel. This is particularly handy for walkers crossing the Petersgrat into the Lötschental. Also via Spiez a good rail service runs the length of the Simmental, serving such places as Oey in the mouth of the Diemtigtal, Zweisimmen and Lenk. Going beyond Zweisimmen on a separate line trains also run to Gstaad, which town has rail access with Montreux through the scenic Pays d'Enhaut.

Yellow Postbuses are seen almost everywhere there is a motorable road in Switzerland. As the name suggests they are run by the postal service (they also carry mail) and are as predictably punctual as are the railways. The region covered by this guide is admirably served, with practically every village having a bus route to it - if not a Postbus, then it will be a vehicle owned by a private company licensed by the postal service. In village centres the main Postbus collecting point will be outside the post office (PTT). In outlying areas railway stations will also have a PTT bus stop, and there are certain strategic points without habitation in some valleys where passengers may be picked up on request. Look for the PTT *Haltestelle* sign. Other than at these specific points, passengers should buy their tickets in advance at a post office. By pre-purchasing tickets this way the driver will be able to maintain his schedule.

Various incentives are available to holiday makers planning to use either rail or Postbus in Switzerland. The Swiss Holiday Card is one. Available for periods of four, eight or fifteen days, or for one month, this ticket allows unlimited travel throughout the country by almost every train, boat or Postbus, and discounts on a number of cableways. Enquire for full details at the Swiss National Tourist Office.

Locally in the Bernese Alps there is a regional holiday pass available for use over a fifteen day period on all trains, boats, buses and cableways. Again, details will be available from the SNTO.

In addition to the network of rail and Postbus services already referred to, a number of resorts have assorted cable-cars, chair-lifts, gondola lifts etc that the walker can use to his advantage. Where these occur brief details are given in the text.

ACCOMMODATION

There should be no difficulty in finding suitable accommodation anywhere in the region covered by this book. The Swiss have a long tradition of hotel- keeping, and in the Bernese Alps there is plenty of every standard of lodging to meet the requirements of holiday makers no matter what their financial resources might be. Whilst one often thinks of Switzerland as being an expensive country to stay in, it is quite possible to enjoy a very fine walking holiday there without spending a small fortune. There are campsites a-plenty, as well as youth hostels and moderately-priced *pensions*. There are various *matratzenlagers* (inns with dormitory-style accommodation) that would suit the pockets of those who are happy with spartan sociability, and there are the extremely grand hotels for those without wallet restrictions. There are also, of course, hundreds of intermediate hotels and *gasthofs* and, in a number of resorts, a growing list of chalets or apartments available for short-term rent.

And there are the mountain huts.

For valley-based accommodation the tourist information office of each small town or village will be able to supply a list giving the full range available, from the cheapest to the most expensive. Swiss National Tourist Offices should also be able to give ready information. SNTO offices normally stock the guidebook published by the Swiss Hotel Association which gives addresses, rates, amenities etc of some 2,700 hotels and pensions throughout the country. There is a smaller edition published which covers details of just those hotels and *pensions* in the Bernese Alps.

Camping: Official campsites exist in many of the region's valleys. Some of these offer rather basic facilities, while others have not only first-class toilet and washing blocks, but also provide laundry and drying rooms. But do not automatically assume that because campers are provided for in one of the larger resorts its facilities will reflect the affluence of the area. The converse is often true. Some of the smaller, lesser-known villages, however, take a pride in the provision of their campsites, and the holiday-maker will appreciate the standards they offer. Mention is made within this book where campsites exist, but comments as to the facilities provided are limited, since these may change from year to year.

Off-site camping is officially discouraged in Switzerland. Bearing in mind the limited amount of land available for pasture or hay-making, this is perhaps understandable. Uncontrolled camping could do considerable damage to a peasant farmer's short season crop of meadowland hay. Above the tree-line, though, the backpacker may find a suitably remote corner far from any alp which could accommodate a small tent for a short stay. In such cases the practice may go unnoticed or without comment. Should you choose to take advantage of such a wilderness camp, please be discreet, take care not to foul water supplies and pack all litter away with you.

Youth Hostels: At the time of writing there are several youth hostels in the Bernese Alps belonging to the SJH *(Schweizerischen Jugendherbergen)*, which is in turn affiliated to the International Youth Hostel Federation. Anyone holding a current membership card of the Hostels Association of his own country can therefore use hostels in Switzerland, provided there is sufficient space available. Priority is given to members below the age of twenty-five. Visitors wishing to take advantage of hostels in the Bernese Alps are advised to join their home organisation before setting out. Emergency international membership is possible to arrange in Switzerland, but this is far more expensive than joining at home.

   Dormitory accommodation is offered in all youth hostels. In some, smaller twin-bedded rooms may be available, but should not be expected. Meals may be provided at some, but not all of them, and those regular hostel-users in the U.K. will be disappointed to find that self-catering facilities are not of the same standard as at YHA or SYHA hostels.

Matratzenlagers: Similar to the gîtes d'étape of France, *matratzenlagers* offer basic dormitory accommodation and are located in assorted buildings - on farms, in the attic of rustic mountain inns or even in the basement of a hotel annexe. Facilities offered vary enormously. I have experienced superb self-catering kitchens and unlimited access to hot showers in some, and inn meals and a trough of cold running water in others. Prices are generally much lower than those charged in hotels or *gasthofs*, and more or less in line with youth hostels, but without the necessity of membership. There are a number of *matratzenlagers* within the Bernese Alps, but they are not publicised to any degree. If interested ask specifically at the local tourist information office for details of any in the vicinity.

Mountain Huts: Primarily huts belonging to the SAC *(Schweizer Alpen Club)* are intended as overnight shelters for climbers preparing for an ascent of a neighbouring peak. Several walks described within these pages visit such huts as interesting destinations. Some require a very long approach and it will be necessary to stay overnight, in which case their use by walkers is acceptable.

Those familiar with the mountain hut system in the Alps will need to read no farther, but for first-time users a few words might be considered helpful. Firstly, mountain huts (*hütte, refuge* or *cabane*) vary considerably in their standards of accommodation and degree of comfort, if not in the basic facilities provided. In recent years many SAC huts have been substantially renovated, improved and enlarged. Those prospective hut users who have only read of the primitive conditions experienced in the past will be surprised by some of these improvements. But it should be stressed that they are not evident in all huts.

Sleeping quarters are invariably of the dormitory variety; in most cases upon a large communal platform with a plentiful supply of mattresses, blankets and pillows. There is no segregation of the sexes. If the hut is busy - and most will be in the height of the summer season - this type of sleeping arrangement can very soon lose any attraction it might otherwise be deemed to have. On arrival at the hut and finding sufficient room, it is best to lay claim to your bedspace whilst there is light.

Most huts have a guardian who will allocate bedspace and often provide meals. These can be either substantial in quantity and quality, or meagre and uninteresting, depending upon the interest and enthusiasm of the man (or woman) in charge. Bottled drinks are usually for sale. In some cases there is no natural drinking water available, and the guardian will sell it by the litre. Water at the washroom tap is seldom acceptable for drinking.

Staying in mountain huts is not cheap. The buildings are expensive to build and maintain, and the cost of supplying them with food and equipment is aggravated by the distance everything must be carried from the valley. Formerly supplied by mule or by porter, these days foodstuffs are normally brought by helicopter. Hence the relatively high charges made. But if you plan to undertake one or two multi-day tours in the mountains, the special atmosphere that comes from staying overnight in such remote lodgings will make the experience worthwhile.

MOUNTAIN FLOWERS

Any mountain walking holiday undertaken in the Bernese Alps between June and October will be enlivened by the company of flowers. No matter what degree of interest or knowledge one normally has in wild flowers, few could fail to be moved by the sight of the Alps in bloom. All Switzerland may lay claim to a bounty of alpine plants, and the Bernese Alps will be no exception.

This is no place to describe in depth all the flowers one is likely to meet, nor could it possibly set out to identify particular species. Anyone sufficiently interested in putting a name to those seen in a meadow or rock crevice are advised to consult one of several handy books on the market that deal with them. Some of these will be found in bookshops in the main tourist areas. However, a word or two of a more general tone might be of some use.

The Bernese Alps display all the main habitats and zones of mountain flowers, from low-lying, lush alpine meadows to more sparse yet flower-rich higher alps where cattle are grazed in summer. There are the forests with open glades; warm outcrops of rock in the lower regions and high slabs riven with crevices that are sometimes wet with ice-melt and sometimes dry from the winds or sunshine. There are screes and marshy meadows and acid bogs, and the raw moraines pushed to one side by the glaciers that nature has begun to soften into wild gardens. Whilst the geology of the region is some- what complicated there is a preponderance of limestone, which is good for a variety of flowering plants.

Early in the season as snow melts from the meadows and the grass is still short, soldanellas and crocuses flush the hillsides with colour. Primroses and primulas, gentians and cowslips are all likely to be found as pastures warm under the sun. There will be anemones, St Bruno's and martagon lilies and a rich collection of orchids, and as summer comes into its own alpenroses, the dwarf rhododendron, blaze across the high alps.

Rocky outcrops will display delicate harebells and the dark blue globularias. Stonecrops and houseleeks, common in British rock gardens, are found in many areas, while among the damp rock faces the lovely yellow mountain saxifrage is found in company with

21

various shades of viola.

Screes may appear drab and lifeless from a distance, but on closer inspection will be found to contain a good selection of plants, including the purple saxifrage, moss campion and glacier buttercup. Among the moraines it is not unusual to find alpine rosebay happily growing on the mountain's rubbish tip.

Almost every region covered by this guide will repay the seeker of alpine flowers. Grindelwald, of course, with its wide variety of habitats close to hand, is one of the best. Wengen too has much to commend it, especially in the early summer when its meadows are rampant with colour. Kandersteg has some interest near the Öeschinensee, but even more in the Gasterntal or up among the high country leading to the Gemmi Pass. I have also found much of delight on the high rolling grasslands that form a broad ridge between Lenk and Lauenen, where curious hillocks and hollows tell of their limestone ancestry and where a wonderful display of flowering plants brightens summer walks. Another fine flower walk is that which goes from Lauenen to the Gelten hut, and another nearby among the alps of Walliser Wispile.

A number of the plants are protected by law. A list of these varieties is regularly updated and illustrated posters are often displayed in railway stations, hotels and post offices. There are also a

Gentiana kochiana
(Trumpet Gentian)

Rhododendron ferrugineum
(Alpenrose)

few nature reserves and Plant Protection Zones where the picking of flowers is strictly forbidden. So please, walk in the valleys and round the mountains and be inspired by the plants that you see. Study them, photograph them, breathe their heady perfume. But leave them for others to enjoy too.

MOUNTAIN ANIMALS

Of all creatures native to the Alps the marmot (*Marmota marmota*, whose name comes from *Murmeltier* - the alpine mouse of the Romans) is probably the one most likely to be seen by walkers in the Bernese Alps. Colonies of these furry little mammals that grow to the size of a large hare and weigh anything up to ten kilograms, are to be found in many valleys, usually in the upper alps or among boulder slopes where there is plenty of cover for their burrows. Marmots hibernate through the long winter months, emerging in springtime a little scruffy and scrawny-looking and ready to mate. Their young are born during the early summer, and you may be lucky enough to catch sight of two or three kitten-sized creatures romping or playfully fighting in the short grass of the upper hillsides. Often the first indication a walker has of the proximity of a colony is the sound of a shrill warning whistle; a marmot apparently acting as sentry will be seen standing upright and alert before it races off for cover. Sometimes it is not man's presence that gives rise to the warning whistle, but the sight of an eagle or other bird of prey hovering overhead.

Chamois *(Rupicapra rupicapra)* are rarely seen at close quarters, but in the high regions of the mountains, just below the snowline, it is not unusual to spy a small herd picking its way with agile ease over excessively steep terrain. From a distance it is sometimes possible to mistake chamois, with their small curving horns, for female or young ibex. But ibex have a more stocky body and seemingly shorter legs.

Ibex (also known as *bouquetin* or *steinbock*) do not come down to the lower valleys, but remain in very wild terrain. Probably the only time you might see one or more of these sturdy animals is if you visit one of the remote mountain huts. There is a small herd near the Rottal hut.

Whilst female ibex have short horns, the males display a proud pair of scimitar-shaped curving horns marked with a series of knobbles, which they use in battle as they fight for control over their herd. They make a very fine sight, silhouetted against a background of snowfield or glacier.

WEATHER

Mountains make their own weather. This is an old adage that is certainly true of the Bernese Alps. Since the range more or less faces north and is the first of the main mountain areas to collect the weather patterns flooding in across north-west Europe and the low Swiss plains, it also attracts a worse record than most other regions of the Swiss Alps.

Thunderstorms are to be expected, especially in the early summer, at least once or twice during a two-week holiday, when precipitation will almost certainly be in the form of rain below two thousand metres, and possibly snow above that level. However, when the *Fohn* blows there will be clear skies for days at a time (this may occur two or three times a month during the summer), but this is usually succeeded by more rain.

Temperatures are frequently dictated by elevation, whether or not there is a wind blowing, but so too can topographic configuration play an important role in temperature control. Deep valleys and basins may collect cold air at night but, protected from strong winds during the day, their temperature range can be considerable.

Having spent many weeks wandering through the Bernese Alps over several decades I have personally enjoyed more good weather than bad, and a reasonable amount that could be considered indifferent. Hardly a day has occurred when the weather was so foul it was impossible to go walking. Although high country should be avoided when storms threaten, I have had my share of experiences of being caught out, but even these occasions have sometimes repaid me with moments of sheer magic as storm clouds have parted momentarily to reveal a memorable glimpse of a mountain wrapped in swirling mist.

So do not allow the possibility of a few days of rain dissuade you from visiting these wonderful mountains for a walking holiday. Go prepared for the worst and hope for the best. You'll not be disappointed.

NOTES FOR WALKERS

It is to be hoped that this book, in common with others in the series, will be used by casual walkers who may never have ambled through an alpine valley before, as well as by the more experienced mountain wanderer aiming for the snowline. There is something in the Alps for everyone to enjoy, and I am convinced from personal experience that each level has its own spice, its own essential charm. Much of the pleasure of rambling among these mountains comes from the enormous variety of scenery that the paths lead through. That variety may be experienced to some degree even in the lowliest valley, as well as upon the upper hillsides among the very boundaries of heaven and earth. If the wanderer sets out with an eye for the views, for the flowers and shrubs in the meadows, the lichen- embroidered rocks beside the path, for the crystal clarity of the streams and tarns and the dark mystery of the forests, he will never be disappointed with his day.

It should be borne in mind, of course, that the more adventurous the chosen route, the more prepared one must be for it. The following few notes have therefore been put together to help towards that preparation, and so enable you to make the most of your visit to the Bernese Alps. Those who set out on a mountain walking holiday will gain most if they are in fair physical shape upon arrival. The day you begin your holiday in the Bernese Alps is not the time to start thinking about getting fit. Most regular ramblers will understand this and will have been taking walks at home before the holiday, to avoid aching legs and a pounding heart from tackling a strenuous outing without first getting the body and limbs into shape. It is also worth remembering that some of the valley bases are still considerably higher than most city dwellers are used to, and the altitude may demand some adjustments. Don't make the mistake of taking on too much for the first day or so, but instead build up distance and height- gain steadily, day by day. Hopefully you will find sufficient outing suggestions contained within this guide to enable you to enjoy a good day out at any level. Certainly every valley, hillside and grassy ridge has its own unique flavour to sample at will.

The next point to consider will be that of equipment, the choice of which can make or mar a walking holiday. Boots, quite naturally, are of prime importance. They should be well-fitting and comfortable, and broken-in before embracing the Alps. Lightweight boots will see you less weary at the end of the day than the more traditional heavyweight variety. Mediumweight boots are also on the market. These will give a little more support, perhaps, for use on screes, and are likely to offer better waterproof qualities than the ultra-lightweight kind. For low valley walks along beaten-earth paths, strong shoes or trainers should be adequate.

Shorts may well be fine to wear on most summer walks in the Alps, but upon the hillsides and higher, breeches are normally worn. A sudden breeze at 2,500 or 3,000 metres can seem extremely cold, and even the temporary loss of the sun behind a cloud can create a dramatic drop in temperature. Strong winds can arise almost without warning, with heavy rainfall and even snow to face at high altitudes. Be prepared with warm waterproof clothing. At the very least a thick pullover should be worn or carried in the rucksack for low walks. Even when setting out on what is a bright summer morning, a waterproof cagoule and windproof clothing should be packed if you intend going up the mountainside. Headwear and gloves are also advisable.

If one needs to be prepared to face cold and wet weather, the extreme of dazzling sun and unshaded heat can create problems too. Sunglasses will help those prone to headaches caused by the sun, and should in any case be taken as protection against snow glare. Because of ultra-violet rays the alpine light is often excessively bright even on cloudy days, and those with sensitive eyes should on no account leave their sunglasses behind. Sunblock or suncream should be used for skin protection. A lip salve is also useful. All these items are easily obtainable in villages in the Bernese Alps.

A small day sack should be sufficient to contain spare clothing and other necessary items such as first aid kit, map and compass, whistle, torch and spare batteries, water flask and food, on most of the outings except multi-day tours, when overnight equipment will need to be carried.

A word about drinking water in the mountains. Most of the streams seen tumbling down the hillsides should be safe enough to drink from, unless sheep, goats or cows are grazing above. I have personally never experienced any problems arising from drinking directly from mountain streams, but one should treat all such water sources with a certain amount of caution. Perhaps the safest course would be to limit topping up your water bottle to those hewn-out log troughs that are frequently found in valleys and pasturelands. These are filled by spring-fed pipes, and the gushing fountain should be adequately safe to drink from.

For safety's sake, never walk alone on remote trails, on moraine-bank paths or glaciers. For those who prefer to walk in the company of a group and have not made prior arrangements to join an organized walking holiday, several tourist information offices arrange day walks in the company of a qualified leader. These take place throughout the summer and are often free of charge to those staying in the organising resort. Enquire at the information office of your village base for specific details.

PATHS AND WAYMARKS

By far the majority of paths and tracks to be followed will be routes that have been used for centuries by farmers and huntsmen going about their daily business - from alp to alp, or from one valley to the next by way of an ancient pass, or up onto a ridge where chamois might be spotted. A few have been made in comparatively recent times by the local commune, or by a branch of the Swiss Footpath Protection Association (*Schweizerische Arbeitsgemeinschaft für Wanderwege*), or by members of the SAC in order to reach a mountain hut.

Of the officially-maintained paths there are two varieties, both of which are signposted and waymarked by paint flashes: the *Wanderweg* and *Bergweg*. A *Wanderweg* is a path that either remains in the valley itself, or runs along the hillside at a moderate altitude. These are well maintained and graded at a much more gentle angle than the *Bergweg*. They are marked with yellow metal signposts containing the names of major landmark destinations, such as a pass, lake, hut or village, with estimated times given in hours (*Stunden*, or *Std*) and minutes (*Min*). A white plate on these yellow signs gives the name of the immediate locality and, often, the altitude. Along the trail occasional yellow signs or paint flashes on rocks give assurance that you are still on the correct route.

A *Bergweg* is a mountain path which ventures higher and is more demanding than a *Wanderweg*. These paths will usually be rougher, more narrow, and sometimes fading if not in regular use. They are for walkers who should be properly equipped, for they lead to remote areas, often through rugged terrain. Signposting is similar to that for a *Wanderweg* except that the outer sections of the finger post will be painted red and white, and the intermediate paint flashes along the way will also be white-red-white bands. There may well be the occasional cairn to offer additional route- finding aid where the path has faded away or crosses a boulder slope, and in the event of low cloud obscuring the onward route, it is essential to study the area of visibility with great care before venturing on to the next paint flash or stone-built cairn.

SAFETY IN THE MOUNTAINS

Without wishing to be alarmist or over-dramatic, it is the duty of the guidebook writer to draw attention to the dangers that exist in mountain regions for the unwary: a sudden storm, stones dislodged from above, a twisted ankle on a scree-slope etc., each of which could have serious consequences if the party is not prepared to cope with the emergency.

Wandering along a valley path should be harmless enough, but the higher one ventures in the mountains, the more realistic the walker's approach should be. Walk carefully, be properly equipped, take local advice as to weather prospects and plan your day accordingly. Take care not to dislodge stones from the path, for they may well fall onto an unfortunate walker, farmer or animal some way below. Never be too proud to turn back should you find your chosen route takes longer than anticipated, or if it becomes difficult or dangerous. Watch for signs of deteriorating weather and study the map well in conjunction with your compass before visibility is reduced. Think ahead.

In the unhappy event of an accident, stay calm. Should the party be large enough to send for help while someone remains with the injured member, make a careful note of the exact location where the accident victim can be found. If there is a mountain hut nearby, seek assistance there. If a valley habitation is nearer, find a telephone and dial 01 383 11 11. This calls out the Swiss Air Rescue - *but should only be used if absolutely essential.*

The international distress call is a series of six signals (either blasts on a whistle or flashes by torch after dark) spaced evenly for a minute, followed by one minute's pause, then repeated with a further six signals. The reply is three signals per minute, followed by a minute's pause.

Remember, there is no free rescue service in Switzerland and, though remarkably efficient, emergency rescues can be both extremely expensive to mount and costly for the victim or his family. Specialist mountain insurance companies often advertise in the climbing press, and some holiday insurance policies will often include mountain walking in the Alps as one of the acceptable risks - but do check the small print for certain exclusion clauses. Be insured, and be cautious.

GLACIER CROSSING

Very few routes described within these pages venture on or near glaciers. However, one or two do, so a word about icefields and glacier crossing might be considered appropriate.

To the inexperienced, glaciers can be exceedingly dangerous places for the unprepared. Not only the ice itself, riven as it might be with deep crevasses, but the moraine walls on either side, and the glacial slabs immediately below - all should be treated with caution.

Since it is assumed that most walkers using this guide will not be equipped with ice axes, rope or crampons, it should be stressed that on no account should you wander onto any glacier that is snow-covered. Should you have chosen a route that leads across one, and upon arrival find it is so covered, turn back - unless you are properly equipped and experienced. However, some 'dry' glaciers, that is to say, those that are free of snow cover, have trails leading across them, marked by paint flashes on rocks or tin cans, or by cairns built upon them. In such instances it may be safe to proceed across with caution, keeping a wary eye open for crevasses that must be avoided. Always seek the company of someone experienced in glacier work, but if in doubt proceed no further.

Moraine walls are composed of the broken rock and grit that have been spewed to one side by the slowly moving ice. Some of these walls, or banks, rise to gigantic proportions. Some have footpaths marked along them, but unless there is such a path, do not be tempted to climb onto them, for they can be unstable and dangerous.

Sometimes your route may lead below a glacier, and then you will be faced with crossing glacial slabs washed by the streams that flow from the icefield above. These slabs can be extremely slippery, so do take care. Watch out also for any stones that might come clattering down, brought by the streams, or for great chunks of ice breaking away from the glacier's snout. (A short section of the route to the Balmhorn hut in the Gasterntal is exposed to such objective dangers.) Move carefully but quickly to reach safe ground.

But to reiterate an earlier warning: Never be too proud to turn back. If you're unsure, and there's no-one near to hand with experience to help you over, return by an alternative path. The mountains are there for you to enjoy on holiday, not to be threatened by.

All the above is for the exercise of caution. However, glaciers are fascinating places and they can be remarkably beautiful. Do not allow their objective dangers to detract from your appreciation of their form, their colouring or their great industry in carving the mountains and valleys into scenes of wonder. They are an integral part of the alpine kingdom, and their mystery is part of its intrinsic charm.

GRADING OF WALKS

The walks described in this book are designed to help you make the most of your holiday in the Bernese Alps, and since it is intended that walkers of all degrees of commitment will find something of value contained within, it seems that a grading system might be useful to direct readers to the standard of outing of particular interest to them. Since grading is not an exact science the three categories used will cover a fairly wide spectrum.

Grade 1: Suitable for family outings, mostly short distances involved or along gently-graded paths or tracks with little change of height to contend with.

Grade 2: Moderate walking, mostly on clear footpaths; some will be *Wanderweg* paths, others *Bergweg* trails with some altitude gains. Walkers should be adequately shod and equipped.

Grade 3: More strenuous routes on rough paths. Some scrambling may be involved in rare instances. There may be high passes to cross, some glacial involvement (individual routes will be marked in the text) and possibly scree work. Steep ascents and descents and fairly long distances involved. Walkers attempting these routes should be well equipped.

RECOMMENDED MAPS

The Landeskarte der Schweiz (L.S.) series of maps that cover the Bernese Alps are magnificent works of art that will breed excitement in the heart of any map enthusiast. Open any sheet and a picture of the country immediately leaps from the paper. By clever use of shading, contours and colouring, the line of ridges and rock faces, the flow of glaciers and streams, the curve of an amphitheatre, the narrow cut of a glen, the expanse of a lake and the forest cover of a hillside all announce themselves clearly. They are a source of inspiration prior to setting out, and a real pleasure to use in the mountains.

At the head of each valley section of this book a note is given as to the recommended map to use. In every case I have chosen the 1:50,000 series, as this should be adequate for most, if not all, the walks described. (There is superb waymarking on the ground which for the most part does away with the need for greater detail than is found on these sheets.) Clearly, more detail will be found on sheets at 1:25,000 scale, but rather a lot of these would be needed to cover the same area. For much of the region covered we are fortunate in requiring only two sheets: 5004 *Berner Oberland* and 5009 *Gstaad-Adelboden.*

In addition, certain of the tourist information offices in the main resorts publish local sheets that are, in effect, L.S. maps with walking routes overprinted. These may well be worth studying. Ask at the tourist office for their *Wanderkarte.*

USING THE GUIDE

A brief word of explanation is offered about the use of this guide. Distances are given throughout in kilometres and metres, as are heights. (To convert kilometres to miles, divide the distance given by 1.6093; for metres to feet divide the amount given by 0.3048.) These details are taken directly from the map, but in attempting to measure the actual distance of walks I have made the nearest estimation I could. With countless zig-zags it's almost impossible to be exact. Likewise, times are also approximate only and make no allowances for rest stops or photographic interruptions. Invariably these times will be found slow by some walkers, fast by others. By comparing your times with those given here you will soon have an idea of how much we differ and compensate accordingly. Remember though, these routes are not designed for racing, but for a simple enjoyment of fine mountain scenery and in order to absorb the maximum of mountain experience.

In descriptions of routes, directions 'left' and 'right' apply to the direction of travel, whether in ascent, descent or traverse. However, when used with reference to the banks of glaciers or streams, 'left' and 'right' indicate the direction of flow, ie: looking downwards. Where doubts might occur a compass direction is also given.

At Schratteren in the Urbachtal (Route 4 - Haslital).
Chorten on the Unteraargletscher (Route 6).

A note too, about the use of the word 'alp'. Commonly the Alps are taken to mean the chain of mountains spreading in an arc from the Mediterranean to the Julians of Yugoslavia. However, traditionally 'alps' were to the mountain peasants, not the peaks themselves, but those high pastures on which cattle were taken to graze during the summer months on what was known as the transhumance. Some of the walks in this guide wander through 'alp' hamlets, linking the high pastures with all their lush fragrance and idyllic views. They are, indeed, alps among the Alps.

Finally, I have made every effort to check these routes for accuracy and it is to the best of my belief that the guidebook goes into print with all details correct. However, changes are made from time to time; paths are re-routed, certain landmarks altered. Any corrections required to keep the book up-to-date will be made in future printings wherever possible. Should you discover any changes that are necessary, I'd very much appreciate a brief note of the particular route and alteration required. A postcard via the publisher would be gratefully received.

Typical Oberland haybarn

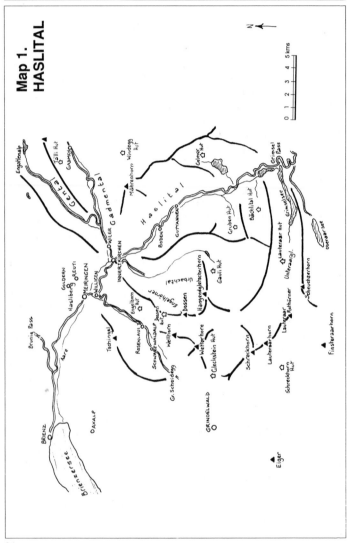

Map 1.
HASLITAL

HASLITAL

Position:	At the eastern end of the Bernese Alps, rising at the Grimsel Pass and draining northwards to the Brienzersee.
Maps:	L.S. 5004 'Berner Oberland' 1:50,000
	L.S. 255 'Sustenpass' 1:50,000
Bases:	Innertkirchen (625m), Gadmen (1,205m),
	Meiringen (595m),
	Hasliberg (1,000-1,100m)
Tourist Information:	
	Verkehrsbüro, 3862 Innertkirchen
	(Tel: 036 71 4338)
	Verkehrsbüro, 3860 Meiringen (Tel: 036 71 4322)
	Verkehrsbüro, 6084 Hasliberg (Tel: 036 71 3222)

As a base for a walking holiday, or as the starting point for an exploration of the Bernese Alps, the flat-bottomed, deeply cut Haslital has much to commend it. It's a broad trough at its lower, northern, end where it curves to meet the gleaming expanse of the Mediterranean-like Brienzersee, but in its upper reaches it has all the raw, barren chill of the high mountains. The Grimsel Pass is measured at 2,165 metres, the Brienzersee a modest 564 metres. Between the two extremes the valley has been created in a series of steps exhibiting a rich variety of landscapes with lush pastures, dazzling cascades, tight gorges and several tributary valleys equally worth wandering into.

In fact the Haslital has been used as a major transit valley for centuries. As early as 1211 the Bernese marched through it and crossed the Grimsel to invade the Valais, but in more peaceful times it was used as an important trade route to Italy. Today there are no fewer than four road passes feeding into the valley: the Brunig, Susten, Grimsel and Grosse Scheidegg - the last-named admittedly open only to Postbuses.

The main peaks which give birth to the glaciers that have carved the valleys feeding into the Haslital are to be found in a great arc to the south. Titlis (3,238m) heads both the lovely Gental and the Gadmental. Then there's the Sustenhorn (3,503m) above the pass of the same name; the big glacial mass of the Winterberg, Tieralplistock and the Gelmerhörner swirling round above the Furka and Grimsel passes. To the west of the Grimsel the Oberaar and Unteraargletschers lead into the arctic-like heartland of the Bernese Alps and the western wall of the Haslital begins with the Bachlistock (3,247m) and Ritzlihorn (3,263m) before being sliced by the peaceful Urbachtal with the Hangendgletscherhorn (3,292m) and the great east-facing slabs of the Engelhörner rising from it.

There's enough here to keep a mountaineer or mountain walker quietly content for many a long day.

General tourists based in the valley will find enough to satisfy a holiday too. There are associations with Sherlock Holmes around Meiringen, for example, for Conan Doyle was sufficiently impressed with the area that he brought the fictitious Holmes here for a final battle with the dastardly Professor Moriarty by the Reichenbach Falls. There is the Aareschlucht too, an imposing narrow limestone gorge with a walkway through it, midway between Meiringen and Innertkirchen. There are yet more lovely cascades to be seen in the Gental which leads to the honeypot of Engstlensee, and a series of cableways that whisk visitors up to the high terrace of Hasliberg and beyond for gentle strolls with memorable views.

To restate the obvious, the Haslital makes a fine start to an exploration of the Bernese Alps for visitors of all persuasions. But perhaps the very best is reserved for the walker.

Main Valley Bases:

INNERTKIRCHEN (625m) lies scattered in the bed of the valley about six kilometres to the south-east of Meiringen in an upper grassy plain. Reached by Postbus, or by train from Interlaken via Meiringen, the village has campsites, six hotels and 150 beds in holiday flats, limited shopping facilities, PTT and tourist information office. There are also modest winter sports facilities represented by a single ski-lift, but cross-country (or *langlauf*) comes into its own here when the snows lie deep. To the east of the village the Susten Pass road cuts away into the Gadmental, which in turn forks soon after with one of its branches delving into the Gental. Innertkirchen, therefore, is conveniently situated to make the most of several very fine walking districts.

GADMEN (1,205m) lies near the head of the valley of the same name, in a green basin below the windings that take the road over the Susten Pass. The village has several fine old wooden chalets; it is served by Postbus and has a campsite and four hotels.

MEIRINGEN (595m) is the main tourist centre of the valley. It's an old town, but little remains of its origins, for two serious fires destroyed much of it in 1879 and 1891. (A total of 293 houses were burned in the two fires.) Napoleon was here in 1810; other visitors have been Conan Doyle, Gertrude Bell, Hilaire Belloc and King Albert of the Belgians. Melchior Anderegg, one of the great mountain guides of the 'Golden Age', had a farm at nearby Zaun. The church, with its fourteenth century Romanesque tower topped by a wooden spire, is worth a visit. Elsewhere, Meiringen is very much a modern resort with no shortage of shops, restaurants, banks, PTT, sports facilities, hotels, youth hostel and tourist information office. The valley's hospital is also situated here. (Tel: 036 72 6161) Meiringen is served by railway from Interlaken and, of course, by Postbus. From the town there is cableway access to Reuti on the green terrace of Hasliberg on the hillside above the resort. In the neighbouring village of Willigen (one kilometre south of the Aare river) *matratzenlager* accommodation is to be had. Enquire at *Hotel Tourist*.

HASLIBERG (1,000-1,100m) above Meiringen consists of a scattered collection of hamlets and houses, a sunny, prosperous terrace made accessible by cableway from the valley, and continuing cableways leading up to Käserstatt and Under Stafel in the high bowl of Mägisalp, and from there to Planplatten - a ski area with splendid views, which also gives plenty of opportunities for the walker. Hasliberg has a dozen hotels and some 300 beds in holiday flats, chalets and farmhouses. It has its own tourist information office.

Other Valley Bases:
Most villages in the Haslital and neighbouring valleys have accommodation of some sort. Of particular interest, mention must be made

of Hotel Engstlenalp (1,834m) at the head of the Gental. Served by Postbus from Meiringen, it makes a very popular excursion with the lake of Engstlensee nearby, the Joch Pass above (accessible by chairlift or footpath), and several very fine walks leading from it. Just below the Grimsel Pass the Grimsel Hospice provides rooms and meals on a site overlooking a bleak dam but with access to the wild heart of the mountains.

To the west of the Haslital, and on the way to the Grosse Scheidegg, several quiet *gasthofs* in the valley that leads to and beyond Rosenlaui offer accommodation in gentle surroundings. Rosenlaui (1,328m) itself has a famous climbing school at the foot of the Engelhörner.

Mountain Huts:
Numerous huts exist in the mountains above the Haslital and surrounding area, few of which will be of interest to walkers, however. The **LAUTERAAR HUT** (2,392m) sits in wonderfully wild country above a junction of glaciers. With places for fifty it is reached in four and a half hours from the Grimsel Hospice along the lakeside at first, then below the Bachlistock and Hienderstock. From it access is gained to a good many climbs and glacier tours.

The **BÄCHLITAL HUT** (2,330m) lies to the north-east of the Lauteraar Hut, under the Alplistock, and is reached from the Grimsel road by a footpath that breaks away from the dammed end of the first lake. It has fifty-six places, twice as many as the **GRUBEN HUT** (2,510m) which is found on the far side of the Diamantstock ridge near the Gruben Glacier. This hut is best approached from the hamlet of Handegg (highest in the Haslital), in about three and a half hours.

The Urbachtal, winding southward from Innertkirchen, has the **GAULI HUT** (2,205m) near its head, on the eastern flanks of the Hangendgletscherhorn, and the **DOSSEN HUT** (2,663m) perched precariously on the high ridge between the peaks of Dossen and Gstellihorn, but which is more often approached from Rosenlaui.

But perhaps the most convenient of all mountain refuges in the region is the **ENGELHÖRNER HUT** (1,901m) which is reached in only an hour and a half from Rosenlaui (along part of the route to the Dossen Hut). This popular hut is owned by the Academic Alpine Club of Bern; it has sixty places and a guardian in weekend residence throughout the summer months.

Of those refuges on the eastern side of the Haslital, there is the **TÄLLI HUT** (1,720m) under the Tällistock, two hours walk from Gadmen; the **GELMER HUT** (2,412m) in rock climbing country to the north of the Grimsel Pass, reached by path from Chüenzentennlen (Point 1,596m) on the Grimsel road; and the **WINDEGG HUT** (1,887m), a small refuge with only places for a dozen on the north side of a col dividing the Triftgletscher from the Gadmental. To reach it involves nearly three hours of walking from the valley. Finally, the **TIERBERGLI HUT** (2,797m) deserves mention for its situation at the base of a rocky island almost completely surrounded by glaciers. It is reached by track and path from the Susten Pass in three and a half hours, can accommodate sixty-seven in its dormitories, and has a guardian during summer weekends.

Route 1:   **Engstlenalp (1,834m) - Schwarzental (1,369m)**

Grade:	**1-2**
Distance:	**5 kilometres**
Height loss:	**465 metres**
Time:	**1½ hours**

Engstlenalp lies at the head of the lovely Gental, in a position reckoned by Professor John Tyndall, the scientific Irishman and a Vice-President of the Alpine Club, as "one of the most charming spots in the Alps." What he wrote in 1866 is still true today.

There's a gentle greenery adorned by a clutch of timber chalets and barns, and the clear blue-green lake of Engstlensee walled to the south by a huge mass of slabs topped with snow and ice leading unerringly from the Mähren and Wendenstöcke, and over the Reissend Nollen to the summit of the Titlis. Cattle graze along the shores of the lake, and much of the area is a designated nature reserve. A track heads up to the lake from the hotel and car park, and when the track narrows to a path the route continues to the Joch Pass (2,207m), and over the other side to eventually reach Engelberg. There is also a chair-lift to the pass from the eastern end of the lake. (See *Central*

Switzerland, a walking guide in the same series as the present book, for additional routes.)

To the south-west of Engstlenalp runs the long, deep valley of the Gental - forested here and there, but with open meadows and tiny hamlets lining the narrow road that climbs through it. As you gaze along the valley from the alp, so eyes are drawn to the magnetic shapes of the big mountains of the Oberland and, most of all, to the Wellhorn and Wetterhorn, seen from here in unmistakable profile.

Postbuses go as far as Engstlenalp from Meiringen and Innertkirchen, and the car park there is often very busy on bright summer days. It is a very popular place with picnic parties. From the alp there are three ways back to the Haslital; this particular route is the shortest and easiest, but is quite delightful and with some spectacular landscape features to enjoy.

From Hotel Engstlenalp cross the approach road and join a path which descends ahead among trees to the south of the road, and keeps to the left of a stream which soon cuts a channel below. It is an easy path to follow, in and out of woods with wild fruits in season and plenty of wild flowers too. There are open glades and rough pastures to cross, and at Point 1,535m (on the map) you pass a tiny huddle of alp huts. The path continues without difficulty, crossing the occasional side stream and with the woods thinning to give more open views into the valley stretching ahead as it falls away in natural terraces, or steps, of pastureland.

Suddenly, near the huts of Under Graben (1,468m) and by a large old sycamore tree, you have a superb view of a collection of cascades showering out of the limestone cliffs ahead and to the left. It is a lovely sight, but it becomes even better as you pass below them.

The path swings to the right, then resumes its former direction to take you beneath the waterfalls, crossing the stream that comes from their united force by way of a footbridge. Shortly after this you cross the valley to the hamlet of Schwarzental (*refreshments*), from which point you can catch a Postbus down to Innertkirchen or Meiringen. (**Note**: Should you wish to walk further through the Gental and, decrying the use of Postbus, prefer to continue walking to Meiringen, the following route outline is suggested. Follow the road down-valley beyond the hamlet of Gentalhütten to a small tarn. A short distance beyond this tarn a signposted track/path heads away from the right-hand side of the road, goes through Gruebi and, waymarked and signposted at intervals, takes you round the mountainside on a modest level above the Haslital and eventually slopes down into Meiringen. Allow an additional three and a half hours from Schwarzental.)

Route 2:	Engstlenalp (1,834m) - Hinderarni (1,459m) - Reuti (1,045m) - Meiringen (595m)	
Grade:	3	
Distance:	16 kilometres	
Height gain:	87 metres	Height loss: 1,239 metres
Time:	4¹/₂-5 hours	

This is a high-level route that follows a belvedere course along the hillside above the Gental, and is used on the classic Alpine Pass Route. There is nothing particularly difficult about this walk, save for its length, and it is the distance, rather than severity, that uprates it to Grade 3. All along the high path there are fine views to enjoy. At first there are temptations to linger in order to gaze back at the mountains walling the upper part of the valley. There are also features in the valley below to study from a distance, and the all-absorbing scene ahead of the Oberland peaks growing larger and more prominent by the minute. By the time you reach Reuti (Hasliberg), you will have a fresh respect for this stunning landscape. From Reuti there is a steep descent through forest to Meiringen, although there is the option of cable-car for those who prefer it.

There will be no possibilities for refreshment (other than fresh water at Underbalm) between Engstlenalp and Reuti, so fill water bottles before setting out, and carry a packed lunch.

Facing the Gental with your back to Hotel Engstlenalp take the path heading to the right (north-west) signposted to Hasliberg-Reuti. It leads past the collection of haybarns and farm buildings of the alp, then swings westward over an undulating hillside below cliffs, with streams flowing and delightful views ahead to the Wetterhorn. You cross a stream and a few paces beyond this begin the belvedere course that leads all the way to Reuti. (Be careful not to be led along the broad path which rises up the hillside ahead to Tannenalp and Melchsee, but take the lower alternative.)

It's a delightful walk; long vistas, wild flowers and shrubs - and peace. It's not a well-walked path, so there is a good chance you will be able to enjoy a certain amount of solitude - a rarity to be savoured.

In places the path is narrow and a little exposed (though never dangerously so); sometimes it fades to a mere trail of brushed grass. Mostly, of course, it is clearly defined and will be seen far ahead rising and falling with the natural contours of the hillside. An hour after setting out you come to the handful of buildings of Baumgarten (1,702m), which has a narrow surfaced road leading to it from the valley. Walk ahead along this road for about 150 metres, and when it makes a sharp turn to the left, leave it in favour of the continuing path ahead.

When the path reaches the solitary farm of Underbalm (1,551m) you can refill water bottles from a gushing spring-fed pipe. The path leads on, and at Hinderarni (1,459m; two hours ten minutes) new panoramas present themselves for inspection as you gaze east to the big snow peaks that crowd the horizon above the unseen Susten Pass, and south, too, to those that neighbour the Grimsel. The way now curves to the right above the Haslital and joins a broad track that heads through patches of forest and out between pastures again.

About twenty minutes before reaching Reuti the track becomes a paved road taking you past a few farms and chalets. Reuti itself has accommodation, refreshments and cable-car access from (and to) Meiringen.

From the entrance to Reuti signposts direct the continuing path across pastures, then into very pleasant forest where the route becomes rather steep on the sharp descent to the valley, which it reaches in Meiringen not far from the centre of town.

Route 3:	Engstlenalp (1,834m) - Tannenalp (1,974m) - Melchsee-Frütt (1,902m)

Grade:	1-2		
Distance:	7 kilometres		
Height gain:	140 metres	Height loss:	72 metres
Time:	2 hours		

This is a popular walk, not too demanding but visually delightful. It begins by using the initial section of Route 2, then crosses the north-western wall of the Gental to enter a high, gently sloping pastureland that leads down to the small resort of Melchsee-Frütt. Down there the valley has patches of limestone pavement and rich alpine flora. There are two lakes in the pastureland and a small alp village (Tannenalp) with youth hostel accommodation. A choice of routes will return you to Engstlenalp.

From Hotel Engstlenalp wander along the path round the western edge of the alp, then veer westward on a clear trail (as for Route 2) which soon takes you across a stream below a cascade. Soon after this the path forks and you keep ahead rising steadily south-west-wards now with views along the Gental. This path makes a rising traverse below the cliffs walling the valley, and brings you above them onto a grassy crest (fine views), and over this to descend slightly towards Tannenalp (one hour, *refreshments, accommodation*).

From Tannenalp bear left along a narrow road, and on coming to the Tannensee (lake) pass round either side of it; path to the left, roadway to the right. Continue downvalley, so to reach Melchsee-Frütt (*accommodation, refreshments, shops*).

To return to Engstlenalp either reverse your outward route (two hours), or head south from the lake at Melchsee and climb up to Balmeregghorn (2,255m) following the line of a cableway. Once on the ridge between the Gental and Melchsee bear left and follow the ridge-path to Tannensee, where you can re-join the outward route back to Engstlenalp.

Other Routes from Engstlenalp:
One of the classic walks from here is along the path to the **JOCH PASS**

(2,207m) in about one hour ten minutes. It is a busy path and somewhat devalued by the close proximity of the chair-lift. But that being said, it is still a fine walk, with the possibility of extending it all the way to **ENGELBERG** - a walk of about four hours from Engstlenalp.

Another good route, somewhat strenuous but very rewarding, is that which crosses the ridge of the Tällistock - the mountain wall dividing the Gental from the Gadmental - and descends to the village of **GADMEN** on the far side. This is a walk of a little over five hours, with the option of breaking it with an overnight stay in the **TÄLLI HUT**.

An extension of Route 3 leads across the **BALMEREGGHORN** to **PLANPLATTEN** and **MEIRINGEN** in six and a half hours. From Engstlenalp to Tannenalp the route is the same as in Route 3, but thereafter the ridge dividing the two valleys is gained and followed south-westwards, beyond the Balmeregghorn to Planplatten Sattel (2,186m) and a choice of continuing routes to Meiringen. There are also cableway options in a number of places along the way. (Grade 3)

Route 4:	Innertkirchen (625m) - Urbachtal - Gauli Hut (2,205m)

Grade:	3
Distance:	13 kilometres
Height gain:	1,580 metres
Time:	6 hours

The Urbachtal slices the mountains south of Innertkirchen. It's a green, level, pastoral valley in places, which rises now and again in gorge-like narrows between high walls of rock. Its western wall is a stupendous flank of limestone - the Engelhörner - which divides the Urbachtal from that of Rosenlaui. This walk wanders all the way through the valley to the stark inner recesses below the drapery of the Gauligletscher which, with other smaller icefields, forms an untamed glacial cirque. In this wild region below the cirque there stands the Gauli Hut, owned by the Bern Section of the SAC and with places for fifty-five in its dormitories. A guardian is in residence only during weekends in summer, but it is open at other times, although if you intend to stay overnight, you should carry food supplies in with you.

From Innertkirchen follow the narrow road which cuts away to the south of the Aare river to Grund, and then climbs in a long series of hairpins among forest, eventually levelling above a rocky cleft to enter the Urbachtal. There are footpath short-cuts in places. The road then crosses the Urbachwasser and heads into the valley proper after about one hour twenty minutes.

Continue along the road heading south-west, passing as you do a long string of farmhouses and haybarns dotted on either side among the meadows. The vast Engelhörner wall on the right is streaked with slender waterfalls and the whole scene is reminiscent of parts of Norway. High above, at the head of the valley, modest glaciers and snowfields may be seen draped from the Hangendgletscherhorn.

The road ends and becomes a stony track. A signpost here gives the Gauli Hut as five hours, the Mattensee three hours fifty minutes; both times perhaps somewhat over-cautious. The track winds up-valley, passes the little hut of Röhrmatten (seen off to the left) and continues as a footpath. Ahead the valley narrows almost to gorge-like proportions and is heavily wooded. The path takes you up into the woods, gaining height steeply in places, then rounds a bend below a solitary cabin at 1,364 metres and eases across a steep gully with a stream pouring through it. (Early in the season this gully may be choked with snow; in which case you must proceed with great caution.) Beyond the gully the way becomes a gentle terrace, now out of the trees but with rampant vegetation for company.

The valley has broadened again, opening with interest and attraction to a wide stream-sliced basin. Shortly after, you come to Schrätteren, a rough pasturage with a handful of alp huts above to the left. The path leads on, crosses the Urbachwasser stream and soon forks. The right-hand branch climbs round the head of the valley and goes up to the Dossen Hut (2,663m), perched high on the ridge leading between Dossen and Gstellihorn and overlooking the Rosenlaui Glacier. The left-hand path is the one to take, for it climbs on over increasingly rough terrain to gain another 300 metres or so before making another fork.

Both the ongoing trails lead to the hut, but the left-hand branch swings round to take the shaft of river-cut valley to visit the hidden tarn of the Mattensee before climbing on to reach the hut. This is perhaps of more interest than the direct route which climbs over the lower reaches of the Tëlligrat (2,222m) before making a steady decending traverse to the hut itself in its lonely position in the rocky glen.

Other Walks in the Urbachtal:
If Route 4 seems to be rather longer or more demanding than you'd care to tackle, don't despair, for the valley is well worth a visit no matter what your demands may be. It is also possible to drive there from Innertkirchen, thus reducing the time and effort otherwise required to explore it. Should you decide to drive into the valley, park with discretion in its lower reaches soon after entering. You should be able to find a space to park just off the road in order not to block it.

By following Route 4 a very pleasant walk may be had to **SCHRÄTTEREN** (allow three to four hours for the walk there and back; Grade 2). Or, if this is still too far, simply wander to **RÖHRMATTEN** and back for an overview of a valley that is practically unique in the Bernese Alps.

Route 5:	Innertkirchen (625m) - Guttannen (1,050m) - Grimsel Hospice (1,980m)

Grade:	2-3
Distance:	19 kilometres
Height gain:	1,355 metres
Time:	6½ hours

The Grimsel Pass has been used for centuries; in times both of war and of peace. It has been used by traders transporting goods from the north of Switzerland to Italy - and vice-versa - and by mountain peasants, hunters, mercenaries and pilgrims. A mule track was the first 'road' to cross it, and when the specially engineered highway (mostly used today) was opened in 1895, there were some 300 horses stabled in Meiringen for use in drawing the postal coaches over it.

Parts of the old mule track through the Haslital are still in evidence, and this walk follows it wherever possible. There are paths in other places, sometimes on the road itself, but from Handegg, midway between Guttannen and the Pass, a *Bergweg* is taken through the wild upper part of the route.

To return to Innertkirchen from the Grimsel Hospice at the end of the walk, take the Postbus.

From the start it is necessary to follow the path which climbs in zig-zags south of Innertkirchen through the woods towards the entrance to the Urbachtal. This leads to the narrow road serving the valley, but almost as soon as the road takes you across the Urbachwasser at Vordertal you strike away on the route signposted to Understock. Here you join a track leading along the upper southern slopes of hillside above the Haslital. In and out of woods it makes a steady traverse of these slopes and eventually brings you to the hamlet of Boden (869m), a little under two hours after setting out.

Go onto the main road here and walk a short distance down-valley to join the old mule track on the true right bank of the Aare, and then follow this upstream. The way now leads uphill to Guttannen, the highest village in the Haslital - Handegg is little more than a hamlet. (Guttannen, noted for its crystals, is actually on the opposite bank, but may be reached by a bridge. Refreshments are available there.)

Beyond Guttannen the route becomes yet more interesting and wild, the mountains crowding overhead. About two and a half kilometres above it the track brings you onto the road and you then walk along this for the next three to four kilometres as far as Handegg, a little over four hours from Innertkirchen. Handegg is the home of a hydro-electric station, the lakes above having been dammed to serve it. Off to the right are seen the cascades of the Handeggfall. Shortly after this you will see a path breaking away from the road on its right-hand side. This is the path to take, and it leads up to the north-western edge of the Raterischbodensee reservoir. Continuing along the path you skirt the western edge of the lake, join the road and come to the Grimsel Hospice overlooking the Grimselsee *(Postbus, accom-modation, refreshments).*

This is an astonishing place; drab yet exciting, eerie but vibrant. There is evidence of past glaciations everywhere. Grey granite slabs scarred by long-gone ice, and the hint of icefields far-off; highways into the heart of the mountains. A wild place it certainly is, and it is interesting to speculate on the influence the region had on the pioneers of mountaineering - and of the study of glaciology - who came this way more than 150 years ago.

See Route 6 below for a route into the heart of the mountains from the Hospice to the Lauteraar Hut.

Other Walks from Innertkirchen:

Walkers based in Innertkirchen need not run short of ideas. There's something here for every taste; short, easy valley strolls and long and arduous mountain trails to follow. The **AARESCHLUCHT** is one of the valley's features and it will no doubt attract many walking visitors. It's a deep and narrow shaded gorge, 1,400 metres long and 200 metres deep with a walkway (fee charged) leading through it. The gorge is open daily between April and the end of October - weather permitting - and on two nights a week in July and August it is floodlit from 9.00pm.

A high route, nearly 1,000 metres above the valley, can be achieved by going from Innertkirchen to Guttannen along a farmers' trail linking several isolated alps. First you climb up to **BLATTENSTOCK** (1,849m), then along the path high on the northern flanks of the valley to **BLATTEN, HOLZHUS** (Holzhausalp; 1,931m) and **STEINHUS** (Steinhausalp; 1,942m) before descending a knee-shattering zig-zag path to Guttannen. This Grade 3 route will take about eight and a half hours to achieve.

There is a long walk to be had through the Gadmental towards the Susten Pass. Three hours along a variety of footpath, track and road will lead to **GADMEN** (Grade 2) in charming scenery. The **GADMENTAL**, served by Postbus from Innertkirchen, or by using Gadmen as a base, has many fine outings worth exploring, among them the two and a half hour walk from Nessental through the alps of Staldi and Birchlaui to the **TÄLLI HUT**. (Grade 2-3) There is also a steep haul up to **SÄTTELI** on the Tällistock ridge for a choice of grand vistas - either to the east to the Sustenhorn and its glacier-clad neighbours, or across the depths of the Gental, or south towards the giants of the Oberland. This Grade 3 route from Furen will require a little over three hours.

Furen (sometimes spelt Führen) is also the starting point for a demanding cross-country route over the mountains to Guttannen, high in the Haslital. This Grade 3 walk goes south from Furen into the valley of the Triftwasser and up to the little alp of Underi Trift. From here one and a half hours will lead to the Windegg Hut, then a scramble south-westwards to gain the **FURTWANGSATTEL** (2,568m) before dropping very steeply to Guttannen. This magnificent route is for experienced mountain trekkers only, and will take between seven and a half and eight hours.

Route 6:   Grimsel Hospice (1,980m) - Lauteraar Hut (2,392m)

Grade:	3		
Distance:	10 kilometres		
Height gain:	483 metres	**Height loss:**	71 metres
Time:	4-4¹/₂ hours		

The Lauteraar Hut sits on a grassy shelf overlooking the Concordia of two major glacier systems; the Lauteraargletscher and the Finsteraargletscher which combine to become the Unteraargletscher. This serves as a highway into the very heart of the Bernese Alps. As their names suggest, the Lauteraar Glacier is headed by the Lauteraarhorn, the Finsteraar Glacier by the Finsteraarhorn. Also in view are the Schreckhorn and Oberaarhorn and an assortment of savage mountain walls and pinnacles. The site of the hut has a link with the pioneering age, for here was set the historic Pavilion Dollfus.

This approach route skirts the dismal-looking Grimselsee, then heads along the rubble-strewn Unteraargletscher through a landscape more reminiscent of the barren Karakoram than of the pastoral Alps. But this raw, monochrome mountainscape has great attraction for many of us, and serves as a direct contrast to that enjoyed on the vast majority of walks included in this guide.

In noting that the route wanders along a glacier, it should be pointed out that this glacier is likely to be roughly carpeted with morainic debris. No crevasses were detected when the walk was researched, but it is important to follow marker poles and cairns (not always easy to see) for the precise up-to-date route. In poor visibility the correct point at which the glacier is left may be difficult to locate.

From the Grimsel Hospice *(Postbus from Meiringen; parking spaces, accommodation, refreshments)* go down a series of steps and cross the top of the dam wall. Climbing up the far side the path takes you high above the northern side of the Grimselsee, through a tunnel and out to steep, shrub-covered hillsides heading west. It's a fine walk, passing below cascades, then bare walls of rock that are popular with climbers, for much of the way among clusters of alpenrose.

At the far end of the lake (about two to two and a half hours) the path leads onto the moraine-covered Unteraargletscher. From here the way is marked with poles and cairns on the northern half of the glacier. The way meanders to pick the easiest route. Along the glacier has been built a huge chorten, complete with prayer flags, which adds to the Himalayan, or Karakoram-like atmosphere.

About an hour or so along the glacier you come to a point where the right-hand wall of the valley has a shallow indent with grass-covered slabs at its western end. Marker poles lead off the glacier here, then with painted waymarks on rocks you pick a route up the rough slopes to find a clear path leading upvalley. Crossing one or two streams you gain the grassy knoll and at last come to the hut, which is not seen until just before you reach it.

The hut has bedspace for fifty and a guardian in residence from mid-June until the end of September when a full meals service is offered (Tel: 036 73 1110). Views are magnificent.

Route 7:	Meiringen (595m) - Lammi (694m) - Innertkirchen (625m)

Grade:	1		
Distance:	4 kilometres		
Height gain:	100 metres	Height loss:	70 metres
Time:	1 hour 15 mins		

This short and easy stroll makes a pleasant half-day outing and is useful at the start of a holiday to gain an idea of how the Haslital develops beyond Meiringen. It adopts a section of the old mule track that once led through the valley and over the Grimsel Pass, and wanders among the woods bordering the Aareschlucht, over the rocky knoll known as the Kirchet.

Heading south-east (ie: up-valley) along Meiringen's main street, the road suddenly breaks away to the right, but another minor street continues ahead towards Sand (in the direction of the town's youth hostel). This soon brings you to the river which you cross by a bridge and, over the Aareschlucht road running parallel with the Aare, take to the old mule track leading into the woods that gird the knoll of Kirchet ahead. The trail forks after a short distance; either branch will do, but the suggestion here is to take the left-hand trail. This leads up to the gasthof Lammi, about forty-five minutes from Meiringen station. You now follow the main valley road downhill until, at a hairpin bend, you can take a footpath leading alongside the river to Innertkirchen. Return to Meiringen may be made by Postbus or by train.

Route 8:	Meiringen (595m) - Rosenlaui (1,328m)

Grade:	2
Distance:	8 kilometres
Height gain:	733 metres
Time:	3 hours

Rosenlaui has a magical ring about it. Snug among the trees at the foot of the Wellhorn on the way to the Grosse Scheidegg, it is very much a climbing centre, with the Swiss National Mountaineering School based here. The walk to it, though steep at first, is none too arduous, and is just one part of the longer classic crossing to Grindelwald. Since much of the valley is hemmed in by steep mountains and forest, it is best to choose a bright day to tackle this outing, otherwise it can seem unnecessarily gloomy.

Leaving Meiringen take the main valley road out of town and across the Aare river to enter the neighbouring village of Willigen. About fifty metres beyond Hotel Tourist turn right along a driveway between a house and a barn. When the driveway ends continue along a grass path rising steeply ahead. It brings you onto a narrow road which you follow briefly before cutting away again on the continuing path. Several times this path leapfrogs the road, but is waymarked with precision so there is little chance of missing it. It leads over pastures and soon reaches the hamlet of Schwendi (792m; 50 mins, *accommodation, refreshments*).

By a combination of footpath and narrow road, gaining height all the time, you enter the heavily forested Reichenbach valley. (The noted Reichenbach Falls are off to the right, hidden from view by the dense forest.) The signposted route takes you past Gasthaus Zwirgi (983m; fifty minutes, *accommodation, refreshments*) and along footpath in forest again until at last being returned to the road. Walking along this you come to another solitary *gasthaus*, Kaltenbrunnen (1,210m; two hours fifteen minutes). (From here a fine four-hour circuit will take you on a diversion over Kaltenbrunnen Alp and up to a rare high moorland - Europe's highest protected upland moor. See p.56.)

By now the gradient has eased and the valley stretches ahead, steep-walled and forested still. Continue along the road now all the way to Rosenlaui. As you approach Gschwantenmad (1,304m; two hours thirty-five minutes) so the valley opens to show the dramatic Wellhorn and the broken snout of the Rosenlaui Glacier ahead. A memorable view. The wall above to the left, partly hidden from the road by trees, is that of the Engelhörner.

Soon after passing the few farm buildings of Gschwantenmad the road is enclosed by trees again and you suddenly come to Rosenlaui (*accommodation, refreshments, Postbus*). This little hamlet consists of a few guest houses, hotel and shop. Nearby is the Gletscherschlucht, a fine glacier-carved gorge with spectacular cascades, and a path cut into the rocks which leads to a viewpoint from which to study the retreating Rosenlaui Glacier. Should you decide to stay overnight here in Rosenlaui, you will find plenty to sustain your interest.

Route 9:   Rosenlaui (1,328m) - Dossen Hut (2,663m)

Grade:	3
Distance:	5 kilometres
Height gain:	1,335 metres
Time:	4¹/₂ hours

This route is only for the sure-footed and those with a steady head for heights. The Dossen Hut is perched on the high ridge to the north of the popular little peak after which it is named (3,138m), and which is usually reached in about thirty minutes from the hut. Some very fine wild mountain scenery is to be enjoyed from here. A guardian is usually in attendance during weekends in summer, when meals will be provided. The hut can sleep sixty-five in its dormitories.

From Rosenlaui follow the road up-valley across the river, and soon after rounding the first hairpin, take the footpath heading off to the left towards the glacier gorge. At the outlet of the gorge the path forks. Cross a bridge on the left and climb steeply through forest, near the top of which the path forks again. The left-hand trail here goes to the Engelhörner Hut without undue difficulty; but we continue heading south, up to a one-time moraine leading to much steeper terrain. The way now is dominated by the turmoil of the Rosenlaui Glacier and towering rock walls. Go along a moraine crest, then up a gully below the Gstellihorn. Over more rough moraine the path skirts to the left of rocks, ascends rock terraces and with the aid of cables brings you onto the ridge. A dramatic place. From here the way along the ridge to the south is clear, and in half an hour you reach the hut.

Among the climbs usually attempted from the hut are the Dossen, Ränfenhorn, Hangendgletscherhorn, Wetterhorn, Rosenhorn and Bärglistock to the south. Needless to say, none of these peaks should be attempted by inexperienced or unequipped walkers.

Route 10:	Meiringen (595m) - Schwarzwaldalp (1,458m) - Grosse Scheidegg (1,962m) - Grindelwald (1,034m)

Grade:	2-3
Distance:	21 kilometres
Height gain:	1,367 metres Height loss: 928 metres
Time:	7¹/₂ hours

This is the classic walker's route to Grindelwald. It's well worth tackling, either in its entirety or, if you consider it a bit too far for one day, by taking the Postbus to Rosenlaui or Schwarzwaldalp and walking from there.

Follow Route 8 as far as Gschwantenmad, then leave the road and take the farm track off to the right across the pastures. A footpath soon leaves this, heads through a collection of trees, across more pasture and rejoins the farm track at Rufenen, an open region of grazing land with fine mountain views. A signpost now directs you away across the meadows on the left in the direction of Broch and Schwarzwaldalp. Meadowland leads to forest, and out again to rejoin the valley road at the hamlet of Broch. Bear right and follow the road a short distance to Schwarzwaldalp (1,454m; 3 hours 35 mins, *accommodation, refreshments*).

A few metres beyond Chalet Schwarzwaldalp leave the road again and follow a path off to the left, signposted to Alpiglen. This pleasant stretch of path takes you over the river among trees and shrubs at the foot of the Wellhorn. You recross the Reichenbach stream again, then go over an area of rough pasture to rejoin the road once more near a farm building. The continuing path is found on the right-hand side of the road, and this takes you up to the Grosse Scheidegg, crossing and recrossing the road as it does.

Grosse Scheidegg (1,962m; 5 hours 20 mins, *accommodation, refreshments*) is a true saddle slung between the Wetterhorn and the insignificant Schwarzhorn. From it you look over the rich basin of meadowland in which Grindelwald is scattered, and across to the

Männlichen ridge. The Eiger is seen side-on; a bleak profile.

The way down to Grindelwald is easy and needs little description. It begins directly below the hotel, but soon offers numerous alternative paths. Most will be signposted and with times given, so you simply take your choice. All will give ever-growing views of the mountains and glaciers for which Grindelwald is justly famous, and will take you past romantic timber chalets and farms brightened with petunias and geraniums at their windows. It's a delightful walk down.

Other Walks from Meiringen:

The proximity of the Hasliberg cableway complex adds much to Meiringen's appeal as a walking centre, but even without exploiting this attractive upland area there will be no shortage of outings to consider. One of the full-day trips is that which makes a high traverse of the southern wall of the valley to the west of the town. It visits the quaint scattered hamlet of **ZAUN**, goes to the terrace of **WIRZENALP** (1,246m) and the secluded tarn of **HINTERBURGSEELI** (1,514m) and on to **KURHAUS AXALP** (1,535m) where the Postbus can be taken down to Brienz. This walk, graded 3 on account of its length and height gain, will take about five hours to complete.

A less strenuous walk, keeping in the bed of the valley throughout, goes to **BRIENZ** by way of **UNTERHEID** and **UNTERBACH** - but choose a day when military jets are not using the airstrip near Unterbach, or you will need plenty of earplugs. This walk, Grade 1, will take about three and a half hours.

On the Hasliberg terrace there is a *Panoramaweg* that leads in three hours from **REUTI** to the **BRÜNIG PASS** by way of **WASSERWENDI**. Higher still, the so-called *Murmeliweg* between **KÄSERSTATT** and **MÄGISALP** (one hour), and the *Giebelweg* which goes from **KÄSERSTATT** to **GIEBEL** and steeply down to **LUNGERN** on the edge of the Lungernsee on the far side of the Brünig Pass. This last is a walk of about three and a half hours. Leaflets are available from the tourist information offices in Meiringen and Hasliberg, which outline some of these possibilities. But even a brief study of the map of the area shows the vast range of outings for walkers of all degrees of commitment here. There should be no time to grow bored.

As for the Reichenbach valley (that which leads to Rosenlaui and on to the Grosse Scheidegg), there are plenty of options here too. One already mentioned is that which goes from **KALTENBRUNNEN** to the high moors above **OBERER STAFEL**. In order to make a loop trip, go to **KALTENBRUNNEN ALP** and up to **OBERER STAFEL** and on a little further to the moorland region on the northern slopes of Tschingel; then return once more to the huts of Oberer Stafel where you veer left to **SEILIALP** (1,465m) to find the trail leading back down into the valley at Kaltenbrunnen once more. This circuit will take about four hours, and you gain something like 600 metres of height over all. Grade 3.

Wetterhorn from above Grindelwald

LÜTSCHENTAL

Position:	To the south-east of Interlaken. The valley begins with Grindelwald's mountain-girt basin and flows roughly west and north to the Brienzersee.
Map:	L.S. 5004 'Berner Oberland' 1:50,000
Bases:	Wilderswil (584m), Grindelwald (1,034m)
Tourist Information:	
	Verkehrsbüro, 3812 Wilderswil (Tel: 036 22 8455)
	Verkehrsbüro, 3818 Grindelwald (Tel: 036 53 1212)

Travelling south out of Interlaken either by road or rail, the first village of note is Wilderswil which sprawls in the open 'gateway' of the steep-walled valley of the Lütschine. Here the shafted mountain slopes are dark with forests, but in certain positions and in certain lights a blaze of snow peak and hanging glacier can be seen far ahead, apparently floating as among the clouds.

The road continues following the true left bank of the river into the narrowing confines of the valley, with the railway on the opposite side. Then, at the hamlet of Zweilütschinen, the valley, road and railway all fork at the confluence of two streams: the Weisse Lütschine coming from the south, the Schwarze Lütschine from the east. The valley of the Weisse (or White) Lütschine becomes known as the Lauterbrunnental, the Schwarze (or Black) Lütschine is the Lütschental with Grindelwald at its head.

The Lütschental is a lovely green scoop that saves its best till last. Daily, through summer and winter alike, cars, coaches and crowded trains wind up the valley in a centuries-old pilgrimage that shows no sign of abating. Grindelwald, of course, is the Mecca. Its peaks and pastures and frowning glaciers create an almost idyllic setting to one of the major resorts of the Alps.

As you draw near so the Wetterhorn comes first into view, immediately recognisable with its turreted summits appearing somewhat like a crown, even though many visitors may not at first recall its name. The valley steepens, then opens out as a huge pastoral

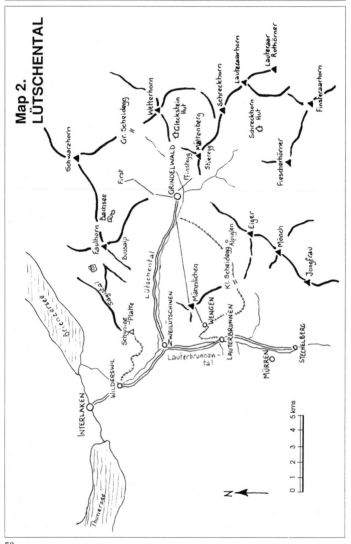

Map 2.
LÜTSCHENTAL

bowl liberally spattered with chalets and haybarns, strung about with cableways and blocked at its head not only by the Wetterhorn, but by the blank-faced Mättenberg which stubs the northern end of the Schreckhorn's ridge, and by the dark brooding walls of the Eiger to the right. Between the Eiger and Mättenberg can be seen the snout of the Unterer Grindelwaldgletscher; between the Mättenberg and the Wetterhorn it is the blue-green motionless cascade of the Oberer Grindelwaldgletscher that holds winter all year through.

These three mountain walls, interspersed with glaciers, are impressive enough in themselves, yet the finest peaks of all in the vicinity may only be seen properly by those prepared to foresake the village streets and immediate pastures of the valley. By going up to Bussalp, Bachsee or onto the easily-gained Faulhorn one of the most beautiful mountain vistas to be had anywhere in Europe is laid out in a panorama of almost unbelievable loveliness. The Schreckhorn, Finsteraarhorn and Fiescherhorn habitually hide themselves shyly behind Grindelwald's immediate backdrop, but from any one of these walkers' viewpoints they become exposed to witness; sharks' teeth of stone and ice, delicate fins that project from gleaming snowfields, walls that shine with glacial armoury, ridges of cream-dashed waves lacing one dreamy summit after another. All this on the horizon. A nearish horizon, but with a foreground of deep rich greenery. Wild flowers and cowbells near to hand, and glaciers draped down the mountains ahead. In such contrasts the very essence of the Alps is spelled out in wonder.

It comes as no surprise then to find that visitors were drawn to this open basin at the head of the Lütschental as long ago as the early eighteenth century. Then it was the glaciers that served as the lure; William Burnet in 1708, Sir Horace Mann in 1723 - who wrote that an exorcist had been employed to halt the advance of the glaciers that were threatening Grindelwald - Thomas Pennant in 1765, William Coxe and Goethe who walked on the ice in 1779. These were but a handful of a steadily-growing stream of visitors, and a hundred years later there was even a colony of English here.

In the early nineteenth century mountaineers became attracted by the peaks themselves. The Finsteraarhorn's lofty summit was first reached in 1829, the Wetterhorn in 1844, the Eiger in 1858 and

Schreckhorn three years later. When Alfred Wills climbed the Wetterhorn during his honeymoon in 1854 he did so unaware at the time that it had already received its first ascent some ten years earlier, and the oft-told account of his climb which appeared in *Wanderings Among the High Alps*, effectively marked the start of the Golden Age of Mountaineering.

More recently, of course, public attention has focussed in grim fascination - inspired no doubt by a certain amount of media myopia - on the Eiger's Nordwand, probably the single major alpine face known to non-mountaineers. Its history has been highlighted sadly by presumed nationalism and public tragedy, yet there have been some magnificent climbing achievements played out upon it. The Eiger is, though, just one piece of the jig-saw; one ornament in the backdrop to some of the best walking to be found anywhere in the Bernese Alps.

Main Valley Bases:

WILDERSWIL (584m) is a busy place in summer, and not only with those staying in the village, for its railway station is the main valley terminus of the Schynige Platte funicular, as well as being one of those that serves the Lauterbrunnen-Wengen-Jungfraujoch-Grindelwald rail system. The village has some interesting features, including a seventeenth century church (re-built in 1673 from a much older place of worship) standing across the river and reached by a covered bridge. A short distance away stands the ruin of a sixteenth century castle, setting of Byron's *Manfred*, and within the village itself there are a few attractive old houses. For accommodation Wilderswil has fifteen hotels and *pensions*, more than 600 beds in holiday flats, and a campsite with superb facilities. One of the benefits of using Wilderswil as a base is its ease of access to so many areas - both in and on the edge of the mountains. Another is its climate which is somewhat less prone to the storms that are attracted to the north-facing mountains up-valley.

GRINDELWALD (1,034m) needs little introduction, its fame has spread far and wide to the extent that in the streets there are now multi-language signs that include even Japanese. It has been used as a mountaineering base for about 150 years, and is now an all-year-round resort as well-known for its skiing as for its summer attractions. There are several cableways of use to walkers. These include the First chair-lift, and the gondola lift to Männlichen (both the longest of their kind in Europe), in addition to the shorter cable-car ride to Pfingstegg. There is the rack-and-pinion railway to Kleine Scheidegg, Postbus to Grosse Scheidegg or to Bussalp, and Europe's highest railway which goes to the Jungfraujoch (3,454m) for an unforgettable view worth capturing on an off-day from walking. It is, however, a very expensive ride. The town is layered on a steep hillside. It has one main street with shops of every kind; there are banks, PTT, restaurants and a large and helpful tourist information office. There is also a mountain guides' bureau which, in addition to providing private guiding services, also arranges climbing and ski-touring tours (*Bergsteigerzentrum, Dorfstrasse, 3818 Grindelwald*). There are numerous sports facilities, including swimming pool, tennis courts etc. Accommodation is available in all degrees of comfort. There are forty-six hotels with almost 2,500 beds, some 7,000 beds in holiday flats; a youth hostel and no less than five campsites.

Mountain Huts:

A number of SAC huts, private inns and small hotels are to be found high in the mountains surrounding Grindelwald. Several of these will naturally be beyond the bounds of most walkers, but some make fine destinations in their own right, either for a there-and-back walk, or as an overnight lodging in a remote or spectacular position. Of these, the **SCHRECKHORN HUT** (2,520m) is worth mentioning for its glorious views and interesting approach. It stands at the base of the western cliffs of the Schreckhorn overlooking the glacier of the Obers Eismeer, between five and six hours' walk from Grindelwald. On the way to it sits the privately-owned **RESTAURANT STIEREGG** (1,650m) with eighteen places available in a *matratzenlager*, and the great Fiescherhörner in full view across the Unterer Grindelwaldgletscher.

The **GLECKSTEIN HUT** (2,317m) is in another memorable position. This 100 place refuge, high above the Oberer Grindelwaldgletscher, is a base for climbers tackling the Wetterhorn and takes something over three hours to reach from Hotel Wetterhorn above Grindelwald. Owned by the Burgdorf Section of the SAC it has a guardian from June to the end of September, during which time meals and drinks are available.

The **MITTELLEGI HUT** is perched like a precarious nest on the superb north-east ridge of the Eiger (the Mittellegi Ridge) and is definitely out of bounds to all but mountaineers. However, tucked just below the summit of the Faulhorn north-west of Grindelwald, **BERGHOTEL FAULHORN** (2,681m) offers eighteen beds and eighty dormitory places, and is ideal for walkers. For over a century there has been an inn here, and it is justifiably popular as a site from which to enjoy the beauties of sunset and sunrise. It is reached from Grindelwald by way of either First and Bachsee, or via Bussalp. Beyond this, on the Schynige Platte path, the small, privately-owned **WEBER HUT** (2,344m; marked as Männdlenen on the map) is snug in a gap on the ridge below the Indri Sägissa, and is well-used by walkers as a refreshment stop on the classic Schynige Platte to Grindelwald walk.

Elsewhere in the vicinity of Grindelwald, accommodation is to be had at **ALPIGLEN** (1,616m) in beds or dormitories below the Eiger, at **KLEINE SCHEIDEGG** with its famous Eiger view (120 beds, 120 dormitory spaces), at nearby **MÄNNLICHEN** and at **GROSSE SCHEIDEGG** in the shadow of the Wetterhorn - also with a choice of bedrooms or *matratzenlager* dormitories.

Route 11:	Schynige Platte (1,987m) - Faulhorn (2,680m) - First (2,167m) - Grindelwald (1,034m)

Grade:	2-3		
Distance:	19 kilometres (15 kilometres to First)		
Height gain:	693 metres	Height loss:	1,646 metres
Time:	6-7 hours		

No book of walks in the Bernese Alps would be complete without this one. It is, quite simply, a classic; one of *the* classic walks of the Alps, and it doesn't matter how often you walk it, nor how many others

Eiger from Schynige Platte

have walked it before you, it is always worth tackling.

Its main feature is the constantly changing panorama. It begins with one of the finest views of all to the Eiger, Mönch, Jungfrau and Lauterbrunnen Breithorn, then changes to a steep overview of the Brienzersee and the northern hills; changes again to one of an intimate little glen, and then grows in glory with the Wetterhorn, Schreckhorn, Finsteraarhorn and Fiescherhorn shimmering in the clear waters of the Bachsee.

But if the views keep changing, so too does the very nature of the walk. Variety is of the essence. But do choose a day with the weather full of promise, for there are long sections away from shelter and it would not be pleasant to be caught out by storm. In any case, you will want clear skies and sunshine to bring out the full wonder of the landscape. Take plenty of film and make an early start in order to have time to dawdle, to study the flowers along the way, and simply to bask in the views. (**Note**: In July and August there are guided tours arranged along this path by moonlight, aiming to capture sunrise from the Faulhorn and having breakfast at the First chair-lift restaurant. Enquire at the tourist information office in Wilderswil for details.)

Take the funicular from Wilderswil to Schynige Platte. (This railway was built in 1893 in order to give visitors the opportunity to admire the breathtaking views.) It is a slow but ever-interesting ride, with passengers glued to the windows in fascination. At Schynige Platte there is an alpine garden with somewhere in the region of 500 species of alpine plants growing in their natural habitats.

From the station at Schynige Platte *(accommodation, refreshments)* a footpath signpost directs you onto the path to the Faulhorn. There is a choice of route to take, but it is advisable to follow signs for the *Panoramaweg*. The way leads initially across rough undulations of pastureland and in just over half an hour brings you to the lip of a cliff that plunges steeply on its northern side. The path is quite safe, but the views down to the Brienzersee are dramatic, while gazing westwards Interlaken is seen far below with the Thunersee shimmering beyond it, and the conical peak of Niesen catching the eye above Spiez.

The path leads on towards the modest Laucherhorn, then skirts below it to cross a slope of scree, soon entering a hidden region of bare limestone ribs and cliffs across a minor col between the Laucherhorn and Ussri Sägissa. This col takes you to the head of the marshy, moorland-like Sägistal with a small tarn at the far end of the valley. This little glen, grazed by sheep, is almost entirely circled by ridges and the path keeps above it along the slopes of the right-hand wall. Much of the way goes along a series of limestone terraces, then veers right, rising gently across more bare ribs of the mountain before coming to a narrow cleft in which is found the tiny Weber Hut (2,344m; *refreshments*) at a junction of paths.

The continuing route takes you past the hut and up a sharp pull, then at an easier angle along the Winteregg ridge with the Faulhorn

Lauterbrunnen Valley from Wengen (Lauterbrunnental).
Breithorn from approach to Mürren (Lauterbrunnental).

Path to Schreckhorn Hut above Grindelwald (Route 25).
Restaurant Stieregg and Fiescherhorn (Routes: 24, 25).

rising ahead and new views opening to the Eiger, Mönch and Jungfrau. It is yet again a superb vantage point from which to study these lovely mountains. Soon the path offers a choice. Either continue directly up to the Faulhorn summit, or break away on the right-hand path which traverses across the face of the mountain, then gives another opportunity to either descend or cut off to the left, also to the summit.

Views from the top of the Faulhorn are certainly worth noting. There is also the prospect of refreshment at the inn there. You then descend to an obvious saddle and bear left, winding down among rocks and over more rough grassy slopes to reach the Bachsee lake with its stunning panorama of big mountains and glaciers. The path skirts the left-hand shoreline of this delightful lake with views drawing you on.

Should you decide to take the chair-lift down to Grindelwald from First, walk ahead along the continuing path that keeps above, and to the left of, a second tarn. It leads directly to the upper station of Europe's longest chair-lift (*refreshments*).

To continue the walk all the way down to Grindelwald (another one to one and a half hours from Bachsee) bear right on the path which goes between the two lakes, then cut off to the left into a deep grassy scoop through which runs the Milibach stream. The path is not always very clear through this, but the way is straightforward enough and it leads to a lone farm on a track near a booming cascade. Bear right and follow this track towards Hotel Waldspitz, with signposts that will soon give a choice of paths down to Grindelwald itself; a descent that is in full view of big mountains once more. Squeezing the day dry with beauty.

Route 12: Wilderswil (584m) - Saxeten (1,103m)

Grade:	2
Distance:	5 kilometres
Height gain:	519 metres
Time:	1 hour 45 minutes

The Saxettal lies to the south-west of Wilderswil and is reached from the village by a winding road served by Postbus. The valley is a hidden glen scooped out by a long-vanished glacier, and is backed by a tremendous amphitheatre formed by the converging ridges of the Lobhörner, Schwalmere and Morgenberghorn. There is one village in the valley, and that is Saxeten, a pretty place in a sheltered position set among pastures and with some interesting walking routes leading from it onto the high encircling ridges. This route makes a pleasant morning's walk, giving time for a picnic in the valley, perhaps wandering to look at the waterfalls, before catching the Postbus down again.

From the railway station (*Bahnhof*) in Wilderswil walk up-valley along the main road and pass the entrance to the campsite on the right. The road forks and you take the right branch (the main road to Grindelwald and Lauterbrunnen is the left branch). On coming to a crossroads continue ahead, now walking along the road to Saxeten. It crosses the Saxetbach river and begins to climb in hairpins in the Sytiwald forest, but a footpath now breaks away from the road and goes below it following the river upstream. The path maintains company with the river through the pine forest, steadily gaining height, and recrosses to the true left bank again by way of a small bridge at 911 metres. From here the way steepens until, emerging from the forest at Usserfeld where another path breaks away to the right, you bear left and wander the short distance into Saxeten (*accommodation, refreshments, Postbus*).

Route 13:	Saxeten (1,103m) - Rengglipass (1,879m) - Morgenberghorn (2,249m)

Grade:	3
Distance:	16 kilometres
Height gain/loss:	1,146 metres
Time:	6 hours

Whether you decide to stay a night or two in Saxeten, or travel to it by road (Postbus from Wilderswil), there are some fine outings to tackle that will make a good contrast to the more popular routes of Grindelwald, Lauterbrunnen or Mürren. One, of course, is to tackle Route 12 in reverse, walking down to Wilderswil in a little under one and a half hours. But a more demanding route goes up to the Rengglipass on the ridge between the Rengghorn and Morgenberghorn, and then along the ridge to the summit of the Morgenberghorn itself. From here - and on the ridge leading to it - superb views are to be had looking over the ridge of the Schwalmere to the big Oberland peaks in the south-east.

The Rengglipass lies in the obvious saddle of the ridge to the south-west of Saxeten. On leaving the village continue directly up-valley for about a kilometre passing the few chalets of Innerfeld, then cut off to the right on a *Bergweg* signposted to the pass, climbing steadily up the hillside and passing several alp huts at Ramsermatten (1,520m), Mittelberg (1,633m) and Innerberg (1,789m) where another path breaks away to the right on a high traverse of the hillside. Ignore this and wander on to reach the pass in about two hours fifteen minutes from Saxeten. Now bear right and follow the ridge without undue difficulty to the summit of the Morgenberghorn, reached in another hour or so.

From the top of the mountain a splendid view looks over the Thunersee and Brienzersee, with Interlaken sprawling between them, and then to the south and east where the Oberland wall runs in a huge undulation of snow, ice and rock, with the Schwalmere ridge marking the middle distance. A very fine viewpoint.

Return to Saxeten by the same route, or make a slight diversion by following the traversing path from Alp Innerberg below the pass, roughly northward as far as the hut of Mittelberg (1,650m - note, this is not the same Mittelberg passed on the upward route) and then descending to Saxeten in the valley.

Route 14:   Wilderswil (584m) - Saxeten (1,103m) - Rengglipass
              (1,879m) - Aeschi (862m)

Grade: 3
Distance: 20 kilometres
Height gain: 1,295 metres   Height loss: 1,017 metres
Time: 7-7½ hours

This is one of the noted long walks from Wilderswil, a full day's traverse of the mountains rising to the west of the village with the crossing of the Rengglipass as its highlight. Initially the way follows the route already described in the two previous itineraries into and through the Saxettal, and on as far as the pass. Then comes a steep descent to the Suldtal and a steady valley walk to the delightful village of Aeschi overlooking the lake of Thun. From Aeschi there are buses to Spiez from which town a train may be caught back to Interlaken and Wilderswil. Refreshments are to be had in Saxeten, before the pass, and in two other places on the descent to Aeschi.

Follow Route 12 to Saxeten, and 13 to the Rengglipass, which is reached in about four hours from Wilderswil. Alternatively, take the Postbus to Saxeten, thereby saving nearly two hours of exercise.

From the pass the way descends steeply on the southern side to an alp hut (Renggli) and, ignoring an alternative route which goes to the right, continues down towards the valley bed. A cluster of alp huts is reached near the foot of the slope (Mittelberg, 1,585m - the second so-named on this walk), and the path veers off to lead down-valley on the right bank of the Latrejebach stream. Continue along the right bank beyond the next alp cluster (Schlieri, 1,427m) until a bridge takes you over to the left bank by the lovely cascade of Pochtenfall (1,260m). Descending steeply again through woods you will reach Suld (1,080m; *refreshments*), once more on the right bank. A quiet road/track now takes you all the way to Aeschi (862m; *accommodation, refreshments*), with its much-loved sixteenth century church which is floodlit in the evening.

Other Walks from Wilderswil and/or Saxeten:
One of the more gentle walks from Wilderswil (Grade 1) heads along

the valley on the true right bank of the Lütschine (east side) to the village of Gsteigwiler, on to Zweilütschinen and through the confines of the Weisse Lütschine to **LAUTERBRUNNEN**. This is a two and a half hour walk, along the valley all the way with river, pasture or forest for company throughout.

There's a short (one and a half hour) ascent from Wilderswil to the viewpoint of **ABENDBERG** (or Aabeberg; 1,135m) which is situated on the spur of mountain almost due west of the village at the end of the long ridge of Darliggrat. This is mostly a woodland walk on a good path (Grade 2), with views along the lakes of Thun and Brienz.

On the eastern side of the valley it is also worth considering the possibility of walking up to **SCHYNIGE PLATTE** (1,987m) on a steep path with increasingly fine views. This Grade 3 route (graded high on account of the height to be gained) will take about four and a half hours, and is worth tackling if you plan to spend a night at the hotel at Schynige Platte prior to walking the classic high route to the Faulhorn and Grindelwald (Route 11 above).

Another splendid viewpoint, this time above the Saxettal, is the promontory of **BÄLLEHÖCHST** (2,095m) which looks eastward into the upper Lütschental to the high peaks above Grindelwald, and southward along the Lauterbrunnen valley to the Jungfrau and its neighbours. This walk goes up-valley on a good track beyond Saxeten to the alp of Unterberg (1,455m), and from there along a *Bergweg* heading north-east up the hillside through Unter Bellen to Bällehöchst. This is also Grade 3, and it will take just over three hours from Saxeten.

Route 15:	Grindelwald (Bussalp: 1,780m) - Faulhorn (2,680m)

Grade:	2-3
Distance:	4 kilometres
Height gain:	900 metres
Time:	2 hours 45 minutes

As has already been noted once or twice, the Faulhorn is one of the classic belvedere viewpoints above Grindelwald. It provides one of the highlights of the walk between Schynige Platte and Grindelwald, and makes a worthy destination on its own count. There are three obvious ways of approaching it from Grindelwald; from Bussalp, upper station of the First chair-lift or from Grosse Scheidegg - the last two going by way of the Bachsee lake. All three routes are described in due course. Bussalp itself is a green and pleasant tilted bowl of pasture reached either by footpath (two and a half hours) or by Postbus from the village. It is better to take an early Postbus in order to spend time enjoying the views, and then make an unhurried descent to the valley via Bachsee and the First chair-lift.

The Postbus journey terminates at Bussalp Mittelläger where there is a restaurant. At once there are grand views to enjoy towards the Eiger, Mönch and Jungfrau, and the long Männlichen ridge marking the valley's limits to the south. Walk up the continuing road to Oberläger (2,020m) where the Faulhorn path begins its climb over pastures and rough slopes ahead. There is no difficulty following the route, although it is a little rough under foot in places, and as you gain height so the eastward panorama unfolds to reveal the Finsteraarhorn and Schreckhorn complementing each other amid a sea of jutting peaks.

In a little under two and a half hours from Mittelläger you come onto a bare saddle (2,553m) below and to the south-east of the Faulhorn. Here you bear left and follow a well-trodden path that winds up to the summit of the mountain, steepening in its final pull, in about twenty minutes. There is a hotel and restaurant tucked just below the summit. From the top you gaze steeply north and west to the Brienzersee and off to the Thunersee. But south and east there is a tremendous vista of snow-capped peaks of immense charm, making the ascent well worthwhile.

(**Note**: To descend, retrace your steps to the saddle below, then bear left to follow a clear path down to the Bachsee, and beyond that to the upper station of the First chair-lift (one hour). Alternatively, to walk all the way down to Grindelwald, see directions given under Route 11.)

Route 16:   Grindelwald (First; 2,167m) - Faulhorn (2,680m) -
             Bussalp (1,780m) - Grindelwald (1,034m)

Grade: 3
Distance: 15 kilometres
Height gain: 513 metres   Height loss: 1,646 metres
Time: 5½ hours

This, the second of our routes to the Faulhorn from Grindelwald, is
the one which is probably taken by most walking visitors. The First
chair-lift is Europe's longest and it rises in four stages from the village
- you do not have to change, however. All the way up superb views
are displayed of the Wetterhorn, but once you leave the chair-lift your
back is turned to the views, so it is necessary to keep stopping on the
path to enjoy the mountains behind you.

The valley station of the chair-lift is found just off the main street
towards the eastern end of the village, midway between the railway
station and the church. It is signposted, of course.

On arrival at the upper station, 1,133 metres higher and thirty
minutes after setting out, a signpost directs you onto the clear path to
Bachsee. At first, when you gaze off to the left, you can see a fine
waterfall gushing in a spout from the gentle Milibach pasture whose
stream drains the Bachsee lakes. There is a colony of marmots
inhabiting the rough hillocks and hollows near the path and you
stand a good chance of seeing some of these creatures as you wander
along. The upper slopes are also popular with paragliding enthusiasts.

About forty-five minutes should be sufficient in order to reach the
Bachsee, and the path is clearly marked all the way. It is a wonderful
view from here too; one of the classic panoramas of the Bernese Alps
as you stand at the northern end of the lake and capture reflections of
the Wetterhorn, Schreckhorn and Finsteraarhorn dancing in it. No
matter how many postcards you may have seen of this view in
Grindelwald, the reality is even better.

Beyond the lake the path begins its ascent of the rough slopes of
grass and rock that lead to the saddle of Gassenboden (2,553m) one
and a half hours from First. Just below the saddle there are the ruins
of a low shelter. Bear right and follow the winding stony path up to

Wetterhorn, above Grindelwald

the Faulhorn summit *(accommodation, refreshments)*.

When you've had enough of the views, tear yourself away and retrace your steps to the saddle, and then go off to the right on a path that takes you down to Bussalp. First to the alp huts of Oberläger, then either on a farm road to Mittelläger, or break away from this onto a steep and narrow path that drops over pastures in a short-cut and reaches the road below the Mittelläger restaurant. If you decide on making the return to Grindelwald by bus, wait at the restaurant. If, however, you choose to walk all the way, wander along the road for a few paces, then cut off to the right on a continuing path that crosses pastures and streams and comes to a track. There are several choices of route between here and Grindelwald, each of which is adequately signposted and waymarked. They all take you through patches of forest with views between the trees to the Männlichen ridge opposite, and the dotted chalets on the green sloping hillsides below. It's a fine walk, and with enough variety to draw out pleasures all the way.

Route 17:	Grindelwald (Grosse Scheidegg; 1,962m) - Bachsee (2,265m) - Faulhorn (2,680m)

Grade:	2-3
Distance:	10 kilometres
Height gain:	303 metres
Time:	3½ hours

This route is known locally as the *Höhenweg 2400*. It is advisable from the start to take a Postbus from Grindelwald to Grosse Scheidegg, as to walk all the way would add about two hours or so to the day.

From Grosse Scheidegg follow a clear track heading northwards along the broad ridge dividing Grindelwald's valley from that of Rosenlaui. On reaching a junction of paths at Gratscharem (2,006m) bear left on a steady contour to cross a few streams as you approach the alp huts of Oberläger. Here there is a choice of route; an upper path that winds round to join the main Bachsee track above First, and the main route which is a continuation of the trail from Grosse Scheidegg. This leads to the First chair-lift station in about one and a half hours from Grosse Scheidegg. Now follow directions as for Route 16 up to the Faulhorn.

Route 18:   Grindelwald (First; 2,167m) - Bachsee (2,265m)

Grade:	1
Distance:	3 kilometres
Height gain:	98 metres
Time:	45 minutes

This route is included in an effort to remind casual holidaymakers that it is not essential to dedicate several hours to an energetic walk in order to capture some of the most magical of views. By riding the First chair-lift and then following the broad and easy path to the Bachsee (described in Route 16 above), a superb morning can be spent without getting out of breath. Take a picnic lunch and laze by the lake with the long views.

For an alternative return to Grindelwald, take the Grosse Scheidegg path from First - described in reverse in Route 17. From Grosse Scheidegg you can catch the Postbus down to Grindelwald.

Route 19:   Grindelwald (First; 2,167m) - Uf Spitzen (2,390m) - Bussalp (1,792m)

Grade:	3		
Distance:	9 kilometres		
Height gain:	223 metres	Height loss:	598 metres
Time:	3 hours		

Between the little hanging valley in which the Bachsee is found, and that of Bussalp, there runs a ridge crest extending south-eastward from the Faulhorn. It has no great peaks projecting from it, but bearing in mind the beauty of the views from both Bachsee and Bussalp, it will be evident that from the elevation of the crest there will be an even more extensive panorama to enjoy. This walk, sometimes known as the *Höhenweg 2200*, links the two hanging valleys by a crossing of that ridge.

From the upper station of the First chair-lift walk along the path to Bachsee, but instead of continuing along the right-hand shore, break away to the left on the footpath that crosses between the two lakes (passing a little hut). The path bears left and soon after forks. The path which goes straight ahead descends into the grasslands split by the Milibach stream, while ours (the main, right-hand trail) begins to rise up the hillside. In a little over half an hour from the lake you will come onto the crest where the path forks again. (Superb views.)

Take the right-hand branch over the top of Uf Spitzen, and then begin the descent, heading west. Above the alp huts of Feld you come to yet another trail junction. Take the right-hand path to make a steady hillside traverse, coming down at last to Oberläger, the upper section of Bussalp. Now follow the track down to Mittelläger where there is a restaurant for refreshment, and the possibility of catching the Postbus back to Grindelwald. (Should you choose to walk down, follow direction signs. It is an easy walk with several options. Allow about two hours.)

Route 20: Grindelwald (First; 2,167m) - Waldspitz (1,918m) - Bussalp (1,792m)

Grade:	2		
Distance:	9 kilometres		
Height gain:	250 metres	Height loss:	375 metres
Time:	3 hours 15 minutes		

Known as *Höhenweg 2000*, this fine but easy walk makes an undulating contour of the sunny lower slopes of the crest running south from the Faulhorn. It is, in fact, a more modest version of Route 19, but with magnificent views practically every step of the way.

From the First chair-lift station take the Bussalp path (uphill), but break away to the left at the first opportunity. A good waymarked path swings round the hillside and zig-zags down among rocks, then crosses pastures to the alp of Bachläger (1,980m). Over a stream the way now broadens and makes a contour of the open hillside - with views ahead to the Eiger - as far as the hotel of Waldspitz *(matratzenlager accommodation, refreshments)*. This part of the walk will take about forty minutes.

The way continues, but instead of following the broad track down to Grindelwald, branch off at a path climbing slightly ahead to the right. It leads round the upper edge of woodland clothing a spur of mountainside, and goes as far as the alp huts of Spillmatten (1,863m); then rises again and heads roughly westward, taking the left-hand trail at a junction (the continuing uphill route goes to Bachsee). Before long you join another route descending from the right (the path taken on Route 19) and follow it ahead to Oberläger. Now walk downhill along the track to Mittelläger, where you find the Bussalp restaurant and Postbus halt for Grindelwald.

Route 21:	Grindelwald (First; 2,167m) - Hagelsee (2,339m) - Häxenseeli (2,464m) - Wildgärst (2,890m) - Grosse Chrinne (2,635m) - First

Grade:	3
Distance:	17 kilometres
Height gain/loss:	723 metres
Time:	5½-6 hours

A long and fairly demanding walk, this explores a wild patch of country, but with plenty of scenic rewards. It goes behind the ridge running roughly eastward from the Bachsee where a couple of wintry tarns are found. There are screes and bleak rock-scapes, but pastures too, and long vistas of magical alpine peaks. There are no opportunities for refreshment, nor for shelter in case of bad weather. In inclement weather with poor visibility there could be difficulties with route finding. Choose a good day, take a packed lunch and a drink, and enjoy the rich and varied terrain along the way.

From the First chair-lift station take the Bachsee path for about thirty minutes until a junction of trails has a signpost pointing right to Hagelsee and Wildgärst. (It also gives directions to Axalp and

Brienz for another long walk.) This path heads up the slopes, passing a small pool (Standseeli) and coming to a modest saddle. The way now descends among boulders round the northern end of the Ritzengratli at about 2,400 metres and heads eastward behind the low rocky ridge.

Hagelsee, draped with snow and adorned with ice even through most of the summer, is passed along its northern shore after about an hour and a half. Continue in the same direction, the route rising and falling here and there among rocks and scree to reach the second tarn, Häxenseeli.

Bergweg waymarks lead on, rising steadily to the saddle of Wart (2,706m) slung between the Schwarzhorn to the right, and Wildgärst to the left. Ahead the mountains curve in an arc to lead the eye into the Rosenlaui valley and off to the Haslital beyond it. *(See note below regarding an alternative return route from here.)*

Bear left and wander up to the summit of the Wildgärst (reached in about three and a half hours after setting out from First) where three ridges converge. Fine panoramas extend in all directions; a contrast of lake and snow-peak, of meadow and glacier, forest and rock wall.

Return to the saddle and back along the route towards Häxenseeli, but halfway to the tarn look for waymarks breaking away left (southeast) and follow these to climb to the little pass of Grosse Chrinne. Emerging on the south side of the Widderfeldgrätli ridge follow a path to the head of the Chrinnenboden ski-lift, and continue all the way back to First.

(**Note:** For an alternative return route from the saddle of Wart, cross over and go down the left-hand side of the Blaugletscher, a small and safe glacier with no need for roped precautions. The descent is steep, however, and continues below the glacier veering south-eastward to cross snow patches, scree and rough grass slopes. The path heads down the left-hand side of the Geissbach stream and comes upon a crossing farm track. Follow this to the right, heading south-west now and soon coming to the alp huts of Oberläger (1,941m). Beyond this you come to another broad track (a farm road) which slopes down to Grosse Scheidegg where you can catch a Postbus for Grindelwald.)

Route 22: **Grindelwald (1,034m) - Hotel Wetterhorn (1,223m)-
Gleckstein Hut (2,317m)**

Grade: 3
Distance: 8 kilometres
Height gain: 1,283 metres
Time: 4 hours 45 minutes

The Gleckstein Hut is situated in a very dramatic position high above
the Oberer Grindelwaldgletscher on the slopes of the Wetterhorn.
This walk to it is a steep and somewhat arduous one, and should not
be tackled by inexperienced walkers.

From Grindelwald's main street walk eastward to pass the church
and continue along the road for about one hour to reach Hotel
Wetterhorn. (This is also served by Postbus, and is as far as private
vehicles are allowed to travel on the road to Grosse Scheidegg.) The
hotel has standard bedrooms and also *matratzenlager* accommodation.

Go past the hotel on the Grosse Scheidegg road, and having
rounded a couple of bends a signposted footpath will be seen
breaking away to the right. This path heads across pastures towards
the steep cliffs of the Wetterhorn rising abruptly ahead, and comes to
a crossing path. (This path has started farther up the road from the
Hotel Wetterhorn, by the farm buildings of Unter Lauchbühl.) Turn
right and follow the *Bergweg* as it works its way up a series of limestone
terraces (the Ischpfad), with occasional handrails for safety. Turning
sharply to the south round a corner at Engi (1,670m) the angle eases,
then steepens again high above the glacier. Steep zig-zags lead up
through rocky bluffs at Schlupf, and on to Schonbuhl and scanty
pastures at 2,151 metres. The final approach, turning first north-east
then to the north-west, continues at a good angle, but by comparison
with the earlier path is easy-going.

The hut overlooks an incredible icy mass as glaciers hang
suspended from high, encircling ridges. Behind it the crags of the
Wetterhorn rise in a confusion of rock, snow and ice. There is a
guardian throughout the summer, and refreshments are available to
visitors. The hut can sleep one hundred in its dormitories.

Return to Grindelwald by the same path, but take care especially on the steep descents. Allow three hours for the return.

Route 23: Grindelwald (Pfingstegg; 1,391m) - Milchbach (1,348m) - Hotel Wetterhorn (1,228m)

Grade: 1
Distance: 3 kilometres
Height loss: 163 metres
Time: 1 hour

The Grindelwald-Pfingstegg cableway, whose lower station is found beside a road just below the village church, whisks you in seven minutes out of the village and onto a belvedere path for easy, but often spectacular walks on a terrace high above the meadows. There are geology trails with rocks and outcrops marked for inspection, and an introductory leaflet is available from the tourist office. There are interesting destinations to aim for too. This walk meanders along the northern slopes of the Mättenberg towards the Oberer Grindelwaldgletscher, visits Halsegg and the Restaurant Milchbach overlooking the glacier, before descending to Hotel Wetterhorn where, for those who prefer not to walk back to the village, there is a Postbus halt.

Having reached the upper station at Pfingstegg turn left and follow the clear and easy path as it makes a steady contour of the hillside, sometimes among trees, often with open views looking onto the pastures and chalets below. In about forty minutes you come to Halsegg and Chalet Milchbach, overlooking the glacier caught, like the frozen river it is, in the gorge it has carved ahead and below the Wetterhorn. Here a descending path goes down through woods directly to Hotel Wetterhorn.

Route 24:	Grindelwald (Pfingstegg; 1,391m) - Stieregg (1,650m)

Grade:	1
Distance:	2.5 kilometres
Height gain:	259 metres
Time:	1 hour

I know of few easier walks in the Alps that give a better close-up view of the high mountains, or of glaciers and snowfields, than this one. It is a real gem of a walk along a path carved out of the steep mountain wall above the glacier gorge of the Unterer Grindelwaldgletscher. There are astonishing views of the eastern (Mittellegi) ridge wall of the Eiger, of the icefalls and glaciers that flow down from the Finsteraarhorn and its great arctic basin, and near-views to the huge ice-plastered face of the Fiescherhorn. Stieregg is a restaurant which occupies a little grassy meadow like an oasis in a sea of ice and snow. It's a sun-trap of a place that is difficult to drag yourself away from.

From the upper station of the Pfingstegg cable-car bear right and follow the well-trodden path at first among trees, then out again as the way curves into the gorge scoured out over countless centuries by the lower Grindelwald glacier. It is an exposed path taking you high above the glacial torrent, but is safeguarded by a fence and fixed cable and is broad enough to enable those tending towards vertigo to move comfortably away from the edge. Then the gorge is passed and the way continues, crosses a stream and leads with some ups and downs over an old moraine, turns a cliff and there, directly ahead, is the Restaurant Stieregg.

Note: To walk all the way from Grindelwald, ignoring the use of the cable-car, will occupy about two hours forty-five minutes and will be graded 2. From the centre of the village walk down to the Pfingstegg cable-car station (Pfingsteggbahn) and continue towards the river. Here a signpost directs you via Auf der Sulz for a gently-graded ascent. At first through forest, then over pasture, the way then steepens between more forest patches before easing to Pfingstegg. From here follow directions as above.

Finsteraarhorn from Schreckhorn hut

Route 25: Grindelwald (Pfingstegg; 1,391m) -
Stieregg (1,650m) - Schreckhorn Hut (2,520m)

Grade:	3
Distance:	7 kilometres
Height gain:	1,129 metres
Time:	4½ hours

This continuation of Route 24 is a much more demanding affair and
it calls for a good head for heights as you scale the Rots Gufer, a band
of cliffs bordering an ice-fall. These cliffs are safeguarded by fixed
ladders, cables and metal pegs and they make an entertaining obstacle
on the way to the Schreckhorn Hut. The hut itself is an ideal destination
for a walk. It sits hunched against the lower rock walls of the
Schreckhorn's broken west face and overlooks a vast sweep of glacier
with the Finsteraarhorn rising like a delicate fin to the south. The

whole walk is a stunning exposé of the forces at work to create a wonderland out of the bare bones of the mountains. It is an outing on which you should pack plenty of film for the camera.

Follow directions outlined on Route 24 as far as Restaurant Stieregg. Continue beyond this to resume over the debris of glacial moraine, the path being diverted here and there where the moraine bank has crumbled away, and after climbing a short pitch by steel ladder, come to a second patch of scanty pastureland with a fascinating view ahead to the ice-fall of the Obers Eismeer. The path leads over grass towards the ice-fall where the cliffs of the Rots Gufer rise to the left of it.

The route up the cliffs is well-marked and made safe with various aids, although caution must always be exercised. Roped parties are not uncommon here, and the additional safeguard of a rope may be helpful as a slip could be serious.

Above the barrier of the Rots Gufer the path continues, easier now, to cross streams and old snow patches. Then you come to a cone of moraine and rocks spreading from the left. There are the ruins of a stone hut and beyond these the way seems to be blocked by converging glaciers. The path forks and you bear left to see the Schreckhorn Hut directly above. The way leads to it along a slope of moraine.

The hut has a guardian in summer residence. Food and drinks may be available then, and there are spaces for ninety in its dormitories. Return to Grindelwald by the same path.

Route 26:   Grindelwald (1,034m) - Männlichen (2,343m)

Grade: 2
Distance: 9 kilometres
Height gain: 1,400 metres   Height loss: 91 metres
Time: 4¹/₂-5 hours

Grindelwald's pastoral basin is contained in the west by a hilltop ridge extending northward from the saddle of Kleine Scheidegg. On the Grindelwald side this ridge sweeps down in green tilted meadows, but on its western side a barrier of cliffs plunges dramatically to the mid-height terrace of Wengen before dropping again into the depths of the Lauterbrunnen valley. This ridge then, effectively divides the valleys of the Weisse Lütschine and the Schwarze Lütschine, and at its northern extremity rises to the knobbly top of Männlichen, a noted viewpoint.

Below the summit to the south there's a variety of cableways and ski tows that rise towards a large hotel and restaurant. The gondola lift that swings up to it from Grindelwald is claimed to be the longest in Europe (6.2km and 1,200m difference in altitude) and it takes about half an hour to ride from the valley at Grund to the upper station in two stages. But there are other, pedestrian, ways to reach Männlichen, of course, that will take much longer, and which will give plenty of opportunities to admire the great Eiger Nordwand rising from the pastures - never seen better than from this walk.

Leave Grindelwald and descend to Grund station in the valley below. (This is the station for the railway to Kleine Scheidegg.) Nearby a narrow tarmac road crosses the river (signpost to various directions, including Männlichen) and rises uphill among pastures and goes past a number of attractive chalets as it does. It would be possible to follow this road (a service road) all the way to the Männlichen hotel, but this would make for uncomfortable walking. Several times clearly marked footpaths break away from it, go through little areas of woodland and across pastureland, rising all the time - sometimes quite steeply. It is not necessary to give precise directions here because of the options available, and the generous amount of signposts at junctions. But as you progress up the hillside, so fine views are to be enjoyed off to the left, where the north face of the Eiger soars in a vast wall above the pastures. The main path veers towards the line of the gondola lift and then heads up the slopes parallel to it.

Once you arrive at the Männlichen hotel (footpaths converge here), bear right and wander along the ridge path to the modest summit. A glorious view is to be had, steeply down to Lauterbrunnen's almost gorge-like valley, and up to the Jungfrau and a whole string of snowy peaks dazzling from the south.

Route 27:	Grindelwald (Männlichen; 2,229m) - Kleine Scheidegg (2,061m)

Grade:	1
Distance:	4.5 kilometres
Height loss:	168 metres
Time:	1 hour 20 minutes

This is one of the busiest walks in the book; a minor classic on account of the direct views to the Eiger's great Nordwand, to the Mönch and Jungfrau and, way off beyond Grindelwald, to the Wetterhorn and Schreckhorn. It's an easy walk, suitable for young and elderly alike, and with transportation available at both ends: gondola lift from Grindelwald, cable-car from Wengen, and train to both places from Kleine Scheidegg. In the early weeks of summer the path takes you among a rich assortment of alpine plants, but please don't be tempted to pick any.

No directions are required beyond simply saying head south on the broad, clearly marked path which takes you along the Grindelwald side of the ridge. It makes a steady curve to round a spur coming from the peaklet of Tschuggen (rising from the ridge), passes below the Lauberhorn (famous for the annual championship downhill ski race held here) and brings you directly to the cosmopolitan complex of hotels and railway station of Kleine Scheidegg - complete with brimming crowds, souvenir stands and alpenhorns. The peace of the mountains will not be found here, but Kleine Scheidegg is, nonetheless, one of those places that all who visit Grindelwald should make a pilgrimage to see.

Route 28:	Grindelwald (Männlichen; 2,229m) - Alpiglen (1,616m) - Grindelwald (1,034m)

Grade:	1-2		
Distance:	12 kilometres		
Height loss:	1,278 metres	Height gain:	83 metres
Time:	3 hours		

As with Route 27, this walk begins at the Männlichen hotel by the upper gondola station and, like that walk, enjoys a privileged view of the Eiger's great north face. In fact you wander directly towards it, then virtually beneath it. Alpiglen is, of course, situated in pastureland at the base of that notorious wall, which is somewhat foreshortened from this angle. The paths are clear, well-trodden and popular; the first, as far as Alpiglen, being known locally as the *Höhenweg 1900*.

Leaving the Männlichen gondola lift take the main, broad path heading south towards Kleine Scheidegg (*Höhenweg 2100*). Break away from this on the first path on the left, reached after 10-15 minutes. Descending past a little pool, follow ahead on a traverse of hillside going south-eastward with the Eiger luring you on. In a little over an hour from Männlichen you will come to the farm buildings of Bustiglen, with views down to Grindelwald and across to the Wetterhorn. Ignoring alternatives continue on the main path as it heads south, then swings round to the east and makes towards the line of the Grindelwald-Kleine Scheidegg railway, which it crosses, and reaches Alpiglen (*accommodation, refreshments*) about forty minutes beyond Bustiglen.

The way down to Grindelwald is straightforward from here. The path leads through forest to a broad track, and this in turn brings you to a steep tarmac footpath among chalets. Steeply down the footpath takes you to the valley bed where you cross the river by one of two bridges and climb up the other side to the main village centre. (About one hour twenty minutes from Alpiglen.)

Route 29:	Grindelwald (1,034m) - Kleine Scheidegg (2,061m) - Wengen (1,275m)

Grade:	2-3		
Distance:	15 kilometres		
Height gain:	1,027 metres	Height loss:	786 metres
Time:	5½ hours		

Crossing the Kleine Scheidegg pass is one of the classic Oberland traverse routes. It is not at all difficult. Neither is it of the same magnitude as the Sefinenfurke above Mürren, Hohtürli between Griesalp and Kandersteg, or Bunderchrinde leading to Adelboden. Those passes are high and somewhat remote, while Kleine Scheidegg is a bustle of train-bound tourists and the path on either side will invariably be trailed by other walkers. What makes this crossing special is the close proximity of so many magnificent high peaks. First, of course, there's the Eiger for company, and looking back from Alpiglen, for example, the Wetterhorn looks very fine. Then, at Kleine Scheidegg, the Mönch is a powerful neighbour, while descending to Wengernalp the glorious Jungfrau rises in snow-draped splendour - tossing down her excesses in avalanche after avalanche on warm summer days. And ahead grows the cock's comb of the Gspaltenhorn across Lauterbrunnen's deep shaft. From Grund the climb to Alpiglen is an extremely steep one. Thereafter the angle eases, and the descent to Wengen from the pass is mostly at a comfortable gradient. Refreshments are available at several places along this route.

Go down from Grindelwald's main street to the station of Grund in the valley below. Cross the river nearby over a bridge with a road leading from it, and bear left immediately on a narrow tarmac track/ path that climbs steeply between chalets, crosses the Kleine Scheidegg railway, and maintains its sharp gradient towards Alpiglen. As the chalets begin to thin out, so the way takes you between hay meadows and pastures, often parallel with the railway.

After an hour or so you go through woods, and in the shade of trees leave the main track where it curves to the right, and continue ahead by a path that brings you out beside the railway line, which you follow to Alpiglen (two hours twenty mins; *accommodation, refreshments*).

From Alpiglen to Kleine Scheidegg a much-trodden track, less steep now, takes you beneath the Eiger's north face, the large hotels at the pass looking out of place in that conflict of grass slope and savage mountain wall. There are no difficulties in finding the way, for Kleine Scheidegg is in full view practically every step. You will arrive there about an hour and a half after leaving Alpiglen.

At Kleine Scheidegg (*accommodation, refreshments*), cross the railway line to the left of the station buildings and descend an easy track beside the railway. A signpost directs you to Wengernalp and

Wengen. The views are dominated now by the Mönch and Jungfrau - lovely they are, too. For thirty minutes the track accompanies the railway, then at Wengernalp (four hours twenty mins; *refreshments*) leave the main track to cut down to the left on a narrow path that crosses a steep and rough patch of pasture heading towards forest. Continue with the path into the trees, and you will shortly come to a track that in turn leads to the sunny level terrace of Mettlenalp. From here there are fine views across to the peak of the Gspaltenhorn above Mürren on its shelf of hillside opposite, and to the Breithorn at the head of Lauterbrunnen's valley. Continue along this track as it curves round a shoulder of hillside. It leads all the way to Wengen, reached in about an hour and ten minutes after leaving Wengernalp.

(For details of Wengen, please refer to the section under the heading: Lauterbrunnental.)

Other Walks from Grindelwald:
In addition to those routes described above, Grindelwald has so many more walks available - and variations of walks - that a fortnight's holiday could easily be spent here without duplicating an outing. One worth considering by fit walkers (a Grade 3 route) goes from the First chair-lift station towards Hagelsee (Route 21), then breaks away to the north to explore the green undulating pre-alpine countryside of **AXALP** (a four-hour walk). A bus goes from here to Brienz, where connections are made for the journey back to Grindelwald.

Another route from First goes north-east to cross the ridge above Grosse Scheidegg, wanders to Krinnenboden (Chrinnenboden) and up to the summit of the **SCHWARZHORN** (2,928m), a near-neighbour of Wildgärst, visited on Route 21. Like its neighbour, this too enjoys a very fine panorama.

An alternative route from **ALPIGLEN** to Grindelwald cuts along the upper edge of meadows at the base of the Eiger, over screes and streams and through forest before dropping to the **GLETSCHERSCHLUCHT**, the gorge carved by the Unterer Grindelwaldgletscher. This four-hour walk is another Grade 3.

The tourist information office in Grindelwald publishes a sheet of suggested walks in the neighbourhood. These are mostly short and easy strolls, but with a few more demanding outings included as well. There are also walking maps available with varying degrees of detail, for those who plan to spend all their holiday here and feel that the expense of a full-scale L.S. map is unnecessary.

Mention should be made of the **JUNGFRAUJOCH**, access to which by the famous railway that tunnels through the Eiger and Mönch is a highlight of the holiday for many visitors to Grindelwald. There are modest ascents possible from that elevated position, but for experienced mountaineers only. The Mönch, for example, may be ascended in about two and a half to three hours from the Jungfraujoch station; the Jungfrau (by a much-crevassed route) in three hours. Most visitors here, of course, are content with the magnificent arctic-style views, or at most with a visit to the **MÖNCHSJOCH HUT** (3,650m), an hour from the station. Those with glacier experience may be tempted by two journeys into the ice-world below the Jungfraujoch. One leads in three hours or so to the **KONKORDIA HUT** (2,850m); a magical place situated above Konkordiaplatz, where four glaciers converge to create the Grosser Aletschgletscher, largest in the Alps. The route to these huts should only be undertaken by experienced - and roped - parties. The other route, also for experienced parties only, goes down to Konkordiaplatz, then up the Grosser Aletschfirn to the **HOLLANDIA HUT** (3,238m) and over the glacial saddle of Lötschenlücke to descend to the Lötschental. This route would occupy about eight hours, but is best broken by a night in the Hollandia Hut, which would give the opportunity for an ascent of the Mittaghorn (3,895m) above the hut to the north-west.

LAUTERBRUNNENTAL

Position:	South-west of the Lütschental (Grindelwald's valley), reached from Interlaken via Wilderswil, heading south at the Zweilütschinen fork.
Map:	L.S. 5004 'Berner Oberland' 1:50,000
Bases:	Lauterbrunnen (795m), Wengen (1,275m), Mürren (1,638m), Gimmelwald (1,380m), Stechelberg (910m)

Tourist information:

Verkehrsbüro, 3822 Lauterbrunnen (Tel: 036 5 1955)
Verkehrsbüro, 3823 Wengen (Tel: 036 55 1414)
Verkehrsbüro, 3825 Mürren (Tel: 036 55 1616)
Verkehrsbüro, 3826 Gimmelwald (Tel: 036 55 381)
Verkehrsbüro, 3824 Stechelberg (Tel: 036 55 1465)

The Lauterbrunnental (or Lauterbrunnen Valley) is one of the finest examples of a glacier-carved valley in all the Alps. A steep-walled, U-shaped cleft, it takes its name from the many feathery waterfalls that shower down its vertical sides, one of which (the Staubbach) is probably the most famous in Switzerland.

Travelling south into the Lauterbrunnental the visitor is at first blinkered by its steep and narrow confines, but the forest withdraws as mountain walls begin to reveal themselves, views gradually unfold and become highlighted by the Breithorn at the very head of the valley. Then the Breithorn's lofty neighbouring peaks - each one snow-draped and girded with hanging glaciers - swell themselves into the scene, topped overall by the beautiful Jungfrau; a superbly proportioned and graceful young lady best seen from one of the green terraces that trim the upper walls of the valley. To the left (east) a terrace is occupied by Wengen, to the right Mürren adorns its own shelf, with Gimmelwald perched on the lip of the slope a little lower. But behind Mürren, and further to the north, is another magnificently set village, Isenfluh, a tiny place enjoying one of the best of all views of the Jungfrau - from its glinting snow crown to its grey stony feet

Map 3.
LAUTERBRUNNENTAL

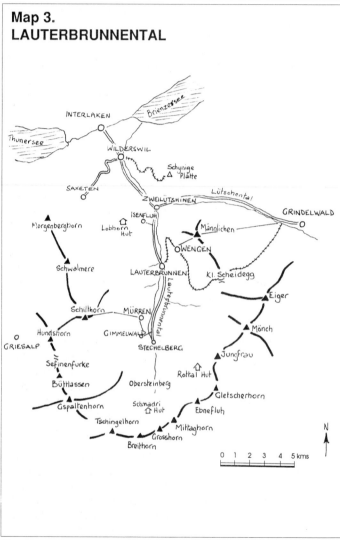

INTERLAKEN

Brienzeesee

Thunersee

WILDERSWIL

Schynige Platte

SAXETEN

ZWEILÜTSCHINEN

Lütschental

GRINDELWALD

ISENFLUH

Lobhorn Hut

Männlichen

Morgenbergliorn

WENGEN

Schwalmere

LAUTERBRUNNEN

Kl. Scheidegg

Schilthorn

MÜRREN

Eiger

Hundshorn

GIMMELWALD

Mönch

GRIESALP

STECHELBERG

Jungfrau

Sefinenfurke

Rottal Hut

Büttlassen

Obersteinberg

Gletscherhorn

Gspaltenhorn

Schmadri Hut

Ebnefluh

Tschingelhorn

Mittaghorn

Grosshorn

Breithorn

N

0 1 2 3 4 5 kms

more than three thousand metres below, seen in one tremendous sweep of the eye.

The Jungfrau's feet rest in the level pastures of Stechelberg where the present valley road ends. South of Stechelberg there are more scanty pastures with dark woods about them, and above these the stony ankles of the mountains, sliced with streams that drain the glaciers and join forces to feed the Weisse Lütschine. This upper basin contains several scenically interesting walks, including a desperately steep haul to the Rottal Hut on the south-western flanks of the Jungfrau.

But the whole valley is a walker's delight; especially on those high terraces above it where alp clusters are inhabited for the summer by peasant farmers grazing their cattle and making cheese. There are mechanical aids to reach these upper regions, too. There are funicular links with Wengen and Mürren, and cableways to the Schilthorn (2,960m) from Stechelberg, Gimmelwald and Mürren and, though possibly only a temporary measure, cable-car from the valley to Isenfluh. (The road which formerly linked it with Lauterbrunnen was cut by avalanche, and at the time of writing has yet to be rebuilt. Until such times as this is reopened, a cableway whisks residents and visitors alike to this otherwise isolated village.)

Main Valley Bases:

LAUTERBRUNNEN (795m) is virtually a one-street thoroughfare with an exceedingly busy railway; a main station on the Interlaken-Wengen-Jungfraujoch line. It has a pretty church with a large bell set before it which is said to have been brought over the mountains from the Lötschental several centuries ago, when the inhabitants of that valley decided to escape the severity of their church rulers in favour of a more relaxed regime in the Lauterbrunnen Valley. This migration involved a number of families - including their cattle - who descended into the Lauterbrunnental by way of the Tschingel Pass and the glaciers that sweep down from the Breithorn. Not far from the lovely slender-spired church Lauterbrunnen has a large car park (also a considerable amount of parking space in a multi-storey near the station) of value to short-stay visitors. There are hotels in the main street, plus *pensions, matratzenlager* accommodation and holiday flats.

There are two very large campsites offering first-rate facilities. The village has several shops, restaurants, banks and a tourist information office. Postbuses run from here to Stechelberg; there are rail links with Interlaken, Wengen, Kleine Scheidegg and Jungfraujoch, and with Mürren via Grütschalp.

WENGEN (1,275m) is noted as much as a winter resort as for its summer attractions, but it is thankfully spared the intrusive mechanisation that so marks many another downhill ski resort. In fact Wengen sits prettily on its shelf, bright with window boxes and with a privileged near-view of the Jungfrau. Reached by funicular from Lauterbrunnen (or by steep woodland paths), it is a traffic-free village - free of traffic, that is, except for a fleet of electrically-powered, softly buzzing vehicles that serve its hotels and shops. There is an abundance of accommodation; twenty-eight hotels and pensions, together with 2,500 beds in holiday flats and chalets. (No camping.) There are plenty of shops, restaurants, banks and a tourist information office; also cinema and discos. A cable-car links Wengen with Männlichen high above, and the railway serves Kleine Scheidegg for the Jungfraujoch, and/or Grindelwald.

MÜRREN (1,638m) complements Wengen and is set upon a sunny perch on the western shelf of mountainside above the valley. Behind it a broad sloping plateau arced around with high mountains makes for fine walking. There are summits to aim for, passes to cross, meadows to amble through. And all the time with astonishing views of Eiger, Mönch and Jungfrau, of the Breithorn and Gspaltenhorn and, from some places, the Wetterhorn way off beyond the Eiger. Like Wengen, Mürren is also famed as a ski resort, and it was here that Arnold Lunn introduced the modern slalom in 1922. It was in Mürren that the Kandahar Ski Club was founded two years later, and the now world-famous 'Inferno' race from the Schilthorn's summit to the depths of Lauterbrunnen had its first outing in 1928. (Arnold Lunn is remembered here with a memorial stone placed in a small garden near the railway station.) But for users of this guidebook there can be no doubt that as a centre for a mountain walking holiday, Mürren takes a lot of beating. Although rather on the expensive side, it has no shortage of accommodation - hotels, holiday apartments and chalets.

Matratzenlager accommodation is available in a couple of rustic mountain inns above the village. There are various shops, banks, restaurants and sporting facilities, and a tourist information office. A cable-car travels from Mürren to the Schilthorn where there is a revolving restaurant enjoying a wonderful panorama; there's also a funicular from the village to Allmendhubel for walking possibilities. The village which, like Wengen, is also traffic-free, is reached by funicular from Lauterbrunnen to Grütschalp and railway from there.

GIMMELWALD (1,380m) is considerably smaller and less developed than its more illustrious neighbour, Mürren, and occupies a steep slope of hillside a short distance below it to the south, near the entrance to the Sefinental. Also traffic-free, a cableway rises to it from Stechelberg. It has minimal accommodation, but is cheaper than Mürren. There are just two *pensions* with thirty beds, holiday flats and a youth hostel, limited shopping facilities, but there is a tourist information office.

STECHELBERG (910m) lies towards the southern end of the valley at the roadhead. A quiet, unobtrusive place, it makes a fine walking centre in its own right with a network of footpaths heading up into the mountains, or along the valley bed. Reached by Postbus from Lauterbrunnen, Stechelberg has hotel and *pension* accommodation, 150 beds in holiday flats, a campsite and the valley station for the cable-car rising to Gimmelwald and the Schilthorn. (There is also a campsite to the north, at Sandbach.)

Other Bases:
To the north of Lauterbrunnen, and lodged on another shelf of hillside above the valley, **ISENFLUH** (1,081m) has pension accommodation, superb views and some grand, if steep, walking country on its doorstep.

Mountain Huts:
There are few mountain huts accessible to walkers based in the Lauterbrunnental, but those that are will reward a visit for the fit. Of particular note is the **ROTTAL HUT** (2,755m) high above Stechelberg, from which it is reached by an excessively steep trail in about five and

a half hours. This hut, owned by the Interlaken Section of the SAC, gazes at the Ebnefluh, Mittaghorn, Grosshorn, Breithorn and Tschingelhorn and their peeling mass of glaciers. There is a herd of ibex resident nearby among the barren rocky slopes above the hut, and some of these often come down to graze in full view.

Also accessible from Stechelberg, the **SCHMADRI HUT** (2,263m) is a small refuge lodged below the glaciers that are draped down the face of the Breithorn. The route to it is usually made via the little tarn of Oberhornsee, but there's an alternative return route via the north-east to enable walkers to enjoy a circular outing.

The **MUTTHORN HUT** (2,901m) is set among glaciers under the little rocky island of the Mutthorn at the head of the Tschingelfirn, south-west of Stechelberg. An amazing site for a hut, about eight hours from Stechelberg, walkers should only attempt to reach it if they are experienced in glacier travel and are well-equipped.

At Boganggen, an alp midway between Gimmelwald and the Sefinenfurke, the **ROTSTOCK HUT** (2,039m) is owned by the Stechelberg Ski Club and has places for fifty-five. It is reached in a little over two hours from Mürren.

The **SCHILTHORN HUT** (2,432m), as its name suggests, serves the peak of the Schilthorn and is found in the little hanging valley of the Engetal below the Schwartzgrat, while further north the **LOBHORN HUT** (1,955m) is reached in three hours from Isenfluh. This small, thirty-place refuge, has a glorious view towards the Jungfrau and is visited on an entertaining walk that goes up to the Sulsseeli tarn. The hut, owned by the Lauterbrunnen Section of the SAC, is normally only available for use by members.

In addition there are various hotels and mountain inns scattered in isolated country above the Lauterbrunnental, in particular at **OBER STEINBERG** (1,778m) above Stechelberg where there is *matratzenlager* accommodation to be had as well as standard bedrooms, and at **SUPPENALP** above Mürren with a couple of rustic mountain inns offering beds and dormitory places.

Route 30:	Isenfluh (1,081m) - Sulsseeli (1,920m) - Lobhorn Hut (1,955m)

Grade:	3
Distance:	5 kilometres
Height gain:	874 metres
Time:	2 hours 45 minutes

Mürren's vista of peaks at the head of the Lauterbrunnental is justifiably famous, and walks are given elsewhere to exploit those panoramas. Less well-known are Isenfluh and Sulwald, yet they too command a magnificent vista of big mountains: Eiger, Mönch and Jungfrau in particular from a high shelf of hillside way above the valley near its junction with that of the Lütschental. This walk makes the most of those views as it visits a 'lost' tarn and an idyllically-situated mountain hut. It's a steep walk that could be eased by taking the cable-car from Isenfluh to Sulwald, thus saving about 560 metres of height and one hour fifteen minutes of walking time.

Note: At the time of writing the road from Lauterbrunnen to Isenfluh is closed. It was cut by avalanche some time ago and its replacement has not yet been built. Information is that this should be complete by the early 1990s, but until that is so you can reach Isenfluh either by temporary cable-car from the valley midway between Lauterbrunnen and Zweilütschinen, by footpath from Zweilütschinen (one hour forty-five minutes), or by way of the funicular Lauterbrunnen-Grütschalp, followed by easy footpath in one hour ten minutes.

Isenfluh is only a small village with limited accommodation and refreshments available. Steep meadows rise above it, while forests cling to the cliffs that plunge into the valley below; views to the Jungfrau are stunning. The path to Sulwald is well-signposted from the village; it climbs through the meadows between farm buildings at a severe gradient from the very start. Soon going through forest the way winds ever-upward with clear directions at all trail junctions. After about one hour fifteen minutes you emerge from the dark shadowed woods onto the open pastures of Sulwald (1,520m), a scattered hamlet of chalets and haybarns with views that will stop you in your tracks.

Follow a narrow roadway past the top station of the Isenfluh cableway and then cut up to the right through more meadows (rich with flowers in the early summer) on the path signposted to Sulsalp and the Lobhorn Hut. It soon enters forest again and climbs on until coming to a clearing where just below you see the alp buildings of Kühbodmen (Chüebodmi on the map). One path drops to it, but we continue uphill and before long leave the forest in favour of a sloping meadowland with ribs of white limestone jutting from it. An obvious saddle is seen ahead, and on the hilltop above it to the right, the Lobhorn Hut can be made out.

Wandering up and across this meadowland yet more extraordinary views will be enjoyed. These include the Wetterhorn, as well as Eiger, Mönch and Jungfrau, and the deep, deep Lauterbrunnental now some 1,200 metres below.

The path, narrow here, goes through the saddle and a little valley beyond following the Sulsbach stream. The smooth rock face of the unfortunately- named peak of Ars rises above to the left, and beyond that the five prongs of the Lobhörner. The path brings you to the alp of Suls (1,910m) with its farmhouse and cattle byres, and then branches to the right, over a bluff, and comes to the lake of Sulsseeli (1,920m; 1 hour 15 minutes from Sulwald).

Go round the right-hand side of the lake and continue on the path for about two minutes, before you cut off to the right (red and white paint flashes) across a grassy bowl, and then you will reach the Lobhorn Hut with its commanding panorama; not only to the well-known Oberland peaks to the south, but south-west to the five fingers of the Lobhörner. It is a delightful situation.

To descend, follow a faint path to the right of the hut. This drops among limestone shelves clustered with gentians in season, then through trees, and comes to the path beside the Sulsbach stream again. Bear left and retrace your upward route. Allow one and a half hours to Isenfluh.

The Jungfrau from Wengen (Lauterbrunnental).
Chalet in Wengen (Routes: 38, 39, 40).

Balmhorn Hut above the Gasterntal (Route 73).
Lac Retaud (Routes: 111,112).

Route 31:	Isenfluh (1,081m) - Bällehöchst (2,095m) - Saxeten (1,103m)

Grade:	3		
Distance:	14 kilometres		
Height gain:	1,014 metres	Height loss:	992 metres
Time:	6 hours		

This long and somewhat tiring day's walk makes a crossing of the mountain ridge that forms an effective divide between the Sulstal and that of the Saxettal (already described under Routes 12-14 - Lütschental section). For those who would prefer to reduce the walking time, cable-car may be used from Isenfluh to Sulwald. There are no refreshment possibilities between Sulwald and Saxeten.

Follow Route 30 as far as the lake of Sulsseeli (1,920m; two and a half hours from Isenfluh), continue on the path along the right-hand (eastern) end, and beyond it to traverse across the north-eastern slopes of the Hoji Sulegg. The path is clear and it rises gently to a saddle midway between Hoji Sulegg and Bällehöchst. Bear right at the saddle and wander to the summit of Bällehöchst (2,095m) which you should reach about one hour twenty minutes from the lake. The views are impressive.

Return to the saddle, then slope down on a continuing path over the Ballenalp, coming first to the huts of Usser Bällen after about half an hour from the summit, then some way lower reach the huts of Hinder Bällen. The path forks. Take the left-hand trail to Underberg (1,455m) in the upper bowl of the Saxettal, where you join the main valley track down to the little village of Saxeten (*accommodation, refreshments*). From here you can take the Postbus down to Wilderswil, and train from there back towards Lauterbrunnen.

Route 32:	Isenfluh (1,081m) - Soustal (1,700m) - Grütschalp (1,486m)

Grade:	3	
Distance:	10 kilometres	
Height gain:	822 metres	**Height loss:** 417 metres
Time:	4-4½ hours	

This is one of those quiet 'back-country' walks that leads into a fine soft valley somewhat off the beaten track, where the daily life of alpine farming goes on without much tourist disturbance. It enjoys many of the long views noted in the two previous routes, but also develops specific viewpoints of its own.

Follow directions towards the alp of Suls (1,910m; two hours twenty minutes) as given in Route 30. Just before reaching it, however, cross the stream flowing through the narrow valley and onto the path on the opposite side. This heads eastward to round a spur of mountain in a lengthy traverse, soon delving among trees and shrubbery with tantalising views every now and then. The path swings round the steep mountainside and into the mouth of the Soustal, but high above it. The trail is muddy in places (apparently it always is), having been regularly churned by cattle.

Continue towards the head of the valley, by now heading south-west and with the revolving restaurant on the summit of the Schilthorn seen clearly some way ahead. (Interesting to speculate on the numbers of visitors crowded up at that point while you have the valley virtually to yourself.) Ignore an alternative path that breaks away to the left to descend into the valley by a series of tight zig-zags, but continue ahead on the main path and wander past the alp buildings of Nater-wengli (1,776m). Beyond these you enter woods again, then the path takes you down easily into the valley.

The Soustal is soft, green and pastoral; a back-country 'lost' valley with isolated farms, a clear-running stream and charming views. At its head the Kilchfluh Pass gives access to the valley of Spiggengrund, which in turn leads to the lovely Kiental.

Once in the Soustal proper wander down it on the left bank of the stream, now heading north-east. Passing the first farm a bridge takes you over to the right bank. (But if you need refreshment, continue on the left bank for about 200 metres beyond the bridge where another farm advertises milk, tea and coffee. This also has a bridge over the stream.) Having gained the right bank continue down-valley but aim half-right across the pasture (there is a faint trail in the grass) towards trees. There are occasional red and white paint flashes for guidance. The path becomes clearer, through trees and out to another farm building at a junction of trails. Go left in the direction of Grütschalp Station which is given as an hour away.

Pass a tarn and more farm buildings below to your left and follow the good clear trail mostly through forest, all the way to Grütschalp. Here you can either take the funicular down to Lauterbrunnen, or follow the signposted path which descends very steeply through forest, and will give another hour's exercise.

Route 33: Lauterbrunnen (795m) - Grütschalp (1,486m)

Grade:	**3**
Distance:	**3 kilometres**
Height gain:	**691 metres**
Time:	**2 hours**

This very steep walk to the first shelf of hillside above Lauterbrunnen to the west is an alternative to the Grütschalp funicular. It is a stiff, lung-stretching pull that should be taken at an easy pace. Practically the whole way is through forest.

The path begins near a bakery in Lauterbrunnen's main street a short distance up-valley from the railway station. It takes you up past a number of houses, over a stream and on a traverse towards the right. Ignore a left-hand alternative, go under the railway and then in tight zig-zags uphill through the forest. After about fifty minutes you will come to Alpweg (1,086m) and a junction of trails. Take the left-hand trail which continues its steep upward route, crossing the funicular again and with more zig-zags eventually brings you to another crossing path. Go right here, crossing the railway yet again, then bear left for the final winding uphill to Grütschalp Station.

Route 34:	Grütschalp (1,486m) - Mürren (1,638m)

Grade:	1
Distance:	4 kilometres
Height gain:	152 metres
Time:	1 hour 10 minutes

A delightful, easy walk, on a good path with magnificent views, this makes a fine introduction for newcomers to the area, a prelude to many walks worth tackling. From Grütschalp to Mürren is the gentlest kind of walking you may hope to find in the Alps - almost without any steep ascent, but with a most exquisite panorama that takes in the Jungfrau, Ebnefluh, Mittaghorn, Grosshorn and Breithorn. There's also the spear wedge of the Eiger and the snowy bulk of the Mönch and, as you draw nearer to Mürren, the lovely Gspaltenhorn too. The valley plunges away in a spectacular gulf; there are forests alive with birdsong and pastures rich in flowers.

Either take the funicular from Lauterbrunnen to Grütschalp, or walk up the steep path as per Route 33. Leaving the upper station cross the railway tracks and take the footpath heading left, signposted to Mürren. No further descriptions are necessary, except to say that at every path junction adequate signs are given and it's almost impossible to lose the way. At Winteregg refreshments are available. For some of the way the path runs parallel with the railway, and eventually brings you directly into Mürren by the station.

Route 35:	Grütschalp (1,486m) - Mürren (1,638m) - Gimmelwald (1,414m) - Stechelberg (910m)

Grade:	2		
Distance:	9 kilometres		
Height gain:	152 metres	Height loss:	728 metres
Time:	2¹/₂ hours		

Another first-rate introductory walk, this would make a good initial outing after arrival in the area. There's nothing difficult about it, although the descent from Gimmelwald to Stechelberg has a few steep stretches to tighten those muscles just above the knees unaccustomed to such gradients. Views are quite breathtaking and there is little doubt that the basic walking time will be considerably exceeded by virtue of the need to keep stopping to gaze in wonder at the scenery.

Take Route 34 as far as Mürren. At the station the street forks ahead. Take the left fork. (For tourist information bear right.) As you wander along the street look for a signpost directing you left towards Gimmelwald. The way soon descends out of the village between steeply sloping meadows, and comes to the time-worn village of Gimmelwald *(accommodation, refreshments)* about half an hour or so from Mürren.

Continue through the village on a path signposted to Stechelberg, passing as you do the *Jugendherberge* (youth hostel) on your left. The path descends very steeply past farms and haybarns, then over a stream flowing through the Sefinental where you bear left. The path continues down, now through forest, and nearly always quite steeply. Eventually it brings you out at Stechelberg, *(accommodation, refreshments)* at the roadhead in the valley. Either catch a Postbus back to Lauterbrunnen, or wander down-valley along the left-bank of the river for a pleasant one and a half hour extension to the walk.

Route 36:   Lauterbrunnen (795m) - Stechelberg (910m)

Grade: 1
Distance: 7 kilometres
Height gain: 115 metres
Time: 1 hour 45 minutes

A very gentle walk that gives plenty of opportunities to enjoy the valley at leisure, with the dazzling smoke of numerous waterfalls cascading from the steep walls, and consistently lovely views of the big peaks ahead. This is especially fine on a summer's evening when the snow peaks at the southern end of the valley catch the alpenglow - although you'll probably have to walk back again as no doubt the last Postbus will have left Stechelberg long before.

Walk along Lauterbrunnen's main street heading south, ignoring the left-hand sweep of the road where it forks just before the village church. The Staubbach Falls are seen showering from the right almost from the start. Continue ahead along a peaceful lane cutting through meadows and passing several attractive chalets, with the Breithorn looking particularly handsome directly before you. At Stegmatten the lane crosses the Weisse Lütschine to join the main valley road, but here you take the riverside footpath, still remaining on the true left bank (west side). Continue to Stechelberg (*accommodation, refreshments, Postbus*).

Route 37:   Lauterbrunnen (795m) - Wengen (1,275m)

Grade:	**2-3**
Distance:	**3 kilometres**
Height gain:	**480 metres**
Time:	**1¹⁄₂ hours**

In many ways this route matches the steep walk from Lauterbrunnen to Grütschalp (Route 33), except that more views are shown through the trees and, just below the village, there's a splendid little alpine meadow that is thick with wild flowers in the early summer. It is a steep walk, though, but an enjoyable alternative to the often-crowded train that winds its way up the hillside.

The walk begins by the railway station in Lauterbrunnen and goes between the station and its nearby multi-storey car park, crosses the river, passes some chalets and begins to climb the hillside. Where there are junctions signposts direct the way. Soon zig-zags gain height in the shade of trees, sometimes with the railway for company. Then the forest gives way to an open meadow and you gaze down across it to the top of the Staubbach Falls.

A fine view. Now Wengen is seen just above you and the way enters the village, still quite steeply, past a number of houses with the Jungfrau gazing down in a gleam of snow and ice.

Route 38:   Wengen (Männlichen; 2,229m) - Wengen (1,275m)

Grade:	2
Distance:	4 kilometres
Height loss:	954 metres
Time:	2 hours

There are a few reasonably level walks to be had from Wengen. These wander along the hillside shelf across pastures and through the woods. There are fine viewpoints to be visited too, but it must be said that with the mountainsides being so steep and high above the Lauterbrunnental, it is inevitable that many of the best outings will require either steep ascents or descents. This is one of them. High above Wengen the Männlichen-Lauberhorn ridge makes a formidable wall, crusted here and there with avalanche protection fences. A path links the village with this ridge, but so steep and arduous is it in places that it may be better to walk it from top to bottom. The views are every bit as enjoyable after all. So the suggestion is to take the cable-car from Wengen to Männlichen, wander from the upper cable-car station to the Männlichen summit (a short and easy stroll), then wander back down to the village. On the way up in the cable-car one gains a tremendous respect for the power of the glaciers that carved Lauterbrunnen's deep, deep valley, while from the Männlichen ridge the great panorama overlooking Grindelwald's green pastoral basin is seen in all its glory - with Wetterhorn, Schreckhorn, Eiger, Mönch and Jungfrau all competing for favour. Männlichen is a great favourite with paragliding enthusiasts, and you may see a number of gaily-coloured parachutes sailing quietly over the valley as you walk.

On leaving the cable-car turn right (left for the Männlichen summit), and before coming to the hotel and restaurant with its fine view, cut through the ridge on a descending path that drops steeply at first, then slopes off a little more easily, beside avalanche fences and beneath the cableway, the valley seeming a very long way down. (At this point you are more than twelve hundred metres above it.) Initially the descent is northward, the gradient quite comfortable. Then the path zig-zags steeply to a junction (Parwengi; 1,864m) and you can either continue northwards again before dropping once more through woods to reach Wengen via the alp huts of Ussri Allmi, or bear left for a longer hillside traverse above the treeline before cutting down to the village. If the latter route is chosen, add another twenty minutes to the overall time.

Route 39:	Wengen (Männlichen; 2,229m) - Kleine Scheidegg (2,061m) - Wengernalp (1,874m) - Wengen (1,275m)

Grade:	2
Distance:	11 kilometres
Height loss:	954 metres
Time:	3 hours

This walk is an adaptation of Routes 27 and 29, both of which were described under the previous chapter covering Grindelwald and the Lütschental, but is given here in order to remind visitors to Wengen of the possibilities available to them. It is a classic of the region.

Ride the Männlichen cable-car from Wengen, and on leaving the upper station turn right and follow the clear, broad path that runs along the left-hand edge of the ridge with the Eiger's great north face directly ahead. You will pass a large hotel and restaurant and the gondola lift that has risen from Grindelwald. The path will invariably be busy, and in the early weeks of summer is bordered by masses of alpine flowers. It makes a long curve round the slopes of Tschuggen, passes below the Lauberhorn and reaches Kleine Scheidegg *(accommodation, refreshments, railway to Grindelwald, Wengen and Jungfraujoch)* after about one hour twenty minutes.

Veer right to cross the railway line just to the left of the main station buildings and follow a broad track that goes down beside the railway. The Mönch and Jungfrau dominate the scene. Just before you reach Wengernalp Station *(refreshments)* half an hour below Kleine Scheidegg, cut off to the left on a steep and narrow path that crosses a rough slope of pasture. You will come to woodland and a track that leads to an open terrace of pasture at Mettlenalp. The track continues now, rounds a spur of hillside and at an easy angle makes a steady approach to Wengen, reached in a little over an hour from Wengernalp.

Route 40:   Wengen (1,275m) - Wengernalp (1,874m)

Grade:	2
Distance:	4 kilometres
Height gain:	599 metres
Time:	2 hours

"Surely the Wengern Alp must be precisely the loveliest place in this world," wrote Leslie Stephen in *The Playground of Europe.* "It is delicious to lie upon the short crisp turf ... to watch a light summer mist driving by, and the great mountains look through its rents at intervals from an apparently impossible height above the clouds."

The Wengernalp is indeed a wonderful place from which to gaze at the great mountains. It is a great place, too, from which to gaze at the avalanches that peel off the face of the Jungfrau almost hourly on a bright summer's afternoon. A splendid place for a picnic; listening to the crickets, catching the rich earthy fragrance of damp turf and wild flowers, feeling the sun on your brow and a mountain breeze in your hair, glorying in the wonder of the high Alps.

Of course, you can ride the railway and capture the same views, the same sensations. But much better it is to earn these gifts by walking to them.

From the railway station in Wengen walk along the street which runs parallel to the Kleine Scheidegg line and on its left-hand side, and then bear right to pass beneath the line and continue past several hotels and flower-bright chalets, steadily gaining height. You soon ease out of the village with the Jungfrau drawing you on. A broad track leads without difficulty or diversion among pastures and through patches of forest, heading roughly southward and rising all the time at a comfortable angle. Rounding a spur of mountain high above the cleft of the Trümmeltal you come to the pastures of Mettlenalp. Here you bear left, taking a path away from the track, over pasture and into woods that lead directly to Wengernalp, with its farm buildings, railway above and big mountains hanging overhead.

Route 41: Stechelberg (910m) - Rottal Hut (2,755m)

Grade:	3
Distance:	6 kilometres
Height gain:	1,845 metres
Time:	5 hours

The Rottal Hut is perched high above the upper basin of the Lauterbrunnental under the south-west arête of the Jungfrau. Its position is remarkable for the beauty of its views. Whilst around the hut there are slopes of boulder and rubble, the little hanging valley of Rottal is cupped in a horseshoe of high peaks adorned with ice. Glaciers hang suspended from the near-vertical walls, cornices make sharp lips to the ridges, while just below the hut more icefields are imperceptibly carving out new valleys, new landscapes for tomorrow.

In order to walk up to the Rottal Hut it is advisable to set out early. It's a very steep path - severe even - and with one section depending on a fixed rope to overcome the obstacle of a gully splitting a sheer rock face. Just below the hut there is also a steep snow slope to negotiate. This is probably the most demanding route in the book, but it is one that is highly recommended to all who are fit, have a head for heights and experience of high mountain wandering. There are some objective dangers to face, though, and it is right to draw the reader's attention to them. Stonefall is a hazard you could face on the ascent of the gully, and the snow slope below the hut could be dangerous in melting - or icy - conditions. If you have an ice axe with you, take it.

The walk begins at the valley roadhead in Stechelberg and follows a broad paved footpath up-valley with the Weisse Lütschine rushing along in its bed to the right. It leads between meadows and trees and after about eight minutes comes to a side stream where a footpath branches off left, signposted to Stufenstein and the Rottal Hut.

It climbs steeply with a number of zig-zags, then bears round to the right on a rising traverse with lovely views ahead to the Breithorn. When you come to an alp hut at 1,585 metres head to the left to enter a broad gully steepening into a tight wedge ahead. Going through a fenced enclosure bear right to cross the stream coming down the

Approach to the Rottal hut

gully. The path then resumes its steep ascent, now with the icefall of the Rottal's glacier seen way above, and the icy face of the Mittaghorn off to the right. The stony wastes are relieved by shelves of pasture, but these soon give way to a wilderness of scree and rock, with vertical crags running in a line above.

The route heads up to the base of those crags and wanders along them to the right until coming to a neat gully with a fixed chain hanging down it. If there are others on the cliffs above, take shelter until all danger of stonefall is passed. The ascent of the gully is straightforward with the aid of the chain and/or fixed ropes, but there are a number of narrow ledges littered with grit and stones.

Once above the gully the path resumes in easy windings up a boulderscape of one-time moraine, then along the crest of a moraine wall above the glacier. Wander along the crest heading east into the Rottal corrie, the hut now seen some way ahead. The path brings you to a wall of rock heading a steep but short snow slope. Cross this slope at its upper edge, then scale a small cliff with another fixed rope and emerging at the top you will see the hut nearby.

The Rottal Hut can officially accommodate forty-six in its dormitories and has a guardian in residence at weekends during the height of the summer season. The descent route is by the same path used on the ascent. Allow three hours from the hut to Stechelberg.

Route 42: Stechelberg (910m) - Ober Steinberg (1,778m)

Grade:	**2**
Distance:	**5 kilometres**
Height gain:	**868 metres**
Time:	**2¹/₂ hours**

Ober Steinberg is a seemingly remote belvedere in the upper basin of the Lauterbrunnen Valley. It is found on the south-western hillsides beaming out at the amphitheatre of peaks that crowd the valley head. To the north-east there's the Jungfrau, to the south the Breithorn and to the south-west the Tschingelhorn with the rock towers of the Lauterbrunnen Wetterhorn standing proud. The outlook is one of glacier and talus, of moraine and pine and alpenrose; a raw vista that has been tamed and tended only in rare patches. There's a mountain inn lodged in seclusion with private beds and *matratzenlager* accommodation, too, and to spend a night there is to grow intimate with the unquiet mystery of the hills.

This walk to it is rather steep in places, but is graded 2 since there is nothing difficult about it; nor is it too long. In several places on the way there are opportunities for refreshment.

From the roadhead wander up-valley to the left of the Weisse Lütschine on a paved path. This rises easily between meadows and woods and soon brings you to a bridge across the river. On the true left bank the path goes over a broad crossing track and continues ahead. (During researches for this guide the track was being developed, but it was not possible then to ascertain what future there is for it. Should it be upgraded, or pushed farther up-valley, it is anticipated that signposts will clearly advertise the footpath route from it.) The onward path again meets the track and follows it winding to the right until after about 200 metres another path breaks off to the right and is signposted to Trachsellauenen.

This path soon crosses rough pasture with a small farm set in it, and ten minutes later comes to Berghaus Trachsellauenen (1,203m; *accommodation, refreshments*). Around it there is a huddle of buildings with a waterfall seen ahead. The trail forks and you take the right-hand branch next to a barn. Wandering through woods you come to another junction of tracks, both signposted to Ober Steinberg. (The right-hand path climbs steeply in zig-zags, the left-hand trail is less frenetic.) Bear left and continue on the path which becomes almost a stairway of rocks among a damp and lush vegetation.

At the next junction continue straight ahead and leave the woods to cross an open area littered with avalanche debris, following the stream into an amphitheatre of mountains - the waterfall seen earlier looking particularly fine as it sprays down the hillside ahead from the lip of a cirque.

Pass the farm of Scheuerboden (1,379m), beyond which a long and steepish climb through more woods brings the path to another junction at Wildegg (1,560m) where you branch right for Ober Steinberg. The final section of the walk (about forty minutes) brings you into the open on a steeply winding path with the inn seen above.

Route 43: Ober Steinberg (1,778m) - Oberhornsee (2,065m)

Grade:	2
Distance:	2.5 kilometres
Height gain:	287 metres
Time:	1 hour 10 minutes

This short walk could easily be tacked onto Route 42 for added interest, if the plan is to do a loop trip from Stechelberg. (See also Route 44 for a continuation from Oberhornsee back to Stechelberg.) Oberhornsee is an attractive little tarn trapped among boulders and green moraine below the turmoil of glaciers that streams from the Tschingel Pass, Tschingelhorn and Breithorn. From it there is an unusual view of the south-western flanks of the Jungfrau. The tarn, and a good proportion of this upper section of the valley, is protected as a nature reserve.

Leaving Hotel Obersteinberg head to the right (south-westward - on the approach path) and at the signpost junction a short distance away bear right again on a splendid hillside traverse that follows a gentle contour across flower-rich slopes, a steep drop on the left and the constant boom of cascades in your ears. After a while the path descends to a stream, the Tschingel Lütschine, crosses it on a wooden bridge and climbs over rough pastures. Steadily gaining height you pass waterfalls and cross more streams, then finally climb up and over a grassy bluff to find the little tarn of Oberhornsee nestling among the boulders. The water is a beautiful deep blue, above are glaciers and moraine banks to provide a wild yet lovely scene.

Route 44:   **Ober Steinberg (1,778m) - Schmadri Hut (2,263m) - Stechelberg (910m)**

Grade:	3		
Distance:	8 kilometres		
Height gain:	485 metres	**Height loss:**	1,353 metres
Time:	6 hours		

This alternative return to Stechelberg is an interesting one that leads through some wild country and visits a small mountain hut. It should be borne in mind though, that there is one section of the route that passes below glacial séracs that from time to time crash down and send their ice chunks across the trail.

Follow Route 43 to the tarn of Oberhornsee. Walk along its northern shore and down to a spongy plain bordered on either side by rocks and grassy bluffs. Turn left and follow the stream northward, on its left bank, until you come to a plank footbridge. Cross the stream and follow paint flashes leading steeply up a slope to a knoll with fine views from the top. Above hang the glaciers with their teetering séracs. Now descend to cross the Schmadribach stream by a second plank footbridge, beyond which the trail climbs among a mixture of pasture and moraine to reach the Schmadri Hut. This is a splendid setting for such a small refuge. The big mountains tower overhead; there are views out to the far valley and over wild terrain. (Owned by the Academic Alpine Club of Bern, the hut has no guardian. It can sleep a dozen.)

The route to Stechelberg descends the upward route for a while, then continues to lose height over stony slopes heading north-eastwards, and across streams on the way to Tanzhubel (1,831m). The trail maintains direction to cross avalanche slopes and more streams on the route to the chalet at Schwand (1,684m) where there is a junction of trails. The right-hand path continues round the hillslopes and eventually descends to Trachsellauenen by a circuitous route. The left-hand path descends a grassy rib in zig-zags, then slopes off to the north to reach Berghaus Trachsellauenen (*accommodation, refreshments*) by a more direct route. From here follow the main valley path to Stechelberg.

Route 45: **Stechelberg (910m) - Ober Steinberg (1,778m) - Stechelberg**

Grade:	**2-3**
Distance:	**9 kilometres**
Height gain/loss:	**868 metres**
Time:	**4½ hours**

Another variation on a theme, this walk is a loop trip that, coupled with a side journey to Oberhornsee (Route 43), or a lengthy lunch stop at the hotel at Ober Steinberg, would make a worthwhile full day's outing.

Follow Route 42 to Obersteinberg (two and a half hours; *accommodation, refreshments*) and continue along the path beyond the hotel heading north-east over pastureland. It soon begins to lose height and in about fifteen minutes you come to Hotel Tschingelhorn (1,678m; *accommodation, refreshments*), a rustic mountain inn standing in an isolated position on the edge of woodland. The path forks here - both options ending at Stechelberg.

Continue ahead into the forest. The trail loses more height, steeply in places, but always clear. Eventually you will come to another junction of tracks. One leads to the Sefinental and Gimmelwald, the other cuts down to Stechelberg. Take the descending path to the right. On the way down you cross an open grassy pastureland bluff with a farm and barn upon it, enjoying delightful views down into the Lauterbrunnental. Shortly after this you rejoin the path used on the upward route and wander down the familiar trail to Stechelberg.

Route 46:	Stechelberg (Gimmelwald; 1,393m) - Tanzbödeli (2,133m) - Ober Steinberg (1,778m) - Trachsellauenen (1,203m) - Stechelberg

Grade:	3		
Distance:	20 kilometres		
Height gain:	740 metres	Height loss:	1,223 metres
Time:	6 hours		

Before leaving Stechelberg and the magical upper region of Ober Steinberg, one more route is deemed worthy of outline. This is considered by some to be one the finest of all high walks in the area, and it certainly lives up to its reputation with regard to its visual attraction. From Stechelberg it is advisable to begin the day with a cable-car ride to Gimmelwald. The valley station for this lies just to the north of the hamlet.

From Gimmelwald cut away south-westward into the Sefinental below the Gspaltenhorn. Cross the stream (the Sefinen Lütschine) and take the path climbing up the southern hillside towards Unter Busenalp (1,780m) and cross round the north-eastern slopes of the Spitzhorn at Tanzbödeli (2,133m; two and a half hours) where a superb full-frontal view is given of the Breithorn. The path then slants easily downhill to Ober Steinberg (three hours fifteen minutes; *accommodation, refreshments*). The descent to Stechelberg is straightforward and continues past Hotel Obersteinberg, drops steeply in places to pass the alp farm of Scheuerboden (1,379m), then through forest to Trachsellauenen (five hours twenty minutes; *accommodation, refreshments*). The continuing path leads easily back to Stechelberg in about forty minutes.

Route 47: Mürren (1,638m) - Sefinental - Stechelberg (910m)

Grade:	2-3		
Distance:	11 kilometres		
Height gain:	362 metres	**Height loss:**	1,090 metres
Time:	4-4¹/₂ hours		

Mürren has one of the finest situations of any village in the Alps. Perched high above the Lauterbrunnental it looks across to a wonderful array of high mountains, one of the most appealing of which is the Gspaltenhorn. This walk takes you beneath it into the romantic Sefinental, then descends through the glen to the woods that take you down into the main valley at Stechelberg.

From Mürren's railway station take the lower of the two main streets and continue through the village to pass the Schilthorn cable-car station. At the south-western end of the resort wander uphill along a tarmac path between sloping meadows. Follow signposts directing the way to Schönegg and Gimmeln. Beyond the farm buildings of Gimmeln (1,815m; forty minutes) the path (no longer surfaced) crosses the Schiltbach stream and comes to a small restaurant. Soon after this you begin to climb a spur of mountain (the minor peak of Brünli) and, having made a partial steep ascent, come to a junction of trails. Take the left-hand path sloping steadily down towards the farm buildings of Oberberg (1,930m).

The way now drops into the Sefinental, passing the alp of Ozen (1,582m), then continues to pass round and above a line of crags to make a safe entry to the glen. Now follow the path along the left bank heading downstream. No further directions are necessary. The way is clear, becoming steep in places as you descend out of the glen through forest and down to Stechelberg *(accommodation, refreshments)*. To return to Mürren take the cable-car whose valley station lies about one kilometre to the north of Stechelberg.

Route 48:   **Mürren (1,638m) - Suppenalp (1,852m) -**
Wasenegg (2,140m) - Gimmeln (1,815m) - Mürren

Grade:	3
Distance:	10 kilometres
Height gain/loss:	502 metres
Time:	4 hours

For spectacular views this walk takes a lot of beating. There are some rather steep sections to it, which tends to uprate it to Grade 3, but some fine level stretches too. There are one or two isolated farms to visit and these are linked by quiet paths. It's not a rugged mountain route, but a high walk on soft turf, with flowers and shrubs for company, and a huge panorama to absorb.

Go through Mürren towards the Schilthorn cable-car station. Just above this you will find a footpath climbing steeply up the left-hand side of a stream (the Mürrenbach) in the direction of Suppenalp. The path maintains its steep gradient well above the village and takes you through patches of woodland to arrive in about half an hour at Berghaus Suppenalp *(matratzenlager accommodation, refreshments).* The berghaus enjoys wonderful views of the Eiger, Mönch and Jungfrau that are quite magical in the evening with the alpenglow on them.

Bear left on a continuing path signposted to Schiltalp. It takes you up across a green hillside and passes beneath the Schilthorn cableway, edges round a bluff and gazes directly at the Gspaltenhorn across the Sefinental. The trail eases along a high pastureland and comes to a hamlet of cheesemakers' huts, Schiltalp (1,951m; one hour). Here you come to a junction of tracks and continue straight ahead in the direction of Boganggen.

A short distance beyond the huts a narrow path breaks away from the main track and goes half-left ahead, contours the hillside and comes to another trail junction by the Schiltbach. (The Schilthorn rises overhead.) Cross the stream and climb the path ahead as it works its way up a steep hillside of lush vegetation and comes onto the ridge of Wasenegg. This is another superb viewpoint, elevated and solitary.

A steady descending traverse takes you down to the south-west, into a broad pastureland with a well-trodden path cutting through it. On joining this path turn left and follow it all the way back to Mürren. As you do so there are views of the Jungfrau and the Eiger seen side-on like a great blade of rock.

Route 49:   Mürren (Allmendhubel; 1,912m) -
Suppenalp (1,852m) - Mürren (1,638m)

Grade:	1-2
Distance:	3 kilometres
Height loss:	274 metres
Time:	45 minutes

Rising above Mürren the Allmendhubel funicular opens up another fine walking area for visitors to this western side of the Lauterbrunnental. Built in 1891 the ride lasts for only four minutes but delivers you onto a belvedere of a shelf with a tremendous panorama laid out before you. Ahead rise all the fabled peaks for which this corner of Switzerland is justifiably noted, while behind lies soft green pasture topped by the Schilthorn.

This particular walk makes a gentle traverse of this green pastureland, passes two mountain inns and then descends steeply back to Mürren. It is only the steepness of the descent from Suppenalp that warrants a grading higher than 1, so for those who would prefer an easy, level stroll, the suggestion is made to make a loop trip from Allmendhubel to Suppenalp and back again.

From the upper Allmendhubel station take the left-hand trail that skirts into the brief scoop of hillside below Birg, then shortly after brings you to the berghaus of Blumental (Sonnenberg; *matratzenlager accommodation, refreshments*). Ignore the route down to Mürren from here and continue across the pastures to reach Pension Flora, Suppenalp (*matratzenlager accommodation, refreshments)* in about twenty minutes from Allmendhubel. Between the inn and a farm building next to it a path descends steeply to Mürren. It goes through woods and down beside a stream and comes to the edge of the village by the Schilthorn cableway.

Route 50:	Mürren (1,638m) - Schilthorn Hut (2,432m) - Schilthorn (2,970m)

Grade:	3
Distance:	7 kilometres
Height gain:	1,332 metres
Time:	4¹/₂ hours

A large number of visitors to Mürren take the cable-car up to the Schilthorn. The beauty of its summit panorama is known far and wide, not only from personal visits, but from the James Bond movie, *On Her Majesty's Secret Service*, that was partially shot there. Since there is such ease of access to the summit, none should imagine that after this long and steep walk to it there will be solitude and peace to be had. But the walk is a challenge - though there's nothing difficult about it - and it enjoys the contrast of gentle pasture with the somewhat bleak prospects afforded by the Engetal, in which sits the Schilthorn Hut. And the views, of course, are always worth earning.

The path to Allmendhubel begins near the sports centre in Mürren's upper street. It climbs up in long windings well to the east of the funicular track, skirts forest and comes onto the Allmendhubel shelf after about an hour. Signposts direct the path ahead in zig-zags up the slopes of the Muttlernhorn and in two hours forty minutes you reach the Schilthorn Hut *(accommodation, refreshments)* with its rather splendid view of the Jungfrau and its immediate neighbours. Through the Engetal, then, between the ridges running west and north from the summit of Birg, and the stony Schwarzgrat above to the right. The Schilthorn tops the valley, with its cable-car swinging between Birg and the actual summit.

Rise to a rocky basin above the Grauseeli (2,511m) tarn, where you find a memorial to Alice Arbuthnot who was killed here by lightning on her honeymoon in 1865, then steeply up to the ridge that takes you onto the Schilthorn's flat crowded top. The views are broad indeed. The great snowy massif of the Blümlisalp is impressive to the south-west, while the whole of the Jungfrau group is displayed in full majesty. Huge mountains with plunging precipices, washed by the silent drifting clouds. (From a point a short distance below the summit to the north-west, Mont Blanc can be picked out among a mass of peaks far off.)

Allow about three and a half hours for the descent by the same route or, better still, follow Route 51 back to Mürren.

Route 51:   Mürren (Schilthorn;2,970m) - Schiltalp (1,948m)
**   Mürrenberg - Mürren (1,638m)**

Grade: 3
Distance: 8 kilometres
Height loss: 1,332 metres
Time: 3 hours

This descent of the Schilthorn is offered as an alternative to using the Engetal route down, and may be used in order to extend Route 50 into a full loop trip, or by those who have chosen to ascend the mountain by cable-car. From the summit to the Grauseeli tarn the route is the same as that for the final ascent taken on the above route, and from the tarn down to Mürren the way follows good clear paths into an increasingly green and pleasant landscape.

From the summit cross the eastern arête of the mountain and descend to the southern end of the Grauseeli tarn between the Schilthorn and Birg (where the middle station of the cableway is perched). From here a well-marked path cuts off to the south and descends the steep inner corrie of the Schilttal, bearing left at a trail junction and crossing the Schiltbach stream where the gradient begins to ease. On an easy traverse of the lower hillside the path takes you through the little hamlet of cheesemakers' huts at Schiltalp where there is another junction of paths. Continue ahead. This path narrows somewhat but remains clear. It leads round a spur of the Schiltgrat, goes beneath the cableway from Mürren and comes to Berghaus Suppenalp *(matratzenlager accommodation, refreshments)*.

It is possible to drop down the hillside here and enter Mürren near its southern limits, but it is better to continue across the open pastures of Blumental (Mürrenberg) where there is another mountain inn *(matratzenlager accommodation, refreshments)* and take the path from here which breaks away to the right and descends steeply to the centre of the village.

Route 52: Mürren (1,638m) - Sefinenfurke (2,612m) - Griesalp (1,407m)

Grade:	3		
Distance:	14 kilometres		
Height gain:	974 metres	Height loss:	1,205 metres
Time:	6½ hours		

The Sefinenfurke is one of the classic non-glacial passes of the Bernese Oberland, its crossing being seen as one of the highlights of the Alpine Pass Route. From Mürren to Griesalp is an arduous stretch, but it's also a very scenic one, and given good weather conditions the Sefinenfurke pass makes a magnificent perch from which to view some of the giants of the Alps.

After a long but acceptably graduated approach over pastureland, the final climb to the pass is steep and tiring, while the initial descent on the western side is severe enough to warrant the use of a fixed rope as a hand rail over a slope of black gritty scree. At the end of the walk Griesalp is a tiny hamlet at the head of the Kiental. It has a variety of accommodation (including *matratzenlagers*), and a Postbus service that goes through the Kiental to Reichenbach in the Frutigtal (the lower Kandertal), where trains may be taken to either Kandersteg or Spiez.

From the station on the edge of Mürren take the lower of the two main streets through the village, and at its southern end wander uphill along a tarmac footpath between sloping meadows and follow signs for Schönegg and Gimmeln. (Views are stunning from the very start.) The paving finishes and a clear path of beaten earth continues. Beyond the few farm buildings of Gimmeln you cross the Schiltbach stream and pass a small restaurant, heading south. Now the trail narrows to climb in a series of zig-zags up a spur of Brünli (a minor peak on the ridge of the Wasenegg). Although it is a steep haul, it is a short one and the path soon eases along the left-hand slopes.

The path now contours across a large area of pasture, grazed in summer by cattle, and eventually brings you to the alp of Boganggen (2,039m; two hours ten minutes, *accommodation, refreshments*), one of whose buildings is the Rotstock Hut owned by the Stechelberg Ski Club.

Ahead lies a large bowl of rough pasture speckled with boulders. Cross to the western side and begin to gain height over grassy hillocks into a wild patch of country. The path continues clearly, if somewhat narrow in places, while ahead a wall of rock is eased in just one place with a saddle - the Sefinenfurke. The way steepens and the final stretch is gained by zig-zagging up a slope of gritty black scree.

The Sefinenfurke is reached about four hours after leaving Mürren. It's a very narrow pass, rocks rising on both sides, the faces to the east and west plunging with some degree of drama. But views are grand. Back the way you have come the Eiger, Mönch and Jungfrau are seen side-on. Go up the rocks of the ridge to the left (south) a short way, and you can gaze on the Blümlisalp massif off to the south-west. A grand vista of Alpine savagery.

Take care on the descent. Use the fixed rope on the initial unstable screes to begin with, after which the way is a mixture of slither and walk. At the foot of the long scree slopes the path resumes across more rough pastures on the right bank of a stream. A little over an hour from the pass you come to the alp hut of Obere Dürrenberg (1,995m; *accommodation, refreshments*) squatting on the bank above the stream. Just below this hut cross the stream and follow the winding path down a steep grassy hillside with fine views up to the Blümlisalp seen across the depths of an imposing valley.

Eventually the path brings you to another small farm, Bürgli, at a junction of valleys. Bear right and cross the stream previously followed from below the pass and take the farm road down towards Griesalp. After a short distance a footpath is signposted away from the road on the left, heading to Griesalp. Take either the footpath or road route. The road is pleasant enough, but so is the path. They will bring you past the group of buildings of Steinenberg, and at last down to the hamlet of Griesalp (*accommodation, refreshments, Postbus*).

Other Walks from the Lauterbrunnental:
A hard multi-day route worth considering is a circuit of the Schilthorn.
This would begin in Mürren or Lauterbrunnen and follows Route 52
to Griesalp. From there go down to **KIENTAL** in the valley of the
same name, then east into the valley of **SPIGGENGRUND** to cross
the **KILCHFLUE PASS** (2,454m) and descend from there to
Lauterbrunnen by way of the **SOUSTAL**. Allow three days for this
superb outing.

Halfway between Lauterbrunnen and Stechelberg a steep pathway
begins which climbs the eastern wall of the valley through the
TRÜMMELTAL. This steep ascent leads out to the lovely Biglenalp,
below Wengernalp, then gives a choice of routes along the hillside to
WENGEN. This, like the above outlined walk, would be graded 3.

On the western shelf of the valley various walks are made
possible by the Allmendhubel funicular in addition to those already
described. Try one of several paths that wander northwards to
GRÜTSCHALP, or the **SOUSTAL**; or from Grütschalp into the Soustal
to ascend the viewpoint of the **BIETENHORN**. There is no shortage
of walking possibilities in and around the Lauterbrunnental. Merely
study the map and all sorts of routes and variations of routes will
announce themselves clearly.

Jungfrau - from high above the Lauterbrunnental

KIENTAL

Position:	West of the Lauterbrunnental, the Kiental rises below the Blümlisalp and flows north-westward into the Frutigtal at Reichenbach above Spiez.
Map:	L.S. 5004 'Berner Oberland' 1:50,000
Bases:	Reichenbach (707m), Kiental (958m), Griesalp (1,407m)

Tourist Information:

Verkehrsbüro, 3713 Reichenbach (Tel: 033 76 2376)
Verkehrsbüro, 3711 Kiental (Tel: 033 76 1010)

The Kiental is one of those quiet, unassuming valleys tucked away off the main tourist circuit, and as such reserves its delights for those with an independent spirit. It is a lovely back-country glen, green, open and pastoral, yet it has its dark defiles too, and at its head the wild torrents, huge walls of rock, and snowfields and glaciers of the Blümlisalp massif. It's a valley of many faces, but each one is full of charm.

The eastern flanks of the Blümlisalp sweep round to form, with the help of the neighbouring Gspaltenhorn and Büttlassen, a tight amphitheatre down which flows the Gamchi Glacier. Below the glacier lies a roughly-moulded terrain that is slowly being tamed by Nature's patience and artistry. On undulating shelves above the main valley stream there are one or two summer-only dairy farms. Pine forests clothe the lower hillsides; waterfalls cascade down raw crags, and as the valley progresses north-westward, so little meadowlands open out, starry with flowers in spring and early summer, adorned with clusters of farms and neat Oberland chalets.

Travelling down-valley Griesalp is the first habitation of note, although a little higher Steinenberg and Golderli both have a few houses. Griesalp is tiny; a square with a few buildings round it - an inn or two and a Postbus halt at the end of the road. Below this hamlet the valley falls steeply and the road fights the gradient with some excessively tight hairpin bends between slabs of rock cleft with

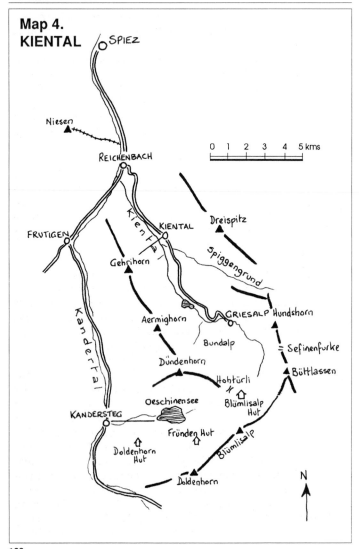

Map 4.
KIENTAL

SPIEZ

Niesen

REICHENBACH

0 1 2 3 4 5 kms

Kiental

KIENTAL

Dreispitz

FRUTIGEN

Gehrihorn

Spiggengrund

Kandertal

Aermighorn

GRIESALP   Hundshorn

Bundalp

Sefinenfurke

Dündenhorn

Hohtürli

Büttlassen

Oeschinensee

Blümlisalp
Hut

KANDERSTEG

Fründen Hut

Blümlisalp

Doldenhorn
Hut

Blümlisalp

Doldenhorn

N

waterfalls. Then the valley eases and there's a lake, the Tschingelsee, spread among the pastures, forest-clad slopes rising to modest craggy peaks on either side.

All this upper part of the valley is known as Gornerngrund, but just before you come to the village of Kiental, roughly two-thirds of the way along the main Kiental valley, another valley flows in from the south-east in a burst of cascades. This is Spiggengrund, a glen serviced by a farm track and with footpaths that lead to a secluded patch of country with prospects for walkers of a high pass or two to cross at its head.

Kiental itself is the only true village in the valley, and then there's not very much to it. It has a pretty church overlooking both village and valley, some pleasant houses and a soft pastoral outlook. It has made few concessions to winter tourism, which is commendable, and the only mechanical aid is a chair-lift rising on the west side of the valley to Ramslauenen, which can be useful to gain height for one or two high-level walks in summer.

After Kiental it's almost as though you're turning your back on the valley, for the road eases along the hillside, rounds a spur and then looks out over the broader Frutigtal, whose upper reaches fork as the Kandertal and Engstligental, respectively noted for the resorts of Kandersteg and Adelboden. And at the foot of the road, where the Kiental joins the Frutigtal, lies the unassuming village of Reichenbach, with the pyramid peak of Niesen rising before it.

The valley, then, is missed by the majority of visitors to the Bernese Alps. It is not for the Kiental to have internationally famous resorts. There are no sumptuous hotels, no intertwining cats' cradles of cableways, their steel towers catching the sun. Instead, a modest landscape where farmers continue with the work of grazing their cattle and making hay untroubled by an overt tourist industry. But there are footpaths a-plenty; walks that will take you hour after hour in the peace of the hills; walks that give a taste of solitude with dream-like views all around. There are arduous long routes that entice you over high passes to east or west, and gentle low-valley strolls to be had alongside merry streams or down to a lake where fishermen stand patient in the cool of early morning. But if it's more stirring sport you're after, the big peaks that block the valley offer climbs on rock, snow or ice. There's rock climbing to be had on crags that never make the glossy magazines, and there are lofty ridges to scramble on, linking one fine summit after another, and the glacier pass of Gamchilücke that leads to the Tschingelfirn (for a devious route to the Lauterbrunnental), the Kanderfirn (for a glacier route to the Gasterntal and Kandersteg) or over the Petersgrat to the Lötschental in canton Valais.

The Kiental may be little-known, but it is much loved by those who have discovered it, and it will certainly repay a few days' exploration.

Main Valley Bases:

REICHENBACH (707m) - not to be confused with the Falls of the same name above Meiringen - no doubt owes its allegiance more to the Frutigtal than to the Kiental, but it sits at the mouth of the latter valley and is on the route of all traffic going into it. It's also set beside the railway from Thun or Interlaken via Spiez, so is additionally important to Kiental economy and communications. The village itself is unimposing yet attractive enough, and is backed by a slope of fine meadows liberally dotted with chalets and farmsteads. To the north-east rises the Niesen, a conical peak with a funicular going from Mülenen to the very summit; it has one of the finest panoramas of any mountain in the Bernese Alps and is well worth visiting. (Better to go either early morning or in the evening. There are footpath routes from it too.) Reichenbach has a few shops and banks, seven hotels and some 300 beds available for rent in apartments or chalets. From the village the Postbus travels through the Kiental to Griesalp.

KIENTAL (958m), according to Baedeker in the 1901 edition of his guide to Switzerland, is 'charmingly situated, and well adapted for a stay of some time.' Ninety years later those sentiments remain true. It's a village of only two hundred inhabitants, and yet it is still the largest community in the valley proper, sitting in the midst of an unspoilt landscape dominated by grass and tree and with the snows of the Blümlisalp shining down from the south. The modern church is most attractive, both within and without, and it makes a photogenic foreground with the big mountains framed beyond. A short distance

Steinenberg, above Griesalp

up-stream the valley is fed by the Spiggebach coming from its own glen above to the left, mostly hidden from the village by a dense covering of forest. The village has just four hotels and pensions, but in addition there are some three hundred beds in holiday flats. In the main street a few shops provide the basic necessities, but the tourist information office is only temporarily manned. A chair-lift swings up the western hillsides to Ramslauenen for winter skiing and summer walking. Kiental is served by Postbus. A large car park is found on the southern outskirts of the village, and a toll is charged to all who wish to drive beyond it to Griesalp.

GRIESALP (1,407m) makes a fine, out-of-the-way base for a walking or mountaineering holiday. It is only a tiny hamlet and yet its three hotels and pensions offer sixty standard beds and 200 spaces in *matratzenlager* dormitories. From the square footpaths branch off to a variety of high mountain destinations, to remote passes, mountain huts, lonely alps and waterfalls. The Postbus terminates here and car parking is forbidden except for *bona fide* hotel guests.

Mountain Huts:
High above the head of the Kiental, lodged in or near the rim of the cirque that spawns it, two SAC huts are found, with a third accessible to mountaineers beyond one of them.

First is the **BLÜMLISALP HUT** (2,837m) above the Hohtürli pass, the saddle in a ridge thrown north of the main Blümlisalp massif. This hut, lodged at the very edge of the glaciers, was recently (1988-89) modified and enlarged. It can sleep more than one hundred in its dormitories, has a restaurant service and there is a guardian in residence throughout the summer. It is reached in about four and a half hours from Griesalp.

On the opposite, eastern, side of the cirque, the **GSPALTENHORN HUT** (2,455m) is reached in about three hours or so from Griesalp. Owned by the Bern Section of the SAC, with spaces for fifty, it is tucked below both Büttlassen and Gspaltenhorn, and to the west of the latter's summit. There are two main routes of approach. One heads directly up-valley from Griesalp, following the Gamchibach to the snout of the glacier, then climbs steeply to the hut; the other cuts round from the Sefinenfurke and skirts the lower edge of the western arête of Büttlassen. The hut has a guardian in charge only through the busy summer weeks, when meals and drinks are available.

The third hut mentioned above is the **MUTTHORN HUT** (2,901m) found to the south of the main Oberland ridge, so far as the Kiental is concerned, yet it is actually perched on the very watershed. This is really out of bounds to all but mountaineers coming from the Kiental, for to approach it requires crossing the Gamchilücke (2,852m) above the Gamchigletscher, then over the glacial Tschingel Pass and across the head of the Kanderfirn; about eight hours from the valley, though more usually approached directly from the Gspaltenhorn Hut. The Mutthorn Hut squats amid a scene of arctic desolation. It can sleep a hundred and has a guardian in residence from the end of June until early September. For those well-equipped and with glacier experience, it can be very useful for an overnight stop on one of several possible high route circuits.

Elsewhere, either in the valley or high above it, there are several little inns or farms with *matratzenlagers* providing accommodation of one sort or another. To the north-east of Kiental village a few metres below the **RENGG PASS**, just below the summit of Wätterlatte, there's a hut with dormitory places for about thirty. This is midway on a cross-ridge walk to the Suldtal, and has fine views north to the Thunersee, and south to the snow-capped mountains.

On the western hillside above Kiental, where the chair-lift terminates, **BERGHAUS RAMSLAUENEN** has eight beds and twenty dormitory places. Above Griesalp **PENSION GOLDERLI** has bedrooms, the **NATURFREUNDHAUS** nearby has room for 120 in its dormitories, and the little alp of **OBERE DÜRRENBERG,** on the way to the Sefinenfurke, can accommodate about fifty. More matratzenlager accommodation is available in the alp of **OBER BUND** on the route to the Hohtürli.

Route 53: Reichenbach (707m) - Engelgiess (990m) - Kiental (958m)

Grade:	1		
Distance:	5 kilometres		
Height gain:	390 metres	**Height loss:**	149 metres
Time:	1 hour 40 minutes		

This easy but pleasant stroll makes a gradual introduction to the Kiental. It wanders between sloping pastures, passes a number of handsome chalets and enjoys bright views.

From Reichenbach walk up the Kiental road to the nearby roadside village of Scharnachtal, which you reach in about twenty minutes. As you enter the village, with houses on the left, the road crosses a stream. Leave the road here and walk up the left-hand side of the stream, over a lane that crosses the path, and ahead on a track making a rising traverse of hillside towards Engelgiess. As you wander along this some lovely views are to be had; neat cropped meadows and big snow-bound mountains rising in the distance, the Frutigtal sliding below between the hills and Niesen marking the northern end of a long ruffled ridge.

From Engelgiess (reached in a little under an hour) continue to rise a little over pastures, pass through some woods and then join a lane which takes you winding downhill towards the buildings marked on the map as Rufene. But at the final hairpin of this lane break away left to follow a track which cuts round the hillside and brings you to the northern end of Kiental *(accommodation, refreshments)*. To return to Reichenbach it is convenient to catch a Postbus.

The Öeschinensee above Kandersteg

Route 54:   Reichenbach (707m) - Gehrihorn (2,130m)

Grade: 3
Distance: 8 kilometres
Height gain: 1,423 metres
Time: 4¹/₂-5 hours

The entrance to the Kiental is guarded in the north-east by the Wätterlatte (2,007m) and to the south-west by the Gehrihorn; modest mountains both, but superb viewpoints. This ascent of the Gehrihorn is straightforward and worth giving a day for.

First head south along the Frutigtal to the village of Kien, then up the hillside behind it to Aris (826m), a small hamlet overlooking the valley. From here the route heads directly up the hillside spur heading south again towards woodland (signposted to Brandweiden and Ober Geerene). By a combination of track and footpath the way leads on to Chüeweid (1,475m - also known as Kuehweide), about two hours or so from Reichenbach.

Ober Geerene lies almost three hundred metres above Chüeweid, but there's nothing difficult about the route to it, although you have a choice of going to left or right from Chüeweid to Bachwald. Ober Geerene (1,766m; *accommodation, refreshments*) is reached about three and a half hours after leaving Reichenbach and from it there are some very fine views. A *Bergweg* leads from here to the summit, climbing steeply up to the northern ridge by which the mountain top is gained. The summit panorama is magnificent.

Descend by the same path, allowing three hours for it or, alternatively, take the descending path from the summit, but instead of breaking away westward from the ridge towards Ober Geerene, continue down the arête and then veer right (eastwards) on a clear path that leads to the chair-lift station at Ramslauenen. From there go down to Kiental for the Postbus back to Reichenbach.

The pass of Voré on border of Canton Bern and Vaud

| Route 55: | Kiental (Ramslauenen; 1,409m) - |
| | Chüeweid (1,475m) - Aris (862m) - Kiental (958m) |

Grade:	2-3	
Distance:	11 kilometres	
Height gain:	640 metres	Height loss: 1,090 metres
Time:	4 hours	

A variation of Route 54 above, this walk is a little less demanding than its predecessor, since most of the way is either downhill or along a steady contour. It makes good use of the chair-lift from Kiental to Ramslauenen, crosses the northern shoulder of the Gehrihorn and descends to the hamlet of Aris. From there a return is made to the Kiental proper by way of an easy lane and track through forest. Refreshments are available at Ober Geerene, above Chüeweid.

From the top of the chair-lift take the uphill path heading west towards the peak of Gehrihorn. It climbs steeply in places, making progress to gain the shoulder of the mountain. After ascending the ridge a short way take the footpath going off to the right and descend towards the clutch of buildings of Ober Geerene (1,769m; *accommodation, refreshments*). Now continue down on the trail marked Chüeweid (or Kühweide), and from there all the way to Aris (862m), a hamlet near the foot of the slope on the left bank of the Kiene river. A narrow road passes through Aris. On coming to this road turn right and walk along it (and the track that continues from its end), through forest and alongside the river all the way back to Kiental.

| Route 56: | Kiental (958m) - Aris (862m) - Frutigen (780m) |

Grade:	1
Distance:	9 kilometres
Height loss:	178 metres
Time:	2¹/₂ hours

This is a valley walk, not unduly demanding yet with an undeniable charm. It follows a track or narrow road all the way and makes for a very pleasant morning's outing.

At the southern (up-valley) end of Kiental village take the street which leads down to cross the river, then immediately bear right on a track that runs parallel with it. Through meadows and woods this track eases its way along the lower slopes of hillside for about four kilometres or so before coming to the little hamlet of Aris in just over an hour from Kiental. Approaching Aris views open out with the broader Frutigtal cutting at right angles ahead and the cone of Niesen rising abruptly to the north-west. Leave the road at the first hairpin bend and contour round the hillside on a track heading south-west to Schwandi, a scattering of chalets and farms where another minor road is joined for the final approach to Frutigen.

To return to Kiental take the train from Frutigen to Reichenbach, and either follow Route 53 or take Postbus from there to Kiental.

Route 57:	Kiental (958m) - Kilchfluh Pass (2,456m) - Grütschalp (1,486m)

Grade:	3		
Distance:	21 kilometres		
Height gain:	1,498 metres	**Height loss:**	970 metres
Time:	7¹/₂ hours		

A long and arduous route, maybe, but a very rewarding one for those who enjoy a feeling of remoteness, of wild country yet with the hand of man never very far away. On this long cross-country trek there are scattered farms, soft pastures and wild corries. The valleys of Spiggengrund to the west of the pass, and the Soustal to the east, complement one another, yet the ultimate destination for walkers tackling this route must surely be Lauterbrunnen below Grütschalp, and the Lauterbrunnental is in stark contrast to that of the Kiental. Taken on its own, this makes a challenging day out. But when combined with Routes 34 (Grütschalp-Mürren) and 52 (Mürren-Griesalp), a superb two-to three-day circuit can be achieved.

Walk south through Kiental and bear left where the road forks on the outskirts of the village, soon to leave the road in favour of a path that slopes up above it ahead to the left. This goes through forest and climbs above waterfalls cascading through a narrow cleft which drains the Spiggengrund valley. Once in this side glen the footpath brings you onto a farm track that crosses to the southern (true left) bank of the Spiggebach and leads deeper into the valley. It's a wildly romantic glen, and as you progress through it, so the tight amphitheatre of mountains at its head appears raw, yet attractive. The pass is detected from a long way off; a saddle in the long ridge that links Schwalmere to Kilchfluh and the Schilthorn.

The way takes you past several farm buildings, between rough pastures and through patches of forest, making steady progress towards the head of the valley. After about three hours the track swings left to cross the stream again, and then soon gives way to a *Bergweg* footpath at the huts of Glütschnessli (1,638m). Now the trail climbs round to the hut of Barenfeld, on to Hohkien (2,027m; three hours forty-five minutes) and then climbs northward for about 500 metres before veering south on a slight descent towards the Kilchfluh Pass. There will invariably be snow patches on the way to it, even in the middle of summer, so take care. The saddle is reached about five hours from Kiental, and a new valley system and long views are spread out before you.

The descent into the Soustal goes down over snow and scree, making for the left-hand side of the Sousbach stream. Once down on pastures follow the stream to the alp hamlet of Oberberg (1,997m) about an hour below the pass, and here you cross to the right bank. Continue in the same direction until joining another path just beyond the farm building of Souslager (1,680m). Now follow the signposted trail veering to the right through forest almost all the way to Grütschalp (about fifty minutes from Souslager). From here either take the funicular down to Lauterbrunnen, or wander down the steep signposted trail. (But you'll probably prefer to ride this last stretch, rather than punish your knees further on such a severe path!)

For details of accommodation etc in Lauterbrunnen, see the previous section headed Lauterbrunnental.

Route 58:   Kiental (958m) - Tschingelsee (1,150m) - Griesalp (1,407m)

Grade: 1
Distance: 7 kilometres
Height gain: 449 metres
Time: 2 hours

An uncomplicated, easy walk, this route follows the road nearly all the way to Griesalp. But since use of the road is restricted, walkers are seldom bothered by much traffic and all the way views are quite lovely.

Leave Kiental heading up-valley, and on the outskirts of the village where the road forks, take the left branch (in fact continuing ahead while the main road drops to the right). Follow this quiet lane to its end and continue on the trail that leads from it, crossing the Spiggebach and soon after rejoin the main Kiental-Griesalp road near the alp huts of Losplatte.

Wander along the road for a further two kilometres, at which point you come to Hotel Alpenruhe (1,141m; *accommodation, refreshments*) about fifty minutes after setting out. Soon beyond the hotel you draw level with the delightful Tschingelsee, fed by the Gamchibach that comes off the glaciers at the head of the valley. At the far end of the lake a good footpath breaks away to the left and zig-zags up between the crags lining the road, and passes near the cascades of the Pochtenfall. Steadily making height the path leads to the track extending from Griesalp (*accommodation, refreshments*). The Postbus may be taken for the return to Kiental.

Route 59:   Kiental (958m) - Hotel Alpenruhe (1,141m) - Mittelbergli (1,458m) - Griesalp (1,407m)

Grade: 2
Distance: 8 kilometres
Height gain: 500 metres
Time: 2¹/₂ hours

A variation of Route 58, this gives rather less road-walking, and after Hotel Alpenruhe takes to the western side of the valley, approaching Griesalp from the south.

Follow Route 58 directions as far as Hotel Alpenruhe (fifty minutes), then cut off to the right on a short road leading across the river. Two paths fork from this; bear left and go up the hillside towards Gurren (1,365m) on a shelf above the lake. The trail continues, crosses a stream, skirts above forest and brings you to Mittelbergli with interesting views. From here to Griesalp the way heads through forest, losing some height, and then reaches the little hamlet by way of the final stretch of road.

Route 60: Griesalp (1,407m) - Gornern (1,440m) - Tschingelsee (1,150m) - Pochtenfall - Griesalp

---

Grade:	1-2
Distance:	5 kilometres
Height gain/loss:	290 metres
Time:	2¹⁄₂-3 hours

Known as the *Bärenpfad*, the first section of this walk is a very popular one and it develops as a circuit that has so much to commend it; the long views down-valley, the gleaming lake, a superb waterfall and an overpowering awareness of the big mountains hovering nearby.

From Griesalp wander up-valley along the continuing road to Golderli where you then turn left to follow a clear track heading north-west along the hillside. It passes a few scattered buildings, enjoys a vista of much beauty along the valley stretching far ahead, then cuts left to zig-zag steeply down a footpath to join the main valley road just north of the Tschingelsee. Here you bear left and wander along the road to a point at the far end of the lake where another footpath breaks away left to climb above the valley past the Pochtenfall. It then veers right and goes easily back to Griesalp. (As a variation, you could stay with the road from the lake all the way back to Griesalp.)

Route 61: Griesalp (1,407m) - Obere Dürrenberg (1,995m) - Sefinenfurke (2,612m)

Grade: 3
Distance: 6 kilometres
Height gain: 1,205 metres
Time: 3¹⁄₂-4 hours

One of the classic walks of the region is this approach to the Sefinenfurke, part of the cross-country route to Mürren and Lauterbrunnen already described in the opposite direction (Route 52).

Continue up-valley along the road out of Griesalp. It takes you to Golderli from where a well-made farm track leads through the pretty huddle of buildings at Steinenberg and on to the alp farm of Burgli (1,620m) on the south bank of the main valley stream. Go left at the farm and take the footpath climbing steeply up the hillside heading east, keeping to the left of another farm some way up the slope, then over a spur to see the little hut of Obere Dürrenberg ahead. To reach this you must cross the stream and continue now on the north side (true right bank). Passing Obere Dürrenberg (one hour fifty minutes; *accommodation, refreshments*) keep to the left of the stream, crossing rough pasture and eventually coming to a steep and daunting slope of scree. Tackle this by zig-zags along its left-hand side. Near the top of the slope the angle steepens and the final haul over shifting black grit is aided by a fixed rope hand rail. The views from the narrow pass are stunning.

To continue as far as Mürren will require a further three hours. The way is straightforward and signposted at all trail junctions. To descend to Griesalp by the way you have come will occupy about two and a half hours.

Route 62:   Griesalp (1,407m) - Burgli (1,620m) - Gspaltenhorn Hut (2,455m)

Grade: 3
Distance: 7 kilometres
Height gain: 1,048 metres
Time: 3 hours 15 minutes

This hut approach takes you into the wild inner recesses of the mountains; away from gentle green pastures and into a raw landscape immediately below the western flanks of the superb Gspaltenhorn, and under the southern cliffs of Büttlassen.

From Griesalp to the alp farm of Burgli (1,620m; forty-five minutes) follow directions given for Route 61. Instead of heading left here, as for the path to Sefinenfurke, continue ahead towards the wild but attractive corrie, keeping above the stream and in a further fifteen minutes you come to Gamchi and a junction of trails (1,673m). (The right-hand trail, which you ignore, goes up to the Hohtürli and the Blümlisalp Hut.) Continue up- valley, but skirt along the left-hand side of the hollow, soon climbing terraces between bands of rock and come to the moraines of the Gamchigletscher.

The path now bears left to ascend roughly eastward in a series of zig-zags under the western arête of Büttlassen with the Gspaltenhorn rising directly ahead. Another path breaks off leftwards (to the Sefinenfurke) but you maintain direction along the northern side of a spur projecting below a hanging glacier, and then head to the right to find the hut situated actually on this spur with a superb outlook.

The Gspaltenhorn Hut can sleep fifty. It has a guardian in residence only during July and August, and at weekends in June and September. If you plan to spend a night there, it is advisable to carry some items of food with you. For the return to Griesalp by the same route, allow about two hours.

Route 63:	Griesalp (1,407m) - Hohtürli (2,778m) - Blümlisalp Hut (2,837m)

Grade:	3
Distance:	6 kilometres
Height gain:	1,430 metres
Time:	4¹⁄₂ hours

Hohtürli is a lofty, wind-scoured saddle on the north-projecting ridge of the Blümlisalp, and from it a sensational view is to be had of nearby glaciers, wave-like ridges and the misty hint of the Kandertal deep below and seemingly far away to the west. Above the saddle stands the Blümlisalp Hut, a comfortable, sturdy lodging from which a good many climbs are made possible. As the destination and high-point of a walk it makes an obvious goal. But the way to it is rough and arduous in places. It is not for the faint-hearted.

Behind Berghaus Griesalp lies a dark stretch of forest. To one side of the building a signpost marks the start of the route, and a path leads to the south into the forest, soon coming onto a track which in turn leads to a farm road. This winds steadily along the edge of the forest and between pastures with the wild-looking mountains frowning ahead. At Unter Bund (1,698m) leave the road and go up a steep grassy path towards an upper shelf of pasture hinted above. You rejoin the farm road and shortly afterwards come to the alp of Ober Bund (1,840m; *accommodation, refreshments*) about one hour fifteen minutes from Griesalp.

Continue along the road for a few hundred metres. It leads into a region of more rucked pastureland where a signpost indicates the start of a footpath which goes up the pastures ahead. It gains height and comes to a steep slope of moraine and black grit, and then fights an uncomfortable way up a spur, with the zig-zags badly eroded by wind and weather.

The obstacle of this black moraine debris is finally overcome and you emerge onto a ridge of grey rock where paint flashes lead on a rising traverse to the right. The way then tucks against the left-hand side of the ridge above a hollow draped with long slips of snow. The path improves, and then begins to climb by a series of rocky shelves,

On the Hohtürli path above Ober Bund

the walls of the ridge overhanging in places. Aided by fixed cable and chains you tackle the final zig-zags to emerge on the pass after about four hours fifteen minutes. The Blümlisalp Hut is seen above to the left. Wander up the slope to it.

For a return to Griesalp allow about two and a half hours, but take special care on the initial descent, and again when tackling the steep slope of grit. Snow is often lying late into summer and at such times the way down can be rendered difficult and potentially dangerous.

Route 64:   **Griesalp (1,407m) - Hohtürli (2,778m) - Kandersteg (1,176m)**

Grade:	3
Distance:	15 kilometres
Height gain:	1,371 metres **Height loss:** 1,602 metres
Time:	7½ hours

Crossing the Hohtürli is one of the great walks of the Bernese Alps. It is a famous route, used by generations of mountain folk as well as by mountaineers and walkers crossing from the Kiental to the Kandertal and vice-versa. It is also the highest crossing on the Alpine Pass Route and one that features in a variety of traverses and circuits. But although it is a crossing that is tackled by a good many each summer, it remains in truth an arduous undertaking.

Take Route 63 from Griesalp to the Hohtürli (four hours fifteen minutes), and descend on the western side by way of a clearly marked path that initially makes the most of well-graded zig-zags over broad slopes of scree. The way continues below the screes along a rocky balcony looking left to a wintry view of glacial tongues perched indelicately above a scoop created by the glaciers of long ago. A descent from this balcony leads onto the crest of a moraine wall, and at the end of this you descend to the right into a rough bowl of pasture dotted with boulders and with a stream winding through. In five and a half to six hours from Griesalp you come to the huts of Ober Bergli (1,981m) and soon after gaze down into the great basin of the Öeschinensee.

A veritable stairway of a path descends to the lake, passing the lower alp of Unter Bergli (1,767m) where the trail veers right, crosses a stream and continues along the northern side of the lake, but some way above it. On coming towards the western end of the Öeschinensee the path slopes down, passes through trees and comes to a collection of hotels and restaurants (1,593m; *accommodation, refreshments*), more than two hours from the pass. A narrow service road leads from the buildings to Kandersteg. It's very steep in places and invariably crowded with holiday makers, but it is the most straightforward way down. In about an hour from the lake you will arrive in the village of Kandersteg *(accommodation, refreshments, Postbus, train)*.

For further details of accommodation and facilities available in Kandersteg, please refer to the following section under the heading Kandertal.

Other Walks from the Kiental:
One cross-country route worth considering from Kiental village heads roughly northward over the Rengg pass and down to the

SULDTAL (four hours, Grade 3), and with an option then of continuing north to **LEISSIGEN** on the shores of the Thunersee, or from Suld head up-valley and cross the **RENGGLIPASS** to **SAXETEN** and **WILDERSWIL** (Route 14 in reverse). By taking this latter option the keen backpacker can see possibilities for extended tours.

A more demanding five-hour route from Kiental to **SULD** goes through the glen of Spiggengrund to cross the pass of **LATREJEFELD** (1,993m). This is another Grade 3 walk. But also by way of Spiggengrund the ascent of the **SCHILTHORN** (2,960m) is made possible. This is a fairly arduous route, Grade 3.

The **PANORAMAWEG KIENTAL-THUNERSEE** is a walk with its own leaflet available from the Kiental tourist office. This five and a half-hour route makes an interesting and scenic traverse of the northern hillsides high above the Frutigtal. On good clear paths and waymarked throughout, this is a highly recommended tour.

Another walk that is being promoted with its own leaflets is the so-called **NORDRAMP**, a high-level path originally created in 1961 and recently up-graded and improved. This five and a half to six-hour route links the Kiental with **KANDERSTEG**. It begins at the chair-lift station of Ramslauenen, crosses the shoulder of the Gehrihorn to Chüeweid (Kuhweid) and traverses southward above the Frutigtal and Kandertal all the way to Kandersteg.

For an interesting two-day approach to Kandersteg, keen walkers could link the two walks outlined immediately above, to create a route from Därligen on the shores of the Thunersee with Kandersteg, overnighting in Kiental.

From **GRIESALP** to **RAMSLAUENEN** a lovely high traversing path wanders the western hillsides for an enjoyable Grade 2 walk of a little over two hours, while those with mountaineering experience need never run short of ideas for all sorts of exploratory expeditions among the surrounding peaks and ridges.

There are, of course, numerous other possible walks in the easier grades that will aid an exploration of this delightful area. The tourist office in Kiental has leaflets giving basic route outlines in German, but with the high standard of waymarking and signposts in the valley and on the hillsides, visitors with only a minimal command of the language should experience no real difficulties.

KANDERTAL

Position: South of Spiez on the Thunersee, the Kandertal is
the upper section of the Frutigtal. The valley
actually rises as the Gasterntal between the main
watershed ridge of the Bernese Alps and the
western peaks of the Blümlisalp massif.

Maps: L.S. 5004 'Berner Oberland' 5009 'Gstaad-
Adelboden' and 264 'Jungfrau' - all at 1:50,000

Bases: Kandersteg (1,176m), Selden/Gasterntal (1,552m)

Tourist Information:
Verkehrsbüro, 3718 Kandersteg (Tel: 033 75 1234)

Frutigtal is the name given to the lower, pastoral valley of the river
Kander, a gentle land of trim chalets set in meadows of green. But as
one travels south through it, so a more grand yet austere scene
beckons. The big snow peaks and stark rock walls that block the
valley soar in an uncompromising sweep of grandeur, setting a
contrast to the lower pastures and flower-filled meadows.

At Frutigen the valley is joined by two distinct branches. From the
south-east flows the Engstligental with Adelboden at its head; to the
south stretches the upper valley of the Kander - the Kandertal - with
Kandersteg a further twelve kilometres away, both valley and
straggling resort known for more than a hundred years for their
mountaineering potential and, much longer, as a noted base from
which to make the crossing of the mountains into the sun-trap of the
Rhône Valley.

The Kandertal is divided from the Engstligental by a long ridge
which terminates at its northern end on the Elsighorn (2,341m). The
southern end of this ridge, however, having been redirected by the
partial intrusion of the Ueschinental, becomes confused beyond the
Steghorn (3,146m) - an outlier of the Wildstrubel massif - where other
spurs and ridges run off to a tangle of rock, snow and ice above the
regionally important Gemmipass.

Opposite this ridge, walling the eastern side of the valley, a long

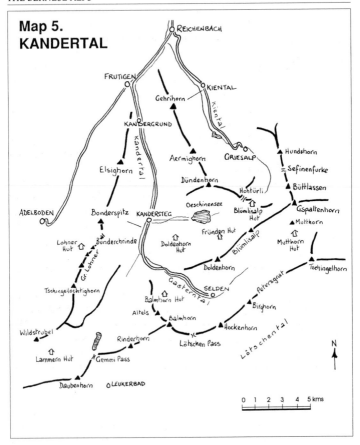

Map 5.
KANDERTAL

line of modest summits rises steadily from the mouth of the Kiental to the Dündenhorn (2,862m), which in itself is linked to the mass of Blümlisalp peaks across the saddle of the Hohtürli. The Dündenhorn and Blümlisalp have between them scoured a deep bowl of an amphitheatre in which shines the Öeschinensee, and it is at the opening of this bowl, where the Öeschibach flows into the Kander, that Kandersteg is to be found.

Continuing south out of Kandersteg the valley appears to be blocked by a massive wall of rock draped with cascades. Above this wall, which is easily gained by cableway, lies the surprisingly gentle upper glen that leads to the Gemmipass and over to the Valais. But to the east of this apparent valley-blocking wall lies a second delightful glen, also secretively hidden by yet another set of rocky walls, and with a mini-gorge at its entrance down which the young Kander pours its way in a tumult of spume, a fury of rush and roar. This gorge is the Klus, the glen it leads to being the Gasterntal, one of the loveliest and least changed of all the valleys in the Bernese Alps.

The Gasterntal is born among the snow and ice of the Kanderfirn, a broad glacial sheet only hinted at from the valley itself. Wandering into the valley, below Altels and Balmhorn to the south and Doldenhorn to the north, one sees undisciplined streams flooding through the edge of woods and across low-lying pasture. Then as you progress deeper into it, beautiful feathery waterfalls spray from the cliffs, meadows open out and are lavish with flowers in early summer, and the pine woods fall back to reveal views to the mountains at its head. Such a glen makes a worthy kindergarten to a valley of distinction.

The Kandertal, with its side glens and upper shelves of alpine meadowland, has plenty to offer the visiting mountain walker or climber. The mountains are big and with a certain grace of form, their flanks abrupt and challenging. Yet they have their soft, feminine aspects too that attract rather than defy, that welcome with gentility. Routes abound for walkers and climbers of all degrees of seriousness. There are short valley strolls, medium-grade outings that visit lonely alps, waterfalls and lakes, and strenuous routes that go up to lofty mountain huts or across high passes and icefields. There is something, indeed, for everyone here.

Main Valley Bases:

KANDERSTEG (1,176m) stretches itself along the valley floor in a long ribbon development of chalets, hotels and shops. By virtue of the railway which now pierces the fifteen-kilometres-long Lötschberg Tunnel through the mountains south of the resort to Goppenstein in the Lötschental, the village is known (briefly) to many more than actually stay here. The heart of the place is situated towards the southern end of the village, not far from the railway station. Here will be found a variety of shops and banks, hotels and restaurants, a PTT and a tourist information office. There is just one public campsite, terraced on the lower hillside to the east of the village on the edge of woods by the chair-lift that serves the Öeschinensee. The campsite has a *matratzenlager* attached to it. Kandersteg has no shortage of accommodation. There are twenty-five hotels and in addition no fewer than 1,000 beds in holiday flats for rent. In winter it is base for the Swiss Nordic Ski Centre, but in summer it becomes a walkers' paradise with more than 300 kilometres of trails to follow, some of which are accessible from a variety of cableways. As well as a chair-lift to the pastures above the Öeschinensee, there's cable-car access to Allmenalp (popular with paragliding enthusiasts) above the valley to the west, and cable-car linked with chair-lift from Eggeschwand (near the entrance to the Gasterntal) to Stock and Sunnbühl to provide easy walking towards the Gemmipass. Kandersteg has its own mountaineering school (Tel: 033 75 1352), a paragliding school (033 75 1917), swimming pool and various other sports facilities. It is also home to an international scout camp.

SELDEN (1,552m) in the Gasterntal has no shops, banks or other facilities beyond two rustic mountain inns (Hotel Steinbock and Hotel Gasterntal- Selden) set in an enchanted landscape. For those who wish to spend a few days or weeks in the unspoilt peace and beauty of the mountains, the Gasterntal makes an ideal base. The valley is banned to private vehicles (other than for permit holders), but a minibus provides a taxi service from Kandersteg railway station as far as Selden. The valley is a veritable flower garden in spring and early summer. It is a joy to explore, with a number of delightful outings to tackle. Both Selden's inns have bedrooms and *matratzenlager* accommodation, as does another timber chalet further up-valley, Berggasthaus Heimritz, and Berghaus Gfällalp too, which is situated almost 300 metres above Selden on the route to the Lötschenpass. (There's also *matratzenlager* for thirty in a hut at the pass itself.) Down-valley, not far from the valley's entrance, Hotel Waldhaus is set in a crescent of woods. This offers standard bedrooms as well as *matratzenlager* accommodation.

Mountain Huts:

In addition to the **BLÜMLISALP HUT** and **MUTTHORN HUT** already described under the Kiental section, there are four SAC refuges in the vicinity of Kandersteg that may be worth visiting. The **LAMMERN HUT** (2,515m) is the first of these. Reached in about six hours from Kandersteg (time which may be reduced by an hour if the Stock cableway system is used), this hut is situated high under the south-eastern glacier bowl of the Wildstrubel, and is approached for much of the way along the Gemmipass route. It can accommodate seventy-eight in its dormitories.

To the north-east of the Wildstrubel rise the twin peaks of Altels and Balmhorn, guarding the entrance to the Gasterntal. Due north of the summit of the Balmhorn is perched the **BALMHORN HUT** (1,955m) with a steeply twisting path rising out of the Gasterntal to reach it. It's only a small hut, sleeping just twenty-eight, but it makes a challenging destination for a day's walk. It is reached in about three and a half hours from Kandersteg and there's a guardian during summer weekends who can provide refreshments.

The **DOLDENHORN HUT** (1,915m) overlooks Kandersteg from the north-west flanks of the peak after which it is named. With places for fifty-four, and a guardian in residence during July and August, this hut was provided by the Emmental section of the Swiss Alpine Club, and has the shortest approach of any mountain hut in the area. (Two and a half hours from the village.)

High above the Öeschinensee the **FRÜNDEN HUT** (2,562m) sits at the foot of the Fründen Glacier on a lip of rock with a spectacular view. This is one of the largest huts in the region, having places for ninety. It is also in the charge of a guardian from June until October, when there are meals and drinks available. This hut is reached by a steep path which takes about four hours.

As for the **BLÜMLISALP HUT** (2,837m), this is found above the Hohtürli Pass to the north-west of the Wilde Frau. The most popular hut for walkers based in Kandersteg, it is reached in five hours, can sleep one hundred in its refurbished dormitories and has a guardian from June until October.

Finally, the **MUTTHORN HUT** (2,901m) is useful for mountaineers and walkers with glacier experience who set out to cross the Petersgrat to the Lötschental. Lost in an arctic world of ice, the Mutthorn Hut is best reached from Selden in the Gasterntal in about four and a half hours. It can sleep one hundred and has a guardian in occupation during the high summer weeks.

Accommodation is also available in a variety of settings beyond the village. Of note are the hotels and berghaus at the **ÖESCHINENSEE** where both standard bedrooms and *matratzrenlagers* are available. On the way to the Gemmipass **BERGHOTEL SCHWARENBACH** can accommodate twenty-five in bedrooms and 120 in *matratzenlagers*, while **HOTEL WILDSTRUBEL** at the pass has twice that number of beds as well as 130 *matratzenlager* places.

Route 65:	Kandersteg (Chair-lift 1,682m) - Öeschinensee (1,593m)

Grade:	1
Distance:	2.5 kilometres
Height loss:	89 metres
Time:	30 minutes

The Öeschinensee is depicted on so many posters around Kandersteg that you almost know what to expect before you actually see it for yourself. But the reality is still worth capturing. This very easy stroll makes good use of a late afternoon when the weather may have been bad and at last there's promise in the sky. Or perhaps you've been travelling to the area and have just arrived and are in need of a little exercise with views to enjoy. Not least, it offers an easy way to reach the lake where you might consider spending the day with a picnic, simply lazing on the edge of the pine woods by the water and gazing at the huge peaks rising from it.

The chair-lift (Sesselbahn Öeschinen) is signposted from the village street and is found on the eastern side of the valley next to the campsite. It is operational from 7.30am until 6.30pm during high summer weeks.

From the upper station a signpost sets you in the right direction, walking eastwards along a broad, well-trodden track through meadows with the Blümlisalp peaks seen in all their splendour ahead. The track soon veers to the right, but you should ignore this and continue ahead on a lesser trail gently contouring between patches of woodland. Ignore a second path which veers away leftwards (a sign points this route to Ober Bergli and the Blümlisalp Hut) and soon after you will come to the buildings at Läger (1,659m). Take the narrow footpath ahead. This takes you down through the woods to the lakeside. Turn right and wander along the shoreline trail that leads to the hotels and restaurants at the western end of the lake, or go left on a rising path that climbs above the northern shore as far as you wish to go. (It is not possible to make a complete circuit of the lake, but there are plenty of idyllic places to enjoy a picnic.) Either wander back to the chair-lift station for a ride down to Kandersteg, or follow the service road that leads from the hotels all the way to the village. If you decide to walk all the way, allow at least an hour for the descent. The road is extremely steep in places, but there are also footpath alternatives.

Route 66:	Kandersteg (1,176m) - Hohtürli (2,778m) - Blümlisalp Hut (2,837m)

Grade:	3
Distance:	10 kilometres
Height gain:	1,661 metres
Time:	5-5^{1}/2 hours

This walk is in part a reverse of Route 65. The way to the hut is, in fact,

147

a rather easier option when tackled from Kandersteg than from Griesalp, but it remains a strenuous day out anyway, and is no less a visual delight. First there are dainty waterfalls cascading down the great slabs of the Doldenhorn as you wander up to the Öeschinensee; then the lake itself - always a joy to gaze on. Above the lake there are rough boulder-strewn pastures with glaciers hanging from the looming peaks of the Blümlisalp, and the path climbs alongside them, on crests of old moraine before finally tackling a long slope of gritty scree. Once at the hut an amazing scene of high alpine splendour is an adequate reward for the time and energy required to get there.

Either take the chair-lift route to the Öeschinensee (Route 65), thus reducing the time required for the walk by about fifty minutes, or follow the service road through the Öeschinental to the east of Kandersteg, rising steeply alongside pine woods to reach the lake in about one hour fifteen minutes *(accommodation, refreshments)*. (If you decide to take the chair-lift there is an alternative path which leaves the main trail just before Läger. It skirts high above the northern side of the Öeschinensee and joins the path from the lake shore at Ober Bergli.)

Wander along the lakeside path which bears left just after the hotels, and continue with it as it begins to rise along a shelf above the northern shore. For a while it hugs the steep cliffs, then leads through shrubs and trees and comes to the alp buildings of Unter Bergli (1,767m). From the upper buildings the continuing path climbs steeply on almost a stairway to emerge on a lip above the Öeschinensee's deep bowl. Soon after, you arrive at Ober Bergli (1,981m; two hours forty-five minutes) set in a rough landscape of boulders.

The way wanders along the right-hand side of a stream, then crosses it and begins to rise once more above the grassy basin towards the moraines thrown up by the retreating glaciers. High above these, glaciers can be seen draped down the face of the various summits of the Blümlisalp massif. Now you go along the crest of a moraine wall, climb to a rocky shelf and come to an upper region of wide scree slopes. The hut can be seen perched on the ridge above. Ascend the screes by a switchback of a trail and come onto the saddle of Hohtürli about five hours after setting out from Kandersteg. Bear right and wander up the final slope to the hut, where you will have earned some refreshment.

To descend to Griesalp at the head of the Kiental on the far side of the Hohtürli, allow two and a half hours. It's a very steep descent and care must be taken over several sections. But for the return to Kandersteg by the same (upward) path, you will need three to three and a half hours.

Route 67: **Kandersteg (1,176m) - Öeschinensee (1,593m) - Fründen Hut (2,562m)**

Grade: 3
Distance: 9 kilometres
Height gain: 1,386 metres
Time: 4 hours

The Fründen Hut is perched on the top of a rocky bluff below the north-west flanks of the Fründenhorn (3,369m), a thousand metres above the Öeschinensee. The Fründen Glacier billows behind the hut, and the views from it are extremely dramatic. This route, though very steep in places, is not difficult, but with so much height to gain from Kandersteg it will be evident that the ascent can be somewhat tiring. The way is always interesting.

Take either the chair-lift route to the Öeschinensee (Route 65), or follow the service road referred to in Route 66 above. The path to the hut is signposted from the hotel/restaurants at the western end of the lake. Cross the little flood plain below the restaurants and follow the path as it meanders south-eastwards among trees and shrubs. After about 200 metres it begins to rise, quite gently at first, then growing a little steeper. It is a clearly marked trail, well-protected with fixed cables where exposed or liable to be greasy when wet. It crosses two fast-flowing streams on plank footbridges, and makes steady progress up the mountainside. The terrain becomes more rough and barren the higher you go, the gradient steepening considerably here and there. Zig-zags become more prolific; then you swing eastwards (left) and climb the final few metres of rocky tower, and suddenly emerge before the hut.

This spectacular situation deserves to be enjoyed at leisure, and if you can spare a night here, it will be a night to remember. Only ten minutes' walk from the hut you can gaze on a veritable maze of séracs and crevasses, and enjoy a wonderful high mountain vista. The hut can accommodate ninety in its dormitories, and has a guardian in residence from June till October.

Allow two to two and a half hours for the return to Kandersteg.

Route 68: Kandersteg (1,176m) - Doldenhorn Hut (1,915m)

Grade:	**2-3**
Distance:	**4.5 kilometres**
Height gain:	**739 metres**
Time:	**2¹/₂ hours**

As the Doldenhorn refuge is the most easily accessible to visitors staying in Kandersteg, this approach makes a reasonably popular outing. It is not very arduous, but it does have some steep sections.

Walk eastward along the road that leaves the main village street in the direction of the Öeschinensee, but leave it when it swings left to cross the Öeschinenbach and instead remain on the right-hand side of the stream. Follow this smaller lane heading into the Öeschinen glen, and after about half an hour a path (signposted to the hut) breaks away to the right and climbs a series of steep and tight zig-zags in order to overcome a rock barrier. Once over this the trail swings to the right, crosses a stream and traverses through woods. A second stream is crossed by a footbridge to a junction of paths. Turn left and climb alongside the stream. This path becomes steeper and then resorts to more zig-zags before the gradient eases, bears left and rises in a north-easterly direction to gain the hut.

Route 69: Kandersteg (1,176m) - Selden (1,552m)

Grade: 1
Distance: 10 kilometres
Height gain: 376 metres
Time: 2¹/₂ hours

This easy walk gives an opportunity to explore the lower reaches of the Gasterntal. (Route 70 below offers an extension as far as the glacier of the Kanderfirn, but is of a higher grade.) It is worth spending the day in the valley, having a picnic and exploring at leisure, and then returning to Kandersteg by minibus. Check the return time and book your seat before setting out, to ensure there will be room for you.

Wander south along the main valley road (it is not very busy beyond the village) as far as Eggeschwand where you find the Stock cable-car station. Branch left through the car park and follow a path into the Klus (or Chluse) gorge. The path climbs through the gorge beside the crashing torrent of the Kander, sometimes dampened by the spray, and emerges at the entrance to the Gasterntal to join the narrow valley service road. Follow this a short distance and cross to the opposite side of the river at a bridge, with a trail leading on to Hotel Waldhaus (1,358m; *accommodation, refreshments*). Continue beyond the hotel following a broad clear track up-valley among trees and over level meadows. When the track forks, bear left to cross the river, then go off to the right on a footpath among trees beside the Kander. This brings you to another crossing track where you turn right to cross the river once more. (Fine views from this bridge.) Now follow the track up-valley all the way to the small group of buildings at Selden (*accommodation, refreshments*).

Route 70:	Selden (1,552m) - Kanderfirn (2,411m)

Grade:	2-3
Distance:	4.5 kilometres
Height gain:	859 metres
Time:	2-2½ hours

From flower meadows to the edge of a glacier, this fine walk passes through several intermediate mountain zones. There are long views down-valley, close views of an icefall, the possibility of seeing marmots and chamois and, in midsummer, a blaze of alpenroses to brighten the day even further. It is one of the noted walks of the Gasterntal, and one that I always find totally satisfying. Taken on its own, using Selden as your base, it will require only half a day, there and back. But if you are staying in Kandersteg a full day will be required, whether you take the morning minibus taxi to Selden or walk there. Perhaps the best way of tackling it, if you are fit, is to make use of the minibus at the start of the day, then return on foot all the way from the Kanderfirn to Kandersteg.

Wander up-valley beyond Selden along the main track as far as the farm of Heimritz (1,632m; *accommodation, refreshments*). The track finishes here and a footpath continues on the left-hand side of the river. It climbs initially through a somewhat desolate region, then enters a higher part of the Gasterntal where lovely natural rock gardens adorn the way; shrubberies of dwarf pine and juniper, and starry flowers among the rocks and tiny 'lawns'. The path then crosses to the opposite side of the Kander, joins another path where you bear left, and goes through more flowery stretches before beginning to climb increasingly rocky slopes. This is marmot country.

The trail leads onto a moraine wall and rises higher towards ice cliffs of the Alpetli Glacier (the lower part of the Kanderfirn). As you gain height so these ice cliffs gleam almost blue in the sunlight. The way is now less sombre as it enters a belt of alpenroses. Gazing back the way you have come there are grand views of the valley with the Balmhorn rising above it. With the aid of zig-zags the path then overcomes a final barrier of rocks and reaches the edge of the glacier.

To vary the descent to Selden return down-valley on the left bank of the stream until you draw level with Berghaus Heimritz. A footbridge takes you across to the right bank. (Allow about one and a half hours to Selden, three hours from the glacier to Kandersteg.)

**Route 71:   Kandersteg (1,176m) - Mutthorn Hut (2,901m) -
                 Petersgrat (3,126m) - Fafleralp/Lötschental (1,788m)**

Grade: 3
Distance: 20 kilometres
Height gain: 1,950 metres (1,570m from Selden)
Height loss: 1,335 metres
Time: 2 days

The Petersgrat crossing is without question one of the classic walks of the Alps. Despite the fact that it traverses the length of a glacier and crosses a high snow- and ice-capped ridge it is a walk and not a climb, but it is a tough one, and one that requires competence and glacier experience. No-one should consider tackling it without the provision of ice-axe, crampons and rope, and the understanding of their correct usage. Given these provisos, this route could be a highlight of any mountain walker's holiday.

The Petersgrat is the remains of a vast ice cap that once covered much of the Bernese Alps, and it separates the Gasterntal from the Lötschental - the latter valley, although being still a part of the Bernese Alps is, in fact, within the canton Valais. To gain the Petersgrat requires the ascent of the Kanderfirn, while its descent to the Lötschental on the southern side initially involves negotiating a steeply-angled ice slope, then an extremely steep and wild glen which eventually gives out to the open splendour of the Lötschental. At all stages of the walk the scenery is glorious. A night is spent in the Mutthorn Hut too, and this gives an opportunity to capture the magic of both evening and early morning in the high mountains.

Either take the minibus taxi from Kandersteg station as far as Selden in the Gasterntal, or follow directions given under Route 69. From Selden to the edge of the glacier is described as Route 70. The path leads alongside the glacier, and when it ends you climb a series of grit-strewn rock terraces to gain the glacier proper. The Kanderfirn rises at a very gentle gradient and should present no major crevasse difficulties. Head straight up the glacier, keeping to the right-hand side. Above to the right a higher level of glacier holds modest ice cliffs; to the left rise the bare cliffs of the Blümlisalp peaks adorned here and there with only small remnants of hanging glaciers.

On reaching the head of the glacier the low crags of the flat-topped Mutthorn stand to the right of the Tschingelpass, with a second glacial saddle between the Mutthorn and Tschingelhorn. The hut is located just over this saddle, tucked against the eastern (right-hand) base of the Mutthorn's low cliffs. So reach the Mutthorn Hut, about two and a half hours from the edge of the Kanderfirn. It occupies an icy world, but the double-peaked Tschingelhorn (3,577m: 3,493m) looks impressive and aloof, and in the evening light glows splendidly.

On leaving the hut in the morning head almost due south towards the Petersgrat, aiming for the right-hand end of the Tschingelhorn's south-west ridge, where the ice folds easily little more than 200 metres above the height of the hut. There are a few crevasses, but they should be detected without problem.

The view from the Petersgrat is magical. It looks directly across the hinted depths of the Lötschental to the Bietschhorn, and far off to encompass almost the complete length of the Pennine Alps from the Dom to Mont Blanc (but without Monte Rosa or the Matterhorn, both of which are hidden by other peaks).

Below the Petersgrat the head of two valleys offer themselves for possible descent. To the left is the Inners Tal, but almost directly below is the Uisters Tal (also known as the Äusseres Faflertal). This second glen is the one to choose. Descend the steep snow and ice slope towards the left-hand side of the head of the glen, and leave the ice in favour of rocks when you can safely do so. Cairns will be seen leading down from the upper glacial slabs. They lead over modest rock bands, down slopes of scree and old snow tongues until at last you reach a proper path well to the left of the stream flowing down into the glen. This path is very steep in its initial stages, but eases lower down. As you progress towards the main Lötschental, the views ahead become increasingly impressive.

Once you reach the mouth of the Uisters Tal bear left on a crossing path and follow this down to Fafleralp *(accommodation, refreshments)* from where you can catch a Postbus down-valley to Goppenstein, and from there take a train through the Lötschberg Tunnel back to Kandersteg.

Route 72: **Kandersteg (1,176m) - Lötschenpass (2,690m) - Ferden/Lötschental (1,375m)**

Grade:	3		
Distance:	20 kilometres		
Height gain:	1,514 metres	**Height loss:**	1,315 metres
Time:	9 hours		

In common with Route 71, this walk makes a crossing of the high dividing ridge between the Gasterntal and Lötschental, and is another classic of its kind; the Lötschenpass (between Balmhorn and Hockenhorn) being the oldest glacier pass in the Bernese Alps, it is very popular as a walking excursion from both north and south sides. As with the Petersgrat crossing there is a glacier to contend with, but with respectful care it should give few problems. If you wish to shorten the walk, take the minibus taxi from Kandersteg station to Selden, thus saving two and a half hours' walking time. Accommodation and refreshments are available at various stages along the way.

Take Route 69 as far as Selden in the Gasterntal. Cross the valley to the south on a footpath signposted to Gfällalp and the Lötschenpass, using a Himalayan-style suspension bridge over the river. The path follows up the right-hand (western) side of a stream, the Leilibach, and is rather steep. Having gained about 300 metres of altitude the way slants up to the building of Gfällalp (1,847m; *accommodation, refreshments*) reached in about one hour from Selden.

The clearly marked trail continues, making steady progress up the hillside heading roughly south-west and with the Leilibach now falling below to the left. About one and a half hours hours from Gfällalp you come to the edge of the Lötschen Glacier. The route

155

across is usually marked with poles; most of the crevasses are easily seen and avoided. On the far side climb a series of rock terraces and in about an hour from the glacier you gain the Lötschenpass (six hours fifteen minutes from Kandersteg). The hut at the pass offers *matratzenlager* accommodation (places for thirty) and refreshments.

At first the descending path is taken at a gentle angle; it leads down to a small tarn or two and then steepens. Views are fine across to the Bietschhorn and out to the Pennine Alps. In one hour fifteen minutes from the pass you come to the alp hamlet of Kummenalp (2,083m; *accommodation, refreshments*) at the mouth of the hanging valley you've been descending. The trail to Ferden drops steeply below Kummenalp, crosses a stream, heads through forest and arrives in the bed of the Lötschental at the neat village *(accommodation, refreshments)* from where there is a Postbus link with Goppenstein. The train back to Kandersteg through the Lötschberg Tunnel may be caught here.

Note: The Lötschental is a real gem of a valley, one of the finest in all Switzerland, and is well worth spending time in. There are some delightful villages, grand mountains walling it, and plenty of opportunities for walks of all grades. For further details and descriptions of some of the best walks the valley has to offer, consult *The Valais - A Walking Guide*, also published by Cicerone Press.

Route 73:	Kandersteg (1,176m) - Gasterntal - Balmhorn Hut (1,955m)

Grade:	3
Distance:	7 kilometres
Height gain:	779 metres
Time:	3¹⁄₂ hours

Another steep walk to a mountain hut of the Swiss Alpine Club, this makes a fine but energetic day out. The Balmhorn Hut, as its name suggests, is perched below the glaciers that adorn the northern flanks of the Balmhorn mountain. It overlooks the lower reaches of the Gasterntal, through which it is approached, and enjoys a privileged

Balmhorn hut signpost in Gasterntal

view from the stalls, as it were, of the wild glacial amphitheatre overhead formed by the converging ridges of the twin peaks that so dominate the southern limits of the Kandertal: Altels and Balmhorn. For much of the way the route is straightforward, if rather steep and narrow and exposed in places. There are sections of fixed cable, others with rough ladders to help overcome certain natural obstacles. And shortly before reaching the hut there is a short (ten-minute) stretch where the path crosses directly below the ice cliffs of the Balmhorn glacier. As is the nature of such ice cliffs, every now and then some break away to create small avalanches and possible stonefall, and the objective danger inherent in this is something all who tackle this walk should be aware of. A notice warning of this danger is positioned on the path as you approach the line of fire.

Follow directions for Route 69 as far as Hotel Waldhaus *(accommodation, refreshments)*. Continue up-valley on the broad main track for another 600 metres or so. As you cross a large open

157

meadowland look for a finely carved wooden figure of a mountaineer on the right. This is the signpost indicating the start of the path to the Balmhorn Hut. The path branches to the right and heads among trees. On coming to the foot of the cliffs the path begins its steep ascent. There are no alternative routes, so simply follow the trail as it makes its way directly up the mountainside. As mentioned above, there are places where fixed cables aid the way; others with sections of rough ladder. Caution is advised for almost always is there a degree of exposure as the path clings precariously to the cliff face.

Eventually the trail leads into a mid-height glacial cirque where the hut can be seen on the far side. High above the glacier's ice cliffs hang ominously. You come to the danger sign, and from here to the hut you should step warily and move fast across moraine, streams and debris. Then, with a sense of relief, come to the hut sitting prettily on its grassy promontory.

The hut can sleep twenty-eight in its dormitory, and a guardian is on duty only at weekends in summer.

Route 74:	Kandersteg (1,176m) - Stock (1,834m) - Gemmipass (2,314m)

Grade: 2
Distance: 15 kilometres
Height gain: 1,138 metres (480 metres if cable-car is used)
Time: 5-5¹/₂ hours (3-3¹/₂ hours with use of cable-car)

The Gemmi is an ancient crossing between the cantons of Bern and Valais, and over the centuries it has been traversed by countless thousands of farmers, traders, pilgrims and tourists. In the early eighteenth century a remarkable staircase of a path was created down the almost perpendicular wall from the pass to Leukerbad; a route that was tackled by mule as well as by men, though accidents were not unknown, as may be guessed by anyone who studies the route today. Nowadays there's cableway access from Leukerbad to the pass, while the route from Kandersteg is similarly eased by mechanical means. Yet despite this taming of the Gemmi and the approach to it, nothing can detract from the sheer splendour of the panorama that greets those who arrive there. From the pass one gazes south to the great chain of the Pennine Alps including Monte Rosa, the Mischabelhörner, Matterhorn, Dent Blanche, Weisshorn and Bouquetins and many, many more. A fabulous view it is, and one that gives a considerable lift to this walk. The curious valley that leads to the pass from the upper station of the Eggeschwand-Stock cable-car is a noted flower garden. Mountains and glaciers wall it, and shortly before reaching the Gemmi you pass alongside the grey limestone-bordered Daubensee. The Wildstrubel rises to the west, Altels and Balmhorn to the east.

Leaving Kandersteg wander up-valley as far as Eggeschwand where the cable-car swings up to Stock. There are two footpath routes for those who prefer to walk all the way; both entail very steep sections as outlined below.

Option 1: Continue along the road beyond the cable-car station until it makes a hairpin bend to the left to enter the Gasterntal. The footpath to Stock begins at this bend and works its way among trees and shrubbery, climbing very steeply and in two and a half hours from Kandersteg arrives at the upper cable-car station. (A chair-lift continues from the upper station to Sunnbühl.)

Option 2: From the car park by the Eggeschwand-Stock cableway station walk through the Klus gorge into the Gasterntal as far as Hotel Waldhaus (see Route 69 for details). At the Waldhaus take the path heading off to the right. It takes you up the left-hand side of a narrow cleft on a series of tight zig-zags, the path made safe in places by fixed cable. It works its way ever higher among woods and emerges at last in the upper valley of the Schwarz Bach just south of the Sunnbühl chair-lift station and restaurant. Continue up-valley along a broad clear path.

For those who choose to ride the cable-car, the way from the upper station is straightforward and signposted. It wanders through a region of alpenroses and dwarf pine, following the course of the chair-lift as far as Sunnbühl (1,934m; *refreshments*). Continue up-valley on a well-trodden track. At the alp pasture of Spittelmatte (1,875m) you cross an area devastated in September 1895 by the collapse of part of the western glacier draped down the Altels (seen above to the left) which killed six herdsmen and their cattle. Beyond this the way crosses a stony region and comes to Schwarenbach (2,060m; *accommodation, refreshments*), about four hours from Kandersteg (one and a half hours from Stock). Between Spittelmatte and Hotel Schwarenbach is the cantonal boundary between Bern and Valais.

Leaving Schwarenbach you steadily gain height over rocky ground, come to the shallow Daubensee, sometimes semi-frozen in midsummer, skirt this along its eastern (left-hand) shore, and then climb beyond it for about ten minutes to reach the Gemmipass *(accommodation, refreshments)* with its magnificent views and abundance of wild flowers in the early summer.

Allow four hours for the return to Kandersteg. Should your plan be to continue as far as Leukerbad, however, the way is obvious, if rather dizzy with its staggering number of zig-zags. The walk will take about one hour forty minutes from the pass, the resort seen with a bird's eye view all the way. Or, alternatively, you could take the cableway.

Route 75:	Kandersteg (1,176m) - Stock (1,834m) - Lämmern Hut (2,515m)

Grade:	3
Distance:	18 kilometres
Height gain:	1,339 metres
Time:	6 hours

For those who fancy a night spent in the wilds of the Gemmipass region, the Lämmern Hut (or Lämmerenhütte) offers one option. It is set in grey limestone country to the west of the Gemmipass, under the Lämmerenhorn which is itself embraced by the crescent of snow, ice and rock of the Wildstrubel. The hut, owned by the Angenstein section of the SAC, can sleep seventy-eight in its dormitories.

Follow directions for Route 74 as far as the Daubensee. Take the path along the western (right-hand) side of the lake, go through the Lämmerendalu ravine beyond it and then bear right round a spur, following the stream to the Lämmerenalp (2,296m) where there is a tarn. The trail heads left away from the tarn to make the final ascent to the hut. This is achieved by way of tight zig-zags to gain the shelf below the Lämmerenhorn where the hut rests.

Route 76: **Kandersteg (Allmenalp; 1,732m) -**
Usser Üschene (1,595m) - Kandersteg (1,176m)

Grade: 1-2
Distance: 8 kilometres
Height loss: 556 metres
Time: 2½ hours

On the western hillside above Kandersteg a shallow scooped bowl of rough pasture below the Bunderspitz (2,546m) is occupied by the little alp farm of Allmenalp where visitors can often watch cheese being made. The farm also doubles as a restaurant, and on the terrace one may sit in the sunshine with a lovely view across the valley towards the Öeschinensee and the Blümlisalp peaks. A nearby slope has been adopted as the launching site for a paragliding school, and on most days in summer the sky is brightened by what at first look like gaily coloured butterflies drifting in the breeze. A small, eight-person cable-car serves this green bowl between May and October, and gives inspiration for several worthwhile walks. This is just one of them, a highly recommended, easy walk, it follows a broad track for much of the way, and has constant fine views to indulge in, especially to the twin peaks of Altels and Balmhorn guarding the entrance to the Gasterntal.

The valley station of the cable-car to Allmenalp is found in a meadow to the south-west of the village railway station. The cabin takes only five minutes to gain the upper hillside where initially all paths head in one direction; uphill. After a few metres take the first path branching left. It leads directly to the chalet-farm of Allmenalp (Undere Allme; 1,725m; *refreshments*) and continues, climbing a short section, then becomes a broad track with magnificent views of the mountains heading the Kandertal. The track contours comfortably along the mountainside. You pass the few alp buildings of Ryharts (where a narrow path drops steeply to Kandersteg) and remain with the track as it curves into the mouth of the Üschenental.

The track/farm road winds into the valley, passing several farms, then comes to a junction. Bear left and wander eastwards to leave the valley, and when you see a *Wanderweg* sign on the right as the road descends, break away on this footpath which short-cuts the road route. No specific descriptions of this descent are necessary. It is sufficient to say the trail leads through forest almost all the way down, and finally reaches Eggeschwand in the valley. Now take the footpath heading off to the left which takes you across meadows to the International Scout Camp, and from there an easy, well-signposted path continues alongside the river to deliver you back to Kandersteg railway station.

Route 77:	Kandersteg (Allmenalp; 1,732m) - Usser Üschene (1,595m) - Tälliseeli (2,405m) - Kandersteg (1,176m)

Grade:	2-3		
Distance:	19 kilometres		
Height gain:	673 metres	Height loss:	1,229 metres
Time:	5½-6 hours		

This full day's walk is an extension of the previous route, for it leads through the Üschenental and visits a tarn trapped beneath the Engstligengrat - a ridge dividing the Üschenental from the attractive Engstligenalp overlooking Adelboden. Above the tarn there is actually a neat pass giving access to Adelboden, but crossing that pass is not for us; the tarn is sufficient. It occupies a grand patch of country and looks up to the Täligletscher which feeds it from the slopes of the Steghorn to the south.

Follow directions as for Route 76 as far as the junction of tracks at the entrance to the Üschenental. This is Usser Üschene. Continue on the track heading deeper into the valley; a very pleasant pastoral glen with lines of crags running above it and the mountains at its head looking mysterious. Stay with the track all the way, passing several clusters of alp farms, and when it finishes at Unterbächen take the footpath leading south-west (veering left from the end of the track). It begins to climb stream-laced rocky slopes, and then eases through a natural gap in the crags that hide the upper section of the glen where the Tälliseeli is located.

Return to Kandersteg by the track to Usser Üschene and then adopt the descent route given under Route 76.

Route 78: **Kandersteg (Allmenalp; 1,732m) - First (2,549m) - Stand (2,320m) - Kandersteg (1,176m)**

Grade:	**3**
Distance:	**10 kilometres**
Height gain:	**817 metres** **Height loss: 1,373 metres**
Time:	**5½-6 hours**

Two summits linked by a good path, followed by a steep descent to the valley, make this a strenuous but very rewarding day out. The summits in question, First and Stand, may not be mountains of great stature, but they have a certain elegance and there's nothing second-rate about the panorama they enjoy. Standing up there on a clear day you can see Mont Blanc far off. The Matterhorn too, and Jungfrau and Eiger. Not forgetting the nearer-to-hand Blümlisalp above the deep jewel of the Öeschinensee. It's a route that demands a good clear day, and if snow is lingering on the high ridges you should retreat unless you're equipped and experienced to cope with any possible hazard.

Take the cable-car to Allmenalp and on arrival walk uphill on a steep path that winds through rough sloping pastures. This is a good flowery stretch, with St Bruno's lily particularly being in evidence in late June/early July. The upper farm of Obere Allme (1,946m) is reached, and above it you must branch right on a path heading north-east. This path leads directly to the building of Steintal (2,027m) where you swing left and climb in gradient-easing loops, then steeper in zig-zags to gain the ridge (the Allmegrat) just below the summit of First.

The continuing route from First to Stand (seen off to the north beyond Howang) avoids a narrow arête. To do so it descends to the western side of the ridge, passes below Howang on a traverse and then by an easy trail up the south-west ridge to the summit of Stand.

Now descend the steep north-west ridge a short distance. The path then bears right, contours below the summit and reaches the Golitschepass (2,180m) - one of the few passes to link the Kandertal with the Engstligental. The path loses height on the eastern side by a series of zig-zags, and in about forty minutes from the pass comes to Golitschealp (1,833m). Veering to the right at the alp building the trail slopes round to cross a prominent stream, passes round a spur, crosses a boulder field and works its way steadily down to the valley.

Route 79:	Kandersteg (1,176m) - Bunderchrinde (2,385m) - Adelboden (1,353m)

Grade:	3		
Distance:	16 kilometres		
Height gain:	1,209 metres	Height loss:	1,032 metres
Time:	6¹/₂-7 hours		

Another classic pass crossing, the Bunderchrinde is a narrow cleft in the high wall of mountains to the west of the Kandertal. It actually links the ridge of the Gross Lohner with that of the Bunderspitz, and offers an interesting way for walkers to travel from the Kandertal to the Engstligental.

The route leaves Kandersteg by the railway station, follows a tarmac footpath to the left (up-valley) running parallel with the railway line, veers right beneath a bridge and crosses the Kander river. Now along a surfaced lane you pass near the Allmenalp cableway and take a footpath alongside the river as far as the International Scout Camp *(Pfadfinder Zentrum)*. Just beyond the buildings a path breaks away to the right and crosses open meadows. On coming to a fork in the path, marked by a signpost midway across one of these meadows, bear right into woods.

The path climbs through the woods, crossing and recrossing a road on short cuts, always gaining height. On coming to the entrance to the Üschenental follow the farm road/track round to the cluster of buildings at Usser Üschene (1,548m) about one hour forty-five minutes from Kandersteg. At the junction of tracks bear left and wander deeper into the valley for about 400 metres. Then head to the right on a grassy path going up the hillside towards a long line of cliffs. The path makes progress without too much effort, then swings left before climbing steeply through a natural fault in the cliffs and bearing right above them.

You then make a steady traverse high above the valley, over rough terrain and with good views off to the right into the Gasterntal. Three hours from setting out you come to the alp huts of Alpschele (2,094m), and have a first real view of the Bunderchrinde above. Pass to the left of the last building and continue on the path as it rises over grass slopes to the north. Instead of wandering up to a green saddle ahead, the trail doubles back to the left and reaches a signpost on the edge of a broad scree slope. The path eases across the screes at a comfortable gradient and brings you directly to the dramatic rocky pass of Bunderchrinde about fifty minutes from the alp.

Descending to the west the path goes steeply down to more screes, then veers towards the right-hand side of a stony corrie. The way is obvious, and it loops down without difficulty to reach a grassy bluff with a cattle byre almost sunken into it (Bunderchumi; 2,098m). The trail descends beyond this and then forks. Break off to the right and cross rough pastures to a farm set a little above a road. Drop to the road and walk along it a short distance to the right. You will come to a second farm, Bonderalp (1,760m; *accommodation, refreshments*) where you have a choice of routes down to Adelboden - both taking one hour forty minutes. A footpath on the left offers a way down over pastures and through woods, while the continuing road twists its way with less commitment down the hillside. Both arrive in the valley to the south of Adelboden. You will then be faced with a last uphill walk to gain the main part of the village.

Other Walks from Kandersteg:
A variation of the crossing of **BUNDERCHRINDE** (Route 79 above) involves going through the pass and down the first section of screes, but then branching away from the Adelboden route to veer to the right under the crags of Chlyne Lohner and sloping up to go through another pass immediately below the **BUNDERSPITZ**, and from there down to Kandersteg via Allmenalp. This, of course, would be Grade 3.

Another crossing to **ADELBODEN** goes through the Üschenental and over the **ENGSTLIGENGRAT**, as an extension of Route 77. Another long, but rewarding Grade 3 walk.

Still on the western side of the valley, a five and a half-hour route crosses the Golitschepass (2,180m) below Stand, and descends to the pretty hamlet of **ACHSETEN** in the Engstligental. Good views and a stretch of lonely countryside; Grade 3.

The well-publicised **HÖHENWEG NORDRAMPE**, mentioned in the Kiental section, is well worth considering too. This makes a traverse of the eastern hillsides above the Kandertal and heads down-valley (but uphill) to Ramslauenen above **KIENTAL**, and could be continued on a subsequent day all the way to the Thunersee. (Enquire at the tourist office for details.)

One superb multi-day route comes down to Kandersteg too, and that is the **WILDSTRUBEL CIRCUIT**, outlined at the end of this book (Route 115: Tour Wildstrubel). A leaflet is available, and week-long guided walking tours are organised round this snowy massif in the summer. Again, enquire at the tourist office for details, prices etc.

ENGSTLIGENTAL

Position: West of the Kandertal, the Engstligental flows
              north-east from the Wildstrubel and joins the
              Kander at Frutigen.
Map: L.S. 5009 'Gstaad-Adelboden' 1:50,000
Base: Adelboden (1,353m)
Tourist Information:
              Verkehrsbüro, 3715 Adelboden (Tel: 033 73 2252)

On entering the Engstligental at Frutigen one of the first impressions
the visitor gains is that the valley seems to grow more narrow,
forested and steep-walled than that of the Frutigtal just left behind,
but farther up-valley at its head this perception changes as the aspect
becomes one of open, sunny benevolence. The road takes its time to
reach that upper region, though, and it winds carefully above the
west bank of the river with numerous streams pouring through
gullies from the long ridge of peaks above. Up there, at mid-height,
little alp huts and hamlets are linked by ancient paths used by
generations of peasant farmers and chamois hunters, and in a few
places little-known passes lead across the mountains to the Diemtigtal
beyond.

   On the eastern side of the valley the Elsighorn marks the northern
end of the ridge that runs from the snowy Wildstrubel; the ridge that
divides the Engstligental from the Kandertal. But as you progress
through the valley, so the Wildstrubel comes into view, impressing
itself upon the valley in a picturesque way.

   The road climbs higher and deeper into the valley and crosses to
the true left bank at Rinderwald to avoid the gorge of Pochtenkessel,
only to return to the western side again after another four kilometres
shortly before reaching Oey where it makes the final steep ascent to
the sunny terrace occupied by Adelboden.

   The head of the valley beyond Adelboden is a large grassy bowl
sub-divided into minor glens and the high plateau of Engstligenalp
which is topped by the Wildstrubel itself. Apart from the Wildstrubel's

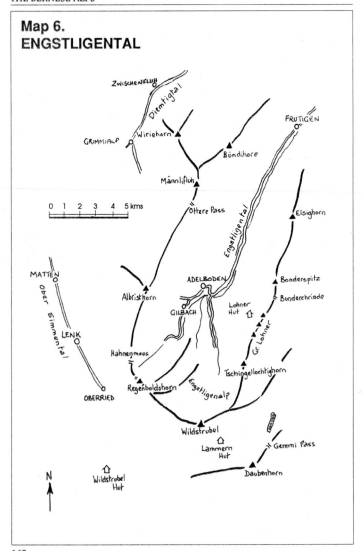

Map 6.
ENGSTLIGENTAL

ZWISCHENFLUH

Diemtigtal

FRUTIGEN

GRIMMIALP
Wiriehorn

Bündihore

Männlifluh

0 1 2 3 4 5 kms

Ottere Pass

Elsighorn

Engstligental

MATTEN

ADELBODEN

Bonderspitz

Ober Simmental

Albristhorn

Bunderchrinde

GILBACH

Lohner Hut

LENK

Gr. Lohner

Hahnegmoos

Tschingellochtighorn

Engstligenalp

OBERRIED

Regenboldshorn

Wildstrubel

Lammern Hut

Gemmi Pass

N

Wildstrubel Hut

Daubenhorn

Wildstrubel, seen from above Adelboden

snow crown and the craggy Lohner group, most of the peaks have plant cover virtually to their summits. Green mountains with easy walkers' passes between them, they offer a friendly, welcoming face and make a direct contrast to the big raw mountains experienced at the head of other Oberland valleys farther to the east. It's a land of pasture and forest, of stunning waterfalls and attractive hidden corners, of clear streams and flower meadows.

This is country for walking in. It's not so much a mountaineer's landscape, other than among a few modest peaks, but there are plenty of opportunities for pedestrian outings of all grades of seriousness, from easy valley strolls to longer circuits and multi-day expeditions into neighbouring valleys. And there's no shortage of accommodation.

Main Valley Base:

ADELBODEN (1,353m) gazes directly across the head of the valley to the Wildstrubel and Lohner ranges. It's a lovely view and one that encourages visitors to go exploring. Adelboden is mainly a ski resort, but summer visitors will nevertheless find plenty to enjoy and as a base for a holiday the village has a lot to offer in the way of shops, restaurants, banks, PTT and, of course, numerous hotels and *pensions*. There are some 7,000 beds in holiday flats, various *matratzenlagers* and two campsites. Reached by train as far as Frutigen and bus from there (fifteen kilometres), it is easily accessible to those without their own transport, while a minibus service relays holiday makers to Unter dem Berg (for Engstligenalp) and Geils (for the Hahnenmoos) to shorten the approach to some fine walking areas. Motorised day visitors are provided for with a large underground car park on the edge of the village. There are cableways (cable-car, chair-lift or gondola) to Engstligenalp, Hahnenmoos and to Tschentenalp (Schwandfeldspitz). Adelboden has open-air swimming and its own mountaineering school. There are a few old buildings in the village and surrounding areas, while the church dates from the fifteenth century. It has a notable sixteenth century mural of the Last Judgement on the outer south wall.

Mountain Huts:

There is only one SAC refuge immediately accessible from Adelboden, and that is the **LOHNER HUT** (2,171m). This is lodged high in a corrie to the east of the village above distinctive rock towers and below the western crags of the Gross Lohner. It has spaces for forty-six, a guardian only at weekends in summer, and is reached by a three-hour walk from Adelboden.

Although there is only one mountain hut in the area, there are plenty of other lodgings scattered about the hillsides away from the village itself where one can spend a night or two in order to capture the alpine ambience. **ENGSTLIGENALP** (1,950m) is of particular interest, of course, and on this plateau beneath the Wildstrubel there's a Berghotel and Berghaus, both of which offer bedrooms and *matratzenlager* accommodation. At **UNTER DEM BERG** (1,400m) below Engstligenalp, Restaurant Steinbock offers dormitory places for twenty.

Elsewhere there's a *pension* as well as *matratzenlager* for 140 at **GILBACH**, (1,430m) up-valley from Adelboden on the way to Hahnenmoos, while **HOTEL HAHNENMOOS** offers both beds and dormitory places. At **BONDERALP** on the way to the Bunderchrinde and Kandersteg there's an alcohol-free restaurant with provision for twenty-five in its dormitories.

Route 80:   Adelboden (1,353m) - Engstligenalp (1,964m)

Grade: 2
Distance: 7 kilometres
Height gain: 611 metres
Time: 3 hours

Engstligenalp is very much a show-piece among the upper reaches of the valley. It's a high-level plateau sliced with streams at the foot of the Wildstrubel. Scattered about the plateau are a number of farms, but there's accommodation to be had here too, and cable-car access from Unter dem Berg. A bus travels from Adelboden along a narrow lane through pastures and as far as Unter dem Berg, so it would be quite easy to reach Engstligenalp virtually without walking at all, but that would be to miss much.

From the main village street above the valley follow signs to the swimming pool and continue down the steep hillside slope until you can cross the river (the Allebach) by bridge to the south side. Then up to Fuhre (Uf der Fure on the map) and the chalets of Boden (1,289m; *accommodation, refreshments*) which you reach in about half an hour. Directly ahead the Wildstrubel, and a great cascading waterfall pouring from the Engstligenalp, lure you along a gentle wooded valley following a narrow lane through flowery meadows.

About two and a half kilometres along this lane it veers left to cross the Engstlige stream and goes to Unter dem Berg and the cable-car to Engstligenalp. Instead of following it here, remain on the right-hand side of the stream and continue through woods towards the lower waterfalls. After about 500 metres swing left, then take the right-hand path (still among woods) at a junction to climb steeply on a mule-track that goes directly beneath the cableway. The path is very steep in places, but it is well-made and there are one or two signposted opportunities to stray slightly to gaze on the magnificent Engstligen Falls, among the finest in Switzerland. The falls have been a Swiss national monument since 1948 and are well worth spending time to gaze on.

The path continues, making height against dark crags, the falls to one side and long views out towards Adelboden and the hills above the village. Then at last you emerge to a sudden open pastureland, a direct contrast to the confines of the last section of climb, and Engstligenalp is spread before you, a crescent of peaks cradling a huge level meadowland - it has no equal anywhere in the Alps. Refreshments and accommodation are both available here.

Route 81:	Adelboden (1,353m) - Unter dem Berg (1,400m) - Hinterberg - Engstligenalp (1,964m)

Grade:	2-3
Distance:	9 kilometres
Height gain:	611 metres
Time:	3¹/₂ hours

This walk is a variation of Route 80. While it misses the opportunity for a close-up view of the Engstligen Falls, the corrie of Hinterberg is the haunt of marmots, chamois and ibex, and there may well be the chance to catch sight of one or more of these animals as you wander through.

The approach is the same as for Route 80, except that you follow the lane all the way to Unter dem Berg *(accommodation, refreshments)*, reached in about one to one and a half hours from Adelboden. Almost opposite the cable-car station a path cuts along the edge of woods, then veers right to go through them and climb in zig-zags, emerging from the trees onto more open ground before swinging south-east to enter Hinterberg. The corrie is formed by the ridge running from the Vorder Lohner to Tschingellochtighorn. Crossing streams the trail now works round the western end of the Artelengrat to be confronted by the great grassland bowl of Engstligenalp.

Route 82:   **Engstligenalp (1,964m) - Engstligengrat (2,623m) -**
                  Rote Kumme (2,620m) - Gemmipass (2,314m)

Grade: 3
Distance: 11 kilometres
Height gain: 770 metres   **Height loss:** 418 metres
Time: 4¹⁄₂ hours

The crossing of the Engstligengrat and Rote Kumme (also known as Rote Chumme) between Engstligenalp and the Gemmipass is one of the classic walks of the area. It is an energetic, though not necessarily difficult route for experienced mountain walkers, but it will require fine settled conditions and good visibility to tackle. Should the weather be at all questionable, do not set out.

Follow the main track running south from the cable-car station on the edge of Engstligenalp, and across the first main stream veer left, heading south-east across the pastureland. The way is clear and on the far side of the pastures it begins to climb up to the ridge above Marbenen. After about two hours twenty minutes you reach a saddle in the Engstligengrat (the Kindbettjoch) to the north of Tierhornli. Cross to the eastern side heading south-east to cut round the head of the Tälli valley. (The Tälliseeli tarn is seen below - this was visited on Route 77 from Kandersteg.) You pass below the Tälli Glacier then climb to the pass of Rote Kumme (one hour from the Engstligengrat).

The Daubensee lies four hundred metres below, and the path descends to it initially by some tight zig-zags and down through a very stony landscape, reaching the lake in forty minutes from the pass. Bear right at the lake and follow it southward, and at the far end where the path divides, take the left fork and wander up to the Gemmipass *(accommodation, refreshments)* for superb views across the Rhône Valley to the chain of the Pennine Alps.

To continue down to Leukerbad either take the cable car, or wander down the stairway of a path (one hour forty minutes). If you plan to spend a night in the Lämmern Hut (see Route 75), allow two hours from the Gemmipass. Allow four hours to return from the Gemmipass to Engstligenalp by the same outward route.

Route 83:	Engstligenalp (1,964m) - Ammertenpass (2,443m) - Lenk (1,068m)

Grade:	3		
Distance:	15 kilometres		
Height gain:	479 metres	Height loss:	1,375 metres
Time:	5½ hours		

This crossing has a good reputation among experienced mountain walkers in Switzerland, but I have no personal experience of the complete route. An outline is given for those who enjoy the challenge of personal discovery, but it should be stressed that this should only be attempted by experienced mountain trekkers. The descent from the pass into the Ammertentali is supposedly a little tricky.

The Ammertenpass is found in the south-western corner of the Engstligenalp, where the Ammertengrat is joined by the ridge linking it with the Rotstock. The path to the pass is clearly marked and will take two hours to ascend from the cable-car station. On the far side of the pass descend with care through the wildly romantic Ammertentali, joining other paths lower down and coming to the spectacular Simmenfälle cascades two and a half hours from the pass. A clear, but often greasy, path leads alongside the stream issuing from the falls and brings you to the floor of the valley at Oberried *(accommodation, refreshments, campsite)*. The continuing path now takes you along the left bank of the stream all the way to Lenk.

Route 84:	Adelboden (1,353m) - Tronegg Grat (1,940m) - Pommernpass (2,055m) - Lenk (1,068m)

Grade:	3
Distance:	18 kilometres

Height gain: 814 metres   **Height loss:** 1,099 metres
Time: 6½-7 hours

One of several routes to Lenk, this makes an interesting day's outing and visits some lonely stretches of countryside on the way. There are no opportunities for refreshment until about an hour from the end of the walk, and few fresh water supplies on the route, so be prepared and carry a full bottle from the start.

Wander downhill along the twisting main road leading out of Adelboden as far as the lower hairpin bend beside a soft drinks factory (*Minerelquelle*, 1,275m). Take the tarmac path/narrow road leading alongside the factory in the direction of Hahnenmoos. On coming to a junction at the river, head to the left and begin to gain height along the narrow road. This leads through pastures and passes farms and chalets. Then you will see a footpath heading off to the right, cutting steeply up through a meadow to short-cut the road. Continue on the footpath and its successors (waymarked most of the way) with fine views down to Adelboden and across the valley to the Lohner peaks.

The path eventually rejoins the road for its final winding to a farm set upon a grassy ridge (Chuenigsbargli, 1,739m). Above the farm a footpath junction bears a signpost giving directions to Hahnenmoos (two hours). Take the path going straight ahead (south) along the right-hand side of the ridge. You pass beneath a mechanical hoist and enter woods, emerging on their far side near a small farm building at 1,802 metres. The path is rather faint here, but it rises steadily and becomes more clear as you gain the ridge once more. This is Tronegg Grat and there are delightful views to the Engstligenalp, its waterfalls and upper snow ridge.

Continue along the Tronegg Grat ridge. The path, however, soon begins to make a steady descending traverse of the western slopes of Fitzer; first among vegetation, then over screes and finally down to the valley floor of the Butschital. Wander up-valley along a farm road. It leads to an upper farm where a *Bergweg* path continues roughly south-westwards to gain a grassy saddle known as Lüegli (2,080m). This is not named on the map, but is situated between the s and h of Regenboldshorn. The continuing footpath takes you on a traverse of the face of Regenboldshorn, and to a junction of paths. Take the upper trail to reach the Pommernpass after about three and a half to four hours.

It is worth straying here to climb the steep slope to the left onto the summit of the Regenboldshorn (fifteen minutes from the pass) for an extensive panorama.

Descending from the pass the path veers left and takes you over steep pastures, past haybarns and farms and down to forest. Signs are for the Simmenfälle, Oberried or Lenk. The way through the forest is clear and on a broad path. The dramatic Simmenfälle is reached in two hours from the pass. Cross a walkway in the full spray of the waterfall and continue down the woodland path to Oberried (1,103m; *accommodation, refreshments, campsite*). If you've walked far enough for one day you can catch a bus from here to Lenk. The footpath route will take an hour. Walk along the road for about 400 metres, then cross the river and head to the right on a pleasant path that leads all the way to Lenk (*accommodation, refreshments, shops etc*).

Route 85: **Adelboden (1,353m) - Hahnenmoos (1,956m) - Lenk (1,068m)**

Grade:	**2**		
Distance:	**12 kilometres**		
Height gain:	**603 metres**	**Height loss:**	**888 metres**
Time:	**4¹/₂ hours**		

The Hahnemoos Pass is an ancient crossing which links the valleys of Lenk (the Ober Simmental) and Engstligental. It was also the site of a local festival that was held centuries ago; a broad grassy saddle where villagers from both valleys used to meet, to take part in trade and to compete in athletic contests. As a result of an epidemic which killed hundreds of Adelboden's inhabitants, the pass was closed for a while in 1669. Nowadays it is again a popular place - winter as well as in summer - thanks to its ease of access. This is by far the simplest route across the mountains to Lenk, and for much of the way it follows quiet surfaced roads among pastureland. The route to the pass is straightforward, wandering through the gentle Geilsbach (or Gilbach) valley, while views on the descent from the saddle are quite beautiful.

Follow the main street out of Adelboden heading south-west until you come to a fork in the road. The left-hand route is the one to take, and it soon leads over an arched bridge and twists into the Geilsbach glen. Forty minutes from setting out you come to the scattered hamlet of Gilbach (1,430m; *accommodation, refreshments*) and continue along the lane with views south to Fitzer and Rotstock, whose interlocking ridge is one which helps contain the Engstligenalp.

Maintain direction deeper into the valley and enjoy the chalets and farms nestling in a green and tranquil landscape around you. When the road forks take the right branch, and 500 metres later when it makes a sharp hairpin bend, leave the road and follow a footpath ahead through woods. This will lead directly to Geilsbuel (1,720m; *refreshments*) where a gondola lift swings up ahead to the Hahnenmoos Pass. Continue to Hahnenmoos using short cuts where possible, and in about forty-five minutes from the large restaurant you will arrive at the pass.

Hahnenmoos *(accommodation, refreshments)* is a crowded place on a bright summer's day, and is reached in about two hours forty-five minutes from Adelboden. The panorama is lovely, and as you wander down the other side, on a clear and easy gravel track, so the views become yet brighter along the Simmental and over to the Weisshorn and its neighbouring glacier.

In a little over half an hour you come to Hotel Büelberg (1,661m; *accommodation, refreshments*), where there is a bus to Lenk. The road here winds down in long loops, but there are some opportunities to make short cuts on footpath now and then. Both road and footpath lead without difficulty all the way to Lenk.

Alternative descent: From Hahnenmoos do not cross over but instead bear left and wander along a clear path rounding the hillside towards the lump of the Regenboldshorn. The trail climbs easily to gain a narrow grassy pass (the Pommernpass; 2,055m) to the right (west) of this peak, and the descent on the far side is the same as that described for Route 84 above.

Route 86:	Adelboden (1,353m) - Bunderchrinde (2,385m)

Grade:	3
Distance:	9 kilometres
Height gain:	1,032 metres
Time:	3¹⁄₂-4 hours

This walk is a partial reverse of Route 79, the cross-country route from Kandersteg. The Bunderchrinde is a narrow pass, a classic nick in the ridge linking the Gross Lohner and the Bunderspitz, and the corrie leading to it is a great place to watch chamois.

Descend the main road out of Adelboden, heading towards Frutigen. At the foot of the lower part of the village is a collection of houses and shops known as Oey, where the Allebach is joined by the Engstlige stream. Shortly before reaching this confluence a road breaks away to the right, crossing the Allebach as it does. Go over the bridge and turn left almost immediately, following a minor road which rises along the hillside, turns a spur and enters the Bunderle (or Bonder) valley. Wander along the road into the valley heading south-east towards the fine steep rise of the Gross Lohner ahead. As you wander deeper into the valley, you pass one or two restaurants.

The road crosses the Bunderle Bach stream and swings north-westward. Soon after a path heads off to the right, signposted to Bunderchrinde and Kandersteg. Follow this uphill, steeply in places, and climbing through forest and over a sloping pasture or two you eventually emerge onto a farm road at Bonderalp (1,760m; *accommodation, refreshments*) a little over two hours from Adelboden. Bear right and walk along the road to a second farm, and there break away to cross the rough pastures on the left, following a narrow path uphill to Bunder Chumi, a couple of huts and cattle byres on a grassy bluff. The path heads round past these and strikes up into a scree-cluttered corrie with the Bunderchrinde seen as a dip in the ridge above. The final climb to it leads up the left-hand side of the corrie, then zig-zags to gain the rocky pass after one hour forty-five minutes from Bonderalp.

Should your plan include continuing to Kandersteg, the descent route is clear and well-marked from the pass. It leads down to the alp hut of Alpschele, and from there into the Usser Uschene valley before plunging through forest to the bed of the Kandertal. Allow about three hours from the pass - whether you go down to Kandersteg, or return to Adelboden.

Other Walks from Adelboden:
The routes described above represent only a small selection of outings available from Adelboden. There are numerous walks of varying degrees of commitment, among them the Grade 3 approach to the **LOHNER HUT** that follows Route 86 as far as Bonderalp, continues along the farm road to Schrickmatten, round the crags at the foot of a ridge coming from the Nünihorn, then up the Zürcher Steps to the hut (three and a half hours).

The ascent of the **BUNDERSPITZ** (2,546m) is a walkers' route (Grade 3 again) that will take about five hours. This too is reached by means of the Bunderchrinde path (Route 86) but diverges from it just below the pass on an alternative trail heading left.

A less-demanding, but also a visually rewarding, walk takes just two hours to ascend from the village to Tschentenegg and **SCHWANDFELDSPITZ** (2,025m) north-west of Adelboden. The route winds up the hillsides near a chair-lift and rewards with lovely views.

One of the recommended long (six-hour) walks heads over the pass of **FURGGELI** (2,336m) to the west of Adelboden and descends through the Farmeltal to **MATTEN** in the Simmental. This should be a very fine walk, Grade 3.

A number of other walks are outlined in a booklet; *Out and About on Foot in Adelboden,* available from the tourist information office.

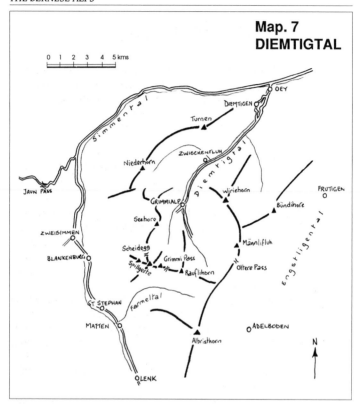

Map. 7
DIEMTIGTAL

0 1 2 3 4 5 kms

OEY

DIEMTIGEN

Turnen

Simmental

ZWISCHENFLUH

Niederhorn

Diemrigtal

Wiriehorn

FRUTIGEN

JAUN PASS

GRIMMIALP

Bündihore

Seehore

ZWEISIMMEN

Männlifluh

Scheidegg

Grimmi Pass

BLANKENBURG

Spillgerte

Oltere Pass

Rauflihorn

ST STEPHAN

Farmeltal

MATTEN

ADELBODEN

Engstligental

Albristhorn

N

OLENK

DIEMTIGTAL

Position: To the north-west of the Engstligental. The valley flows north-eastward from the Spillgerten and joins the Simmental at Oey, west of Spiez.

Map: L.S. 5009 'Gstaad-Adelboden' 1:50,000

Bases: Oey (669m), Diemtigen (809m), Grimmialp (1,220m)

Tourist Information:

Verkehrsbüro, 3753 Oey (Tel: 033 81 2606)

Verkehrsbüro, 3757 Schwenden (Tel: 033 84 1259

The Diemtigtal is a beautiful, peaceful valley that branches unobtrusively to the south of the Simmental, and is therefore largely ignored by the majority of visitors travelling between the Thunersee and Zweisimmen and beyond. But those who do stray into it, and spend time exploring its inner recesses and remote passes, can hardly fail to respond to its charms.

It's a pastoral valley, lush with neat meadows and handsome woods, with unspoilt hamlets scattered along it, and with attractive peaks of medium-height at its head. Although these mountains are of only a modest altitude compared with the better-known Oberland peaks, some of them have very difficult routes to their crowns, while the passes slung to either side make for interesting walks and reveal broad views along the way.

The unspoilt nature of the Diemtigtal is a tribute to its conservation-minded commune, and in 1986 it was awarded the Wakker Prize by the Swiss Heritage Foundation in recognition of the efforts made to preserve the valley's rural heritage and the fine architectural style of its buildings. The ski industry (one of the major threats to mountain landscape and the development of valleys throughout the Alps) has made little impact here, and as a consequence the walker and lover of unsullied hillsides has much to admire and enjoy.

The valley is a dead-end. Or to be precise, two dead-ends, for near its head at Grimmialp it forks; the Senggibach flows from the south-west, the Fildrich from the south-east. Both are closed off by alp-occupied cirques, while down-valley at Zwischenflüh the sub-valley of Meniggrund cuts back to the west.

Few of its summits rise above 2,500 metres, and those that do achieve this height are to be found above the glen of the Fildrich: Männliflue (2,652m) is the highest, the neighbouring Winterhorn (2,608m) is next. There are no glaciers, nor permanent snowfields, but the lovely Spillgerte (2,476m) at the head of the Senggibach (perhaps the finest and most dramatic of all the Diemtigtal peaks), has a splendid wall of rock thrusting northward above the Grimmi pastures. Walkers on their way to the Grimmi Pass can wander in full view of this wall and admire the contrasts of bleak rock and flower-strewn hillsides. North of the Spillgerte rises Seehore (2,281m) whose summit, reached from Grimmialp by a trail coming deviously from the north, commands a broad panorama, while between Spillgerte and Seehore the Fromattgrat has another impressive wall of steep crags overlooking the walkers' pass of Scheidegg.

Most of the hamlets scattered along the valley offer accommodation of some sort or another; and most have interesting walks leading from them. For those visitors without their own transport, the valley is still easily accessible, for there's a railway station at Oey-Diemtigen at its northern end (served by train from either Spiez or Zweisimmen), and a daily Postbus service that meets the train and goes south as far as Grimmialp.

Valley Bases:

OEY (669m) is a village at the entrance to the valley. It has a few shops, PTT, bank, restaurant and railway station. For accommodation there are four hotels with a total of about sixty beds, several holiday flats and a campsite.

DIEMTIGEN (809m) has holiday flats, about thirty beds in three gasthofs and group accommodation in a Naturfreundhaus. It's an architectural gem, with a most interesting priest's house, and the largest private dwelling in the Simmental area, the Grosshaus, dating from the early nineteenth century.

ZWISCHENFLÜH (1,041m), a little over half-way along the valley, has limited accommodation in one hotel and a *pension*, but in addition it has several *matratzenlagers* and three small holiday apartments.

SCHWENDEN/GRIMMIALP (1,163m) near the road-head has a campsite, twenty holiday apartments, four hotels and a number of *matratzenlager* places, and a restaurant. The valley Postbus terminates at Hotel Spillgerten (1,220m), a little above Grimmialp.

There are no mountain huts, as such, in the Diemtigtal.

Route 87:   **Grimmialp (1,220m) - Grimmi Pass (2,057m) - St Stephan (996m)**

Grade:	2-3		
Distance:	13 kilometres		
Height gain:	837 metres	**Height loss:**	1,061 metres
Time:	5-5^{1}/2 hours		

One of the particular pleasures of this walk is the sensation of remoteness that comes from fading footpaths and long views over a barely-habited landscape. It's a green and pleasant route, rich in wild flowers early in the summer, abundant with wild fruits in season, and every metre gained is worth reliving. The Grimmi Pass (also known as Grimmifurggi) is a lush divide, a green saucer of yellow flowers dipped between the Spillgerte Rothorn and the Rauflihorn; a col that links the upper Diemtigtal with the Farmeltal and thence the Ober Simmental. As this is an 'A to B' route transport will be required at one end or the other. If you're staying in the Diemtigtal your return will be by train from St Stephan to Oey via Zweisimmen, and Postbus from Oey. If you have your own transport and are based outside the valley, leave your car in Oey and take a Postbus to Grimmialp to begin the walk, and train from St Stephan at its conclusion. There are no opportunities for refreshment along this route, other than the chance to buy goats' cheese at an alp just below the pass!

   Take the Postbus as far as Hotel Spillgerten (Grimmialp), which is as far as the public road goes. Walk up-valley along the continuing (private) road for a short distance, then fork left on a track that leads through trees and meadows, initially alongside the stream, then to one or two farm buildings. *Bergweg* paint flashes direct a path uphill to another farm where you come onto a track again. This takes you into forest, and you continue to follow this track veering south all the way up to an alp in a rough green undulating bowl with the long and lovely wall of the Spillgerte rising ahead.

The track leads to a lonely little alp building where you can buy goats' cheese. The Grimmi Pass is an obvious saddle seen above to the south, and the path (narrow and faint in places) heads directly to it over hillocks of alpenrose and, before the cattle have been brought up for summer grazing, acres of wild flowers and with streams dancing down. The pass is reached in about three hours from Grimmialp. (Rising to the left is the easy Rauflihorn (2,323m). To gain its summit simply wander up the ridge - about one hour from the pass.)

The steep grass slopes on the southern side of the pass can be very greasy after rain and caution is advised in descending them. Go down to the solitary farm of Obere Bluttlig (1,983m), then continue to a second farm, Untere Bluttlig (1,752m) where the path forks. Take the right branch on a descending traverse that takes you through forest, in and out of gullies and over streams, round an open shoulder of hillside at the alp of Dachbode where you come to a farm track.

Wander along the track, but do not follow it down to the valley. Instead look for a paint flash that leads you away from the track and along a footpath going south-west across meadows to pass a second isolated farm. A line of telegraph poles is the only intrusion on what is otherwise a peaceful and unspoilt pastoral scene. Follow the telegraph poles as far as another farm, now overlooking the Simmental, where you bear left and drop to a farm road. This leads all the way to St Stephan, but there are numerous short-cuts available that lead over meadows and through woods.

The way is clear and well waymarked, and you eventually arrive in St Stephan near the railway station.

Route 88:	Grimmialp (1,220m) - Grimmi Pass (2,057m) - Rauflihorn (2,323m) - Fildrich (1,353m) - Grimmialp

Grade:	3
Distance:	14 kilometres
Height gain/loss:	1,103 metres
Time:	7-7$^{1}/_{2}$ hours

An exhilarating day's wandering, this round trip links the two upper glens of the Diemtigtal via the summit of the Rauflihorn, but should only be tackled by experienced mountain walkers. There's nothing particularly difficult about it, but caution is advised.

Follow directions as far as the Grimmi Pass (three hours) as given for Route 86 above. Now wander up the left-hand grassy ridge to the top of the Rauflihorn in about an hour. The descending path goes steeply down the north-east spur of the mountain (take care) then veers right and left to the Raufli alp (2,119m) in an upper corrie. Continue down to another farm building at a junction of tracks. Bear left on a hillside traverse, then down a spur all the way to the hamlet of Fildrich in the valley bed. Follow the road north, and just beyond Allmi break away left to cross the stream and join a track leading along the western hillside back to Grimmialp.

Route 89:	Grimmialp (1,220m) - Scheidegg (1,991m) - Blankenburg (957m)

Grade:	2-3		
Distance:	11 kilometres		
Height gain:	771 metres	Height loss:	1,034 metres
Time:	5-5$^{1}/_{2}$ hours		

From Hotel Spillgerten at the end of the public road where the Postbus terminates, continue ahead and follow signposts on a graded road leading gently up to Alpetli, a large new-looking alp building, altitude 1,626 metres. There are fine views from here across the valley to the Männliflue ridge beyond which lies the Engstligental.

From Alpetli a trail gradually takes you higher towards an inner hanging valley below the stark rock faces of the Fromattgrat, and to another alp building at 1,794 metres. From here to the pass will occupy about one hour ten minutes, and the way leads through a short corrie, a charming basin embraced by a semi-circle of mountain walls. In the centre of this basin lies a dazzling pool of water in spring and early summer, (it is dry by autumn) above which are stands of old gnarled trees and bushes straddling an ancient rock slide. The alpenroses here are beautiful.

Keep to the left-hand (east) slope as you head up to the pass, for the path almost disappears. You make directly towards the broad bulwark of Hindere Spillgerte; a short ascent over bumpy pasture to the saddle of Scheidegg. From here the whole Spillgerte and Fromattgrat display themselves in a splendid view and make an acceptable reward for those who gain this point. To the west across the forested Betelreid Graben, with the houses of Blankenburg at its confluence with the Simmental, the view goes over low ranges between the Jaun Pass and the Saanen valley, and the long serrated ridge of the Salbelspitzen, Dent de Ruth and the Bern-Vaud borderlands.

From Scheidegg the descent is straightforward, but can be extended slightly for a short detour to the right to visit the alp of Fromatt (1,855m) where you enjoy an extensive view which includes the Jaun Pass, the Wildhorn and the projecting tops at the western end of the Plaine Morte. The path goes through forest and over pasture and finally joins a road alongside the Betelreid Graben stream into the village of Blankenburg (one hour forty minutes from the pass).

Trains go from Blankenburg southward to Lenk or north to Zweisimmen and on to Oey for a return to the Diemtigtal.

Other Walks in the Diemtigtal:

The three routes described above are clearly just a small sample of what is available in the Diemtigtal. From Schwenden/Grimmialp paths lead west then north to climb to a hidden upper pastureland with the lake of **SEEBERGSEE** nestling in it. From here you can either cross the saddle of Luegle and descend to **BOLTIGEN** or **ZWEISIMMEN** in the Simmental, or make a steady descent of the pastures to **ZWISCHENFLÜH** back in the Diemtigtal for a circular walk of considerable charm.

Another pass crossing takes you over the **GRIMMI** (as for Route 87), but instead of wandering westward to the Simmental, branch off east to the head of the Farmeltal and over the **FURGGELI** to **ADELBODEN**. A long route, this would be a Grade 3, of course.

Further down-valley walks can be had from most of the hamlets. **ZWISCHENFLÜH** offers a variety of circular routes on both sides of the valley. A four-hour circuit of the **SCHWARZENBERG** to the east is one possibility; a route round the back of the **HOHMAD** to the alp of **WIRIE** and return through the valley, is another.

ENTSCHWIL, a village to the north of the Schwarzenberg, is another hidden base from which to tackle more circular walks, a little shorter in length than those at some of the higher hamlets, while both **HORBODEN** and **DIEMTIGEN** provide a variety of half-day and full-day walks to suit. A brochure is available from the valley's tourist information office.

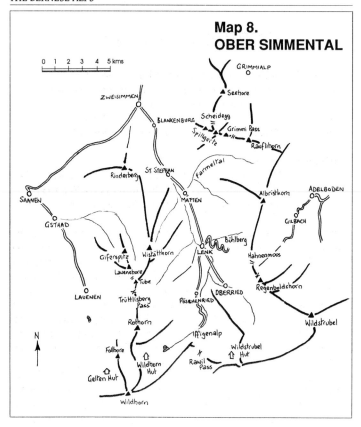

Map 8.
OBER SIMMENTAL

0 1 2 3 4 5 kms

GRIMMIALP

ZWEISIMMEN

Seehore

BLANKENBURG

Scheidegg

Grimmi Pass

Spillgerte

Rauflihorn

Rinderberg

ST. STEPHAN

Farmeltal

ADELBODEN

Albristhorn

SAANEN

MATTEN

GSTAAD

GILBACH

Bühlberg

Giferspitz

Wistätthorn

LENK

Hahnenmoos

Lauenehore

Tube

Regenboldshorn

LAUENEN

Trütthisberg Pass

Pöschenried

OBERRIED

Rothorn

Wildstrubel

Iffigenalp

N

Föllhore

Wildhorn Hut

Wildstrubel Hut

Gelten Hut

Ranil Pass

Wildhorn

OBER SIMMENTAL

Position:	South-west of the Diemtigtal. The Ober Simmental is the upper part of the long and important Simmental valley.
Map:	L.S. 5009 'Gstaad-Adelboden' 1:50,000
Bases:	Zweisimmen (941m), St Stephan (993m), Lenk (1,068m)

Tourist Information:

Verkehrsbüro, 3770 Zweisimmen (Tel: 030 2 1133)
Verkehrsbüro, 3772 St Stephan (Tel: 030 2 1951)
Verkehrsbüro, 3775 Lenk (Tel: 030 3 1595)

Noted for its finely decorated wooden houses and for its cattle, the Simmental is an important valley of communication between the lakes of Geneva and Thun with the cross-country link between the two being completed by either Col du Pillon or the Jaun Pass. It's a great arcing bow of a valley, broad and sunny in places, dark and narrow in others where the river comes foaming through in a series of wild tormented cataracts. Much of the valley is delightfully pastoral; most of its mountains are snow-free and wooded to a regular height, but towards its head these mountains grow in stature and promise, and there is good walking to be had on their smooth grass slopes.

The valley is arbitrarily divided into two; the Nieder Simmental being the lower region from the foot of the Jaun Pass eastwards to the Lake of Thun, the Ober Simmental covering all the valley south of Boltigen. Zweisimmen is the main town, being situated in a broad basin at the confluence of the Kleine Simme (coming from the hills above Saanenmoser) and the main Simme which begins its life among the glaciers of the Wildstrubel above Lenk. The river itself is a favourite of canoeists, but it has plenty of wild stretches to put it out of bounds to novices.

Above Lenk, or to be more precise above Oberried, a great knot of mountains breaks out of the Wildstrubel's Glacier de la Plaine Morte. Seen from a distance the snow and ice of this region gleams

Lenk and its attractive lake

like a beckoning tiara, but from the valley pastures in the southern Simmental, only a jumble of heights and a blue run of long ridge systems reveal themselves. There are hinted inner recesses that draw the mists of evening, while their grassy flanks are speckled with haybarns and secluded alpine farms. To east and west the ridges quickly lose height to allow easy crossings to be made from one valley to the next. These ridges grow broad and pastoral. Cattle graze them. Flowers waver in the summer breeze. Footpaths meander round boggy patches or circumnavigate limestone pits and curious hummocks. And the views hold a walker's breath with pleasure.

Lenk is the highest resort. Once known mainly as a spa, it has now entered the list of mainstream alpine resorts with a growing ski industry, although it has contained both its size and ambition to modest proportions. In summer it is both a walking and, to a lesser degree, a mountaineering centre with ease of access via road or rail from central Switzerland or the west.

Travelling north away from Lenk, away from the higher mountains, the next village you come to is Matten at the mouth of the Farmeltal, from which point there is access by foot over the Grimmi Pass to the Diemtigtal. Then comes St Stephan, spread across the floor of the valley with its leaning towards light industry.

Just before reaching Zweisimmen, Blankenburg crouches on the eastern side of the valley. Both road and railway curve round to serve it, but the river twists away, as though reluctant to be joined by the Betelreid Gruben. Zweisimmen, by contrast with other villages in the valley, is a teeming place with crowded streets and a certain air of authority hanging over it. From the south-west comes the Saanen road alongside the Kleine Simme, then it's a long run north, the road and railway almost ignoring Mannried and Grubenwald, tucked on the east side of the river. But Weissenbach lines the road, as does Reidenbach at the foot of the Jaun Pass. Then a kink in the valley curves it to the north-east and there sits Boltigen, with the Nieder Simmental shafting darkly towards the east.

The valley as a whole has much of interest for the general tourist, while the walker will find plenty to appeal, in particular in the upper reaches of the Ober Simmental where footpaths lead into landscapes of great beauty.

Main Valley Bases:

ZWEISIMMEN (941m) is ideally situated as a holiday base for those with their own transport, since there are many neighbouring areas accessible by car. (It also has good public transport services.) As the main village in the valley (it may be considered almost a town by comparison with others in the region), it has many fine wooden buildings characteristic of the Simmental, a museum of local crafts and a fifteenth century church containing murals and a fine timber ceiling. There are several good walks to be had from here, including an ascent of the Hundsrugg for superb views to Mont Blanc, Grand Combin and many of the big Oberland peaks to the south-east. A gondola lift goes up to the Rinderberg to the south; another fine viewpoint. For accommodation there are some fourteen hotels containing 350 beds, more than 1,000 beds to rent in holiday apartments, *matratzenlagers*, and two campsites. There are plenty of

191

shops, restaurants, banks, PTT and a busy railway station (trains to Gstaad, Lenk or Spiez). There is also a tourist information office whose promotion of the walking potential of the area extends to the presentation of a walker's badge to those who complete a certain number of local walks during their stay.

ST STEPHAN (996m) is much less obvious as a centre than either Zweisimmen or Lenk, but it has four hotels with a total of eighty-five beds, together with 400 beds in holiday apartments and group facilities for about 200. The local church dates from the fifteenth century and has an eighteenth century organ. As a village it has few shopping facilities, but is served by rail on the line midway between Zweisimmen and Lenk.

LENK (1,068m) is a busy and attractive little resort of 2,280 residents situated in level pastures and with green hills rising to east and west. Outliers of the Wildstrubel rise to the south, and the valley forks just outside the village to create a choice of walking areas to explore. Lenk has a fair selection of shops and restaurants. It has banks, PTT and tourist information office. There are twenty hotels and pensions with almost 1,000 beds, with an additional 5,000 beds in holiday flats and chalets. A campsite is found at the head of the valley at Oberried. There is an open-air swimming pool for non-walking days, and a gondola lift system leading to Betelberg (Leiterli) on the western hillsides with a wide selection of walking trails accessible from it.

Mountain Huts:
Two SAC huts are within reach of walkers from Lenk; the **WILDHORN** and **WILDSTRUBEL HUTS**. The first, the **WILDHORN** (2,301m), is set in a stony landscape above the Iffigsee to the north-east of the mountain from which it takes its name. It's a fine hut with one hundred places and a guardian during July and August when meals and drinks are available. Reached in five hours directly from Lenk, or in three hours from Iffigenalp which is in itself accessible by car or bus from Lenk.

There are two **WILDSTRUBEL HUTS** (2,793m) standing side by side beneath the Weisshorn, one of the peaklets above the western edge of the Plaine Morte. With places for seventy-six and a guardian in occupation during the main summer weeks of July and August, they are owned by the Bern section of the SAC and accessible from the road-head at Iffigenalp in four and a half hours.

Hotel accommodation is also available at **IFFIGENALP** (1,586m), **OBERRIED** (1,103m), and **BÜELBERG** (1,661m)

Route 90:	Zweisimmen (941m) - Garstatt (858m) - Weissenbach (842m) - Boltigen (818)

Grade:	1		
Distance:	10 kilometres		
Height gain:	39 metres	Height loss:	162 metres
Time:	2-2½ hours		

This gentle valley walk gives an opportunity to visit several small Simmental villages, passing old timbered farmhouses, cutting through pastures and following the course of the river northward. Initially there are views of the ruined Mannenberg castle on the opposite bank of the river on the outskirts of Mannried.

From the centre of Zweisimmen take the minor road heading north to Obegg, which is reached in about twenty minutes. From here a track branches half-right ahead and cuts off towards the river, joining a service road running parallel with the main valley road. This ends and a footpath continues ahead along the hillside to Laubegg (961m). Crossing the railway you come to Garstatt and go over to the right bank of the river. The trail now follows the river to Weissenbach, most of which village is on the opposite bank, and continues to Boltigen. Here you cross again to the left bank to gain the village proper *(accommodation, refreshments)*. The train may be caught from here back to Zweisimmen.

Other Walks from Zweisimmen:
As has been mentioned before, Zweisimmen makes a good base for a holiday and there are numerous possibilities for walks leading from it. The tourist information office will provide further details, but the following outline suggestions immediately come to mind. Study of

the map and local brochures will provide more ideas.

Another obvious valley walk goes in the opposite direction to that given above as Route 90. This leads along the true left bank (west side) of the Simme and goes to **RIED, SCHADAULI** and **LENK** in three hours fifteen minutes. (Grade 1)

A more taxing outing crosses the river to **MANNRIED** and goes north-east up the hillside to **MEIENBERG** and on to the hidden tarn of **SEEBERGSEE** (1,831m) in a little over three and a half hours. An alternative return may be made by going south-west to **STIERBERG** and down to **OBERRIED** in another three hours, making a good six and a half-hour circuit of Grade 3.

By use of the gondola lift to **RINDERBERG** a three and a half-hour crossing to **GSTAAD** can be achieved. This gives an opportunity for a lovely ridge-walk along the **GANDLOUENEGRAT** (2,078m), followed by a very high-level traverse of the southern flanks of **HORNTUBE** and **HORNFLUE** with spectacular views much of the way. This also warrants Grade 3.

Views from **HUNDSRUGG** (2,047m) have already been mentioned. They include not only the big Oberland peaks, but Mont Blanc too. A steep walk from Zweisimmen via **HEIMCHUEWEID** and **NUJEBERG**, on a combination of footpath and farm road, leads you there in three and a half to four hours. Grade 3 again.

Walks from St Stephan:
Midway between Zweisimmen and Lenk, St Stephan sits on the edge of an area that is also worth exploring on foot. The neat side valley of the Farmeltal to the east is particularly worth wandering into. A long (six and a half-hour) walk takes you through the **FARMELTAL** and over the pass of **FURGGELI** (2,336m) to **ADELBODEN**. This strenuous route will be Grade 3. But even without extending the walk as far as the pass, the valley is still worth wandering in.

An easy valley walk along the east side of the river, linking the villages of **MATTEN, GUETEBRUNNE** and **LENK** makes a gentle morning's outing (two and a half hours) at Grade 1.

On the far side of the valley to the south, the viewpoint of the **FLOSCHHORN** (2,079m) may be reached by path in three and a half to four hours. The route goes via **MATTEN**, then across the river and up the north spur of the mountain, passing through two or three small alps on the way.

Route 91:	Lenk (Büelberg; 1,661m) - Hahnenmoos (1,956m) - Metschstand (2,099m) - Lenk (1,068m)

Grade:	2-3	
Distance:	9 kilometres	
Height gain:	438 metres	Height loss: 1,031 metres
Time:	3½ hours	

Metschstand is a prominent viewpoint above the broad grassy saddle of Hahnenmoos, the classic crossing point between Lenk and Adelboden. (See Route 85 under Engstligental section.) This route to the summit followed by a long walk down to Lenk can be a little tiring on the legs, but is not at all difficult. It is better to begin the outing by taking a local bus from Lenk up to Hotel Büelberg.

From Büelberg wander along the gravel track to Hahnenmoos (*accommodation, refreshments*), and then bear right, soon to gain a grassy ridge between Point 2,013m and Metschstand. The main path continues round towards the Pommernpass, but our route breaks off to the right and climbs steeply to the summit of Metschstand (one and a half hours). A splendid panorama includes the Wildstrubel, the Plaine Morte glacier basin, Wildhorn and a great splay of ridges containing blue-tinted valleys.

The descending path goes down the west spur beside a ski-lift, bears left at a junction and then resumes towards the valley by a series of farm tracks and footpaths. Follow signs to Metsch, which is reached in one hour fifteen minutes from the summit. There is a cableway link with the valley here, but continuing tracks lead easily down to Lenk.

Route 92:	Lenk (Büelberg; 1,661m) - Hahnenmoos (1,956m) - Pommernpass (2,055m) - Oberried (1,103m)

Grade:	2-3		
Distance:	8 kilometres		
Height gain:	394 metres	Height loss:	952 metres
Time:	3¹⁄₂ hours		

This is a variation of the previous route, an alternative loop giving walkers the opportunity to enjoy long views and the dramatic Simmenfälle cascades. A bus is taken from Lenk to Hotel Büelberg, and at the end of the walk another from Oberried down-valley to Lenk.

From Büelberg follow the track easily up to the Hahnenmoos Pass. Bear right and walk along the east side of the green ridge on a clear path that takes you to the saddle of the Pommernpass immediately below the lump of Regenboldshorn (2,193m). It is worth making a slight diversion to scamper up to the summit of this peak from the pass. It's a steep but easy footpath and it will take only ten to fifteen minutes to reach the top.

Return to the pass and go down the south side. There are two paths. Take the left-hand trail and then descend steeply over grass slopes to reach a farm building at 1,766 metres. Follow signs for the Simmenfälle. The path will lead past one or two more farms and on to a track through woods. Without difficulty you come to the waterfalls, seen pouring in a cloud of spray from a cleft on your left. Cross the walkway in the full spray and continue down a dirt path among trees following the Simme stream all the way to Oberried (*accommodation, refreshments*). The bus to Lenk is taken from the restaurant at the roadhead.

Route 93:	Lenk (Iffigenalp; 1,586m) - Iffigsee (2,065m)

Grade:	2
Distance:	4 kilometres
Height gain:	479 metres
Time:	2 hours

Iffigsee

South of Lenk the Simme is joined by the Iffigbach, a substantial tributary coming from the south-west. The valley through which this tributary flows has a narrow road leading through it from Lenk as far as the Iffigenalp. This road is two-way as far as Färiche (1,210m), but from there to Iffigenalp vehicles are subjected to a timed one-way system with access restricted to fifteen minutes every hour. It is possible to drive to Iffigenalp, but there is also a service bus from Lenk.

The walk to the lake of Iffigsee is a steep one in places, but wandering through the valley is most pleasant, while the lake itself is a deep well set amid wild-looking mountain scenery. It makes a popular destination for picnic parties.

From the large car park at Hotel Iffigenalp follow a clear track up-valley with the jutting peaklets on the Seeschnide ridge to the south-west drawing the eye. The way crosses the Iffigbach stream a couple of times, and on the approach to the alp hut of Groppi (1,741m) the track narrows to a path. Pass to the right of the hut and continue, soon winding up a long grassy cone. At the top of this cone the path levels out, goes through a rocky defile and emerges above the deep blue Iffigsee. The shoreline at the far north-western corner is most inviting and attractive, and is accessible.

See Route 94 below for an extension to the Wildhorn Hut. Allow one hour for the return to Iffigenalp.

Route 94:	Lenk (Iffigenalp; 1,586m) - Iffigsee (2,065m) - Wildhorn Hut (2,301m)

Grade:	2-3
Distance:	6 kilometres
Height gain:	715 metres
Time:	3 hours

Perched on a rocky knoll in wild and desolate surroundings, the Wildhorn Hut makes an interesting destination for a walk. In the main summer weeks of July and August there are refreshments available at the hut, so it is tempting to make a round trip, arriving in

The Wildhorn hut

time for lunch with a view of a raw mountain landscape outside.

Take Route 93 as far as the Iffigsee and continue along the path above the northern shore until you come to a junction of trails. Take the left-hand path and descend to an isolated building above the lake and continue on the path as it climbs over grass-covered bluffs to the south-west. In places the path is a little vague, but it eventually brings you into a desolate stony valley with long scree slopes draped through it. The path works its way through the valley, steadily gaining height and with the hut showing itself ahead. The final ascent is up a rocky slope dotted with alpine flowers.

The Wildhorn Hut is base for climbs on several surrounding mountains: Wildhorn, Schneidehorn, Iffigenhorn, Niessenhorn etc. It can sleep a hundred in its dormitories.

Route 95: Lenk (Leiterli; 1,943m) - Tungel Pass (2,084m) - Wildhorn Hut (2,301m) - Iffigenalp (1,586m)

Grade:	3		
Distance:	16 kilometres		
Height gain:	438 metres	Height loss:	795 metres
Time:	6 hours		

On the western hillsides above Lenk the Betelberg gondola lift gives access to a network of footpaths, a wonderland of trails leading over high pastures rich in wild flowers and with gentle views in all directions. Leiterli is the top station of this lift, and one of the longest routes from it is this one to the Wildhorn Hut and down to Iffigenalp for the bus back to Lenk.

Buy a one-way ticket (*Bergfahrt*) on the gondola lift to Leiterli and take the broad signposted path directly uphill to Gumeli and the Stüblenipass, the latter (1,992m) reached in a little under one and a half hours from the gondola lift. Keeping to the east side of the ridge the path now rises over the Arbigrat below the Fürflue, and continues heading south to reach (in two and a half hours from Leiterli) the Tungel Pass. Bear left and work your way in zig-zags up to Point 2,381m, the highest part of the walk.

Veering left the path now slopes down towards the Iffigsee, but you soon break away to the right (signpost) on a stony route that curves round a shoulder of the Niesenhorn and traverses steep grass slopes above the hanging valley containing the Wildhorn Hut. Caution should be exercised on the last stretch of this path before dropping into the valley below the hut. The hut is reached after four hours fifteen minutes. Refreshments are available here during July and August when the guardian is in residence.

Descend the scree-ridden valley below the hut and go round the western side of the Iffigsee (thirty minutes from the hut), then climb the path leading past a solitary building and join another path above it. Bear right and follow this without diversion all the way down to Iffigenalp (*accommodation, refreshments*). A bus goes from the car park below the hotel back to Lenk. Alternatively it will take another two hours to walk down to the village.

Route 96:	Lenk (Leiterli; 1,943m) - Trüttlisberg Pass (2,038m)-Lauenen (1,241m)

Grade:	2		
Distance:	9 kilometres		
Height gain:	95 metres	Height loss:	797 metres
Time:	3 hours		

A fine, easy walk over the ridge of mountains separating the Ober Simmental and the Lauenental, this is a true delight of far views and flowers. The Betelberg gondola lift begins the day with a ride to the top station at Leiterli. From here to the pass the trail follows an almost horizontal course along a ridge, first on one side, then on the other, with lovely views over to the Hahnenmoos and into the craggy combes of the Wildhorn and Wildstrubel. (For those who choose to disregard the cableway and prefer to walk all the way from Lenk to Lauenen, see Route 97 below.)

Leaving the gondola lift take the broad route signposted to Lauenen. It rounds the lump of Leiterli itself and continues on the south side of the ridge. The direct route to Lauenen crosses the Stüblenipass, but the more interesting way forks right, in the direction of the Trüttlisberg Pass. The trail cuts below Stübleni above spiny limestone ribs at the head of the Wallbach valley. Mount easily to the rocky ridge which proves to be an exciting tight-rope path among a mass of mini-craters, pass a small shelter hut and descend left to join the path from the Trüttlisberg Pass.

The descent route is straightforward. The trail takes you over steep pastures and on past a number of farms and barns (Vordere-Trüttlisberg; 1,818m). From here the path becomes a farm track which leads to a metalled road. Turn right. You can either follow this road all the way down to Lauenen, or take the footpath left which you soon come to. This gives a pleasant descent through pastures and small patches of woodland, passes trim chalets and at last arrives in Lauenen (*accommodation, refreshments, shops etc*).

Route 97:	Lenk (1,068m) - Trüttlisberg Pass (2,038m) - Lauenen (1,241m)

Grade:	2-3	
Distance:	14 kilometres	
Height gain:	970 metres	Height loss: 797 metres
Time:	5-5½ hours	

From Lenk to Lauenen over the Trüttlisberg Pass is a walk of almost constant pasture or forest. It's a limestone country bright with flowers, and near the pass there are curious hillocks and hollows from which huge panoramas gaze off to the main crest of the Bernese Alps in the south. It is not a difficult route at all, and is only given a partial Grade 3 on account of its length.

In the main square in Lenk a large signpost board includes initial directions for the Trüttlisberg Pass. Cross to the Hotel Kreuz and continue along the road beyond for about 400 metres, then head left on a more narrow road parallel with the Wallbach stream. When it curves to the left leave the road in favour of a path heading into forest.

The way climbs steeply alongside the stream, then up a series of ladders and stone stairways with waterfalls to one side. Then you emerge from the trees an hour after setting out, near Berghaus Wallegg (1,325m; *refreshments*). Turn right and walk up the right-hand side of a sloping meadow for about one hundred metres, then take a footpath heading into the woods once more. Keep along this path for some way. After crossing the stream on a sturdy bridge you come out of the woods and reach a farm track where you turn left.

The track crosses a streambed, then you bear right on a path climbing a rough hillside. It takes you past several isolated farms, the last of which is Ober Lochberg (1,910m), three hours from Lenk. Just beyond this farm the way forks. Take the left-hand branch over a stream, and then continue up towards the saddle passing a small hut on the way. Trüttlisberg Pass is reached about three and a half hours after setting out. It is marked by a signpost, and the views are quite delightful.

Over the pass bear left and follow a slightly rising path to another junction where you begin the descent to Lauenen. This is straightforward, and is described in Route 96 above.

Route 98: **Lenk (1,068m) - Trüttlisberg Pass (2,038m) -**
Turbachal - Gstaad (1,050m)

Grade:	3		
Distance:	24 kilometres		
Height gain:	970 metres	**Height loss:**	988 metres
Time:	7¹/₂ hours		

A long day's walking but an utterly delightful one, it leads through
a glorious pastoral countryside. First, the way to the Trüttlisberg Pass
wanders through flower meadows with long views. Then it traverses
round to a second easy pass before dropping into the lush green
Turbachtal that takes you all the way down to Gstaad. Parts of this
walk may be a little boggy, and around one or two farms it's not
unusual to find a quagmire of churned mud after rain. But mostly the
paths are well-drained and easy to follow.

Follow Route 97 as far as the Trüttlisberg Pass, but instead of
crossing over towards Lauenen, bear right and, rising a little, cut
round the left-hand side of a peaklet named Tube (2,107m) and make
for an obvious saddle between it and the steeper Lauenehore seen
ahead. Once at this saddle (1,986m) a narrow path descends to the
right towards a lone farm building and continues on the west side of
the sweeping corrie, boggy in places but with plenty of flowers. As
you lose height so the path takes you past cattle byres and hay barns,
over side streams and eventually leads to a bridge to aid the crossing
to the right bank of the main Turbach stream. A farm track leads on
and eventually becomes a surfaced road that goes all the way down
to Gstaad.

However, there is an alternative (signposted) footpath route after
a while. This crosses back to the left bank of the stream and gains
height initially as it traverses the steep hillside. It is an interesting
path, climbing and falling through forest, over pastures, crossing
curious stiles and passing occasional haybarns. The path is not
universally clear, but a route is practicable - with care. You will finally
come to a surfaced road that leads directly to Gstaad.

Other Walks from Lenk:

There's no shortage of walks heading out of Lenk. Some are gentle valley strolls: up-valley to **OBERRIED** and the **SIMMENFÄLLE**, for example (Grade 1); or a little more demanding stroll that leads to the **IFFIGFALL**, midway between Färiche and Iffigenalp.

There are long and arduous pass crossings, like that over the **RAWILPASS** (2,429m) to **LAC DE TSEUZIER** and down to the Rhône Valley at **SION**. This is a twelve-hour walk, but it's possible to use public transport to Iffigenalp, and down from Lac de Tseuzier. The **WILDSTRUBEL HUT** will be a six or seven-hour walk also via Iffigenalp, and this uses part of the route to the Rawilpass.

The tourist information office in the village has a selection of leaflets and brochures that the visiting walker will find useful, in particular one entitled *Hiker's Breviary* with several routes outlined.

LAUENENTAL

Position: West of the Ober Simmental, the Lauenental flows
               north from the base of the Wildhorn to Gstaad
               where it connects with the Saane and Turbach
               valleys.
Map: L.S. 5009 'Gstaad-Adelboden' 1:50,000
Bases: Gstaad (1,050m), Lauenen (1,241m)
Tourist Information:
               Verkehrsbüro, 3780 Gstaad (Tel: 030 4 1055)
               Verkehrsbüro, 3782 Lauenen (Tel: 030 5 3330)

The Lauenental is a short, green and beautiful valley. As you travel
into it from Gstaad, so the Wildhorn massif beckons from the south
with a ridge of snow and ice to complement the neat, shorn hillsides
and trim patches of forest that lead to it. And it is this contrast of
formidable grandeur and tended gentility that helps to invest the
whole area with an atmosphere of welcome.

There's only one village in the valley. Lauenen is a pretty place set
among the meadows; in a shallow scoop of pasture like a hammock
slung between the mountains, and like a hammock it gives an air of
comfort, a tease of calm relaxation. South of the village the Lauenental
has its marshy regions where streams flow from the hillsides and
seep among trees and damp meadows, and at the road-head there's
a charming lake, the Lauenensee, one of the loveliest in all the Bernese
Alps with its reed- and grass-fringed edges casting a deep green tint
across the shallows.

Above the lake, above a forest-clad rise, a superb little glen (a
nature reserve) is flush with flowers and highlighted by a great water
spout - the Geltenschuss. Rise above that and you'll find a secretive
hollow basin fed by numerous streams and cascades pouring from
the glaciers that hang down the face of the Wildhorn (3,248m) and
Arpelistock (3,035m). It's a magical place, full of beauty, grandeur
and romance.

On either side of Lauenen, to east and west, the hills grow to broad

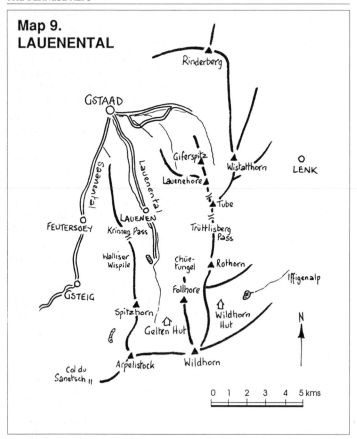

**Map 9.
LAUENENTAL**

Rinderberg

GSTAAD

Saanental

Lauenental

Giferspitz

Wistatthorn

LENK

Lauenehore

FEUTERSOEY

Tube

LAUENEN

Krinnen Pass

Trüttlisberg
Pass

Walliser
Wispile

Chüe-
rungel

Rothorn

Iffigenalp

Follhore

GSTEIG

Spitzhorn

Wildhorn
Hut

N

Gelten Hut

Col du
Sanetsch

Arpelistock

Wildhorn

0 1 2 3 4 5 kms

and easy ridges. On the eastern hillside there are one or two alp hamlets settled among tender rucked terraces open to the sun, while above them the crest of the ridge eases to high pasture. On the west the ridge is a little lower (it doesn't touch 2,000 metres until Chlys Hüri, the last rocky eminence projecting from the Arpelistock) and for much of its length forest reaches right to the top. On both sides there are gentle passes: to the east the Trüttlisberg and Stüblenipass leading over to Lenk, and the Turli and Turnelsattel to Gstaad via the Turbachtal, while to the west the Krinnen (or Chrine) gives easy access to Gsteig at the foot of Les Diablerets.

Moving north away from Lauenen and downstream towards sophisticated Gstaad, the valley narrows slightly. On its western side the crest remains largely forested, while above to the east the mountains have grown somewhat, rising well above the tree-line and offering ridge-walks of open splendour. The Wasserngrat, running north-west from the Lauenehore (2,477m), is well-known for its high belvedere footpath (accessible by cableway from Gstaad) that gives a walk in the sky with a stunning panorama of high mountains and deep green valleys.

On the very edge of Gstaad the Lauibach stream that started out as the Geltenbach and Tungelbach among the glaciers to the south, flows into the Turbach and becomes the Saane, the river that gives its name to a whole region; Saanenland.

Valley Bases:

GSTAAD (1,050m) is very much the St Moritz of the Bernese Oberland, a place of 'other world' sophistication, where personalities of sport and screen gather when the snows fall and the mountains are transformed into ski playgrounds. In the summer it is famed as the venue for the Swiss Open Tennis Championships, and of cultural extravaganzas such as the Alpengala and the Yehudi Menuhin Festival held in the Mauritius Church in nearby Saanen. The small, rather austere chapel of St Nicholas dates from 1402 and is worth a visit. But Gstaad also has access to a wide choice of mountain areas, and with a variety of cableways in close proximity, walkers are able to reach various high points and begin their outings from them. As a holiday base, Gstaad is very much a fashionable resort focussing on

Wildhorn massif above Lauenen

one long main street lined with an assortment of shops and restaurants. There are banks, PTT, a tourist information office and good public transport services with Postbus to Lauenen in the south and Gsteig and Col du Pillon in the south-west, and railway links with towns as far apart as Montreux and Thun by way of the MOB (*Montreux-Oberland Bahn*). The resort has only 2,500 permanent residents, but it can accommodate another 1,000 in its thirteen hotels, and 1,500 in holiday apartments. The nearest campsite is in Saanen.

LAUENEN (1,241m) is quite different to Gstaad. It's a small, pretty village with an unpretentious street and a number of lovely old timbered buildings characteristic of the region, one of which (dated 1765) is a gem of local craftsmanship. The sixteenth century church provides a central focal point, while from almost every corner one gazes south to the Wildhorn. Along the street are a few general stores, PTT and the tourist information office. There are only two hotels with a total of forty-four beds, but an additional 150 beds may be rented in holiday flats. The old schoolhouse has *matratzenlager* accommodation for about a hundred.

Mountain Huts:

The **GELTEN HUT** (2,008m) is the only SAC refuge immediately accessible from the valley, although the **WILDHORN HUT** may also be reached in about five hours from Lauenen. As for the Gelten Hut, this commands a wonderful situation to the north-west of the Wildhorn set above the Geltenschuss waterfalls. It not only has the high mountains as a backdrop, but a fine view along the Lauenental. The approach walk takes about three and a half hours and is a sheer delight. The hut can sleep eighty-seven in its dormitories. Provided by the Oldenhorn Section (Gstaad) of the SAC, it has a guardian in residence for about five weeks in the middle of summer, and at weekends at other times.

Route 99:   **Gstaad (1,050m) -Turbachtal - Turli (1,986m) - Lauenen (1,241m)**

Grade:	3		
Distance:	16 kilometres		
Height gain:	936 metres	**Height loss:**	745 metres
Time:	5¹⁄₂ hours		

One of the many pleasant aspects of this walk is the joy of being drawn deeper into the peaceful Turbachtal. The route leads all the way through it, from its entrance on the edge of bustling Gstaad, to the grassy saddle at its very head between the Lauenehore and Tube. The Turbachtal really is a lovely glen, and this exploration of it makes an ideal day out. Return to Gstaad may be made by Postbus from Lauenen.

  Set out from the heart of Gstaad on the road signposted to Lauenen. The Turbachtal soon breaks away to the left and you follow the road into it. Not long after entering you pass the valley station of the Wasserngrat cableway. The road winds on into the valley, keeping on the left-hand side of the Turbach stream. At a sharp hairpin bend it's possible to leave the road and continue straight ahead on a short cut, rejoining it later. When the surfaced road ends a farm track continues for a considerable distance, steadily gaining height with the stream for company. After about two and a half hours from Gstaad you come to a bridge at Steineberg (1,560m) and cross to the true left bank. Passing a farm at 1,647 metres (Marchli) a footpath continues and rises towards the head of the valley where an obvious saddle is seen to the south. The way becomes a little boggy in places and the path is faint at times. Make towards an alp building just below the saddle, and then beyond it to gain the pass of Turli (1,986m) after about four hours fifteen minutes.

Lauenen lies almost directly below to the west, and the path down to it takes you past the alp of Hindere Trüttlisberg, over pasture and through patches of forest on an easy yet delightful descent, and in a little over an hour from the pass you arrive in the village.

**Route 100:   Gstaad (Wasserngrat; 1,936m) -
Trüttlisberg Pass (2,038m) - Lauenen (1,241m)**

Grade:	2		
Distance:	13 kilometres		
Height gain:	267 metres	Height loss:	962 metres
Time:	4 hours 15 minutes		

The Wasserngrat-Brüeschegrat is one of the classic belvederes of the area. Reached by mechanical aid (gondola and chair-lift) from the Turbachtal, thus saving a steep two and a half-hour walk from Gstaad, this high footpath follows a ridge south with tremendous views to the Wildhorn and Les Diablerets before traversing the face of the Lauenehore and reaching the Trüttlisberg Pass for the descent to Lauenen.

Either walk into the Turbachtal for the Wasserngrat cableway, or take a Postbus. From the upper chair-lift station the footpath is well-signposted and heavily used, if narrow in places. It heads south, keeping on the right-hand side of the crest, rising steadily to the high point of Wandeliflue (2,203m) with magnetic views all the way. The Lauenental is a long drop below, but the big mountains appear much closer than they really are. Here and there are bench seats for resting.

After Wandeliflue you descend to a saddle (Turnelsattel; 2,086m) at the head of the little Turnelsbach glen, reached about one and a half hours from the chair-lift. Continue along the ridge a short distance until you come to a junction of paths. One rises steeply ahead up the west ridge of the Lauenehore, the other makes a traverse of its south face. Take the traversing path, and on regaining the opposite ridge go down to a second grassy saddle (Turli; 1,986m), this one above the Turbachtal. (It is possible to bear right here and descend to Lauenen.) Continue ahead towards the peaklet of Tube and follow the path round to the Trüttlisberg Pass, reached in about an hour from the Turnelsattel.

The signpost here directs the way down to Lauenen. It is an easy, straightforward descent, briefly described under Route 96.

Route 101:	Gstaad (Wasserngrat; 1,936m) - Lauenehorn (2,477m) - Giferspitz (2,542m) - Gstaad (1,050m)

Grade:	3		
Distance:	15 kilometres		
Height gain:	606 metres	Height loss:	1,492 metres
Time:	6 hours		

An extension of Route 100, and a more demanding one, this is a long switchback of a walk, maintaining a high route until the steep descent is tackled from just beyond the summit of the Giferspitz. This outing achieves a tour round the high walls that embrace the Turnelsbach glen, and as a reward the views are remarkable for their breadth and extent. The two and a half-hour descent to Gstaad can be rather tiring.

Take Route 100 from Wasserngrat as far as the Turnelsattel, the 2,086 metre pass to the west of the Lauenehore. Instead of traversing the face of the mountain, as for the previous route, continue on the path that climbs the west ridge to the summit, reached in an hour from the saddle. The route now strikes northward above crags, descends to Point 2,391m, then climbs round the east side of the ridge to pass just below the summit of the Giferspitz. Regaining the ridge you come to Point 2,376m and descend the steep north ridge. Care should be exercised here, particularly after rain. The path takes you down between strips of forest to an alp at 1,659 metres where you have a choice of routes down to Gstaad. One continues down to Bargli and Turbach. Another branches left, rises a little, then traverses from one alp hut to another, to Zingrisberg and then down to Scheidbach where a narrow road takes you down to Gstaad.

Other Walks from Gstaad:

In addition to the cableway to Wasserngrat, the gondola lift to **EGGLI** (1,559m) to the west of the resort opens up another high-level walking area; fine alpine meadows, long views (especially fine to the Gummfluh) and a network of paths worth exploring. One such leads south-westwards with the Gummfluh drawing you on, then from the saddle of **WILD BODEN** (1,651m) traverses below the peak and descends into the valley of **MEIELSGRUND** which you then follow all the way back to Gstaad.

An alternative, which takes you out of Canton Bern and into the Vaudois Alps, goes beyond **WILD BODEN**, traverses below the south-east face of **GUMMFLUH** and crosses the **COL DE JABLE** (1,884m) to **L'ETIVAZ**.

And then there's the gondola lift to the south that gives access to the **HÖHI WISPILE**. This is the ridge that forms the western wall to the Lauenental, and is the eastern limit of the upper Saanen valley. One of the best walks along this ridge starts at the upper cableway station of **STAND** (1,915m) (memorable views to Les Diablerets) and heads south for almost one and a half hours to reach the **KRINNEN PASS** (1,659m), and descends from there through forest and over pasture to **LAUENEN**. (This walk is described in reverse from Lauenen as Route 107.)

Perhaps the easiest (and certainly one of the shortest) walks is the valley stroll that links **GSTAAD** with **FEUTERSOEY** and **GSTEIG**. It heads south through the upper Saanen valley, a cradle of pastureland with the huge mass of Les Diablerets rising ahead above the Col du Pillon. A walk of about two hours forty-five minutes. Grade 1.

There are, of course, many more possibilities. Study the map for ideas, or ask at the tourist information office for a copy of their *Saanenland Excursions Panorama*.

Route 102:   Lauenen (1,241m) - Lauenensee (1,381m)

Grade: 1
Distance: 4 kilometres
Height gain: 159 metres
Time: 1 hour 10 minutes

For a gentle introduction to the seductive nature of the Lauenental no walk could be better designed than this one. It is short and easy, yet what it offers is a series of views showing the pastoral beauty of the region. It winds among meadows, passes attractive chalets and old farms, gazes on the high mountains that block the valley, and comes down to the tranquil shores of the Lauenensee tarn. There's a restaurant at the far end and you can sit on a grassy knoll outside with a cool drink in your hand and plan your next excursion into the very mountains that rise so temptingly to the south. (The tarn is also served by Postbus. But those who ride it miss much.)

From Lauenen walk along the road heading up-valley towards the Wildhorn. Just outside the village a signpost directs our route along a narrow side road forking right. It winds easily uphill past several fine chalets set in steep meadows, and eventually deteriorates to a track. Continue along it, now heading through forest and out again to pass more farm buildings and chalets. There are lovely views to the mountains ahead. Then the track begins to lose height and you suddenly have a view overlooking the Lauenensee between a screen of trees. Wander down and along its left-hand shoreline to find the restaurant at the far end on the left.

Route 103:   Lauenen (1,241m) - Geltenschuss -
Gelten Hut (2,008m)

Grade: 2-3
Distance: 7 kilometres
Height gain: 767 metres
Time: 3½ hours

This must be one of the most pleasant hut approach walks in the Bernese Alps. It's not at all difficult or dangerous. There are no raw screes, no rock slabs to scale by use of ladders or fixed ropes. Instead there's a well-graded path all the way. It leads unerringly into a magnificent series of varied and multi-coloured landscapes. Part of the route goes through a nature reserve. Through meadows lush with flowers and up past a pair of huge cascading waterfalls, above rise the big snow and ice drapes of the Wildhorn massif, circling round as in an embrace. Then at last you come over a steep grassy knoll and find the Gelten Hut perched in a commanding position with a deep and secret bowl of pasture between it and the glaciers. It's a great place for a picnic.

Follow directions for Route 102 as far as the Lauenensee. At the southern end of the lake take a track among trees, then break away left on a *Bergweg* path which climbs steeply through forest and finally emerges to a delightful open pasturage with the cascades of the Geltenschuss pouring down ahead. A cornflower-blue stream hurries through the meadows and a wooden bridge takes you over to the west side. This is a nature reserve (the alp of Feisseberg) and is rich in alpine flowers.

The path heads through this lovely pastureland aiming towards the waterfalls, then bears right to climb the south-west slopes in long switchbacks, crosses a stream and, climbing still, ducks behind a waterfall. Alpenroses clamber over the hillside and there are superb views to enjoy. The path veers to the right and wanders alongside the Geltenbach. The stream here has bored great holes and swirls in the limestone. Once more you cross the stream to the left-hand side and climb a little farther, now over a large grassy bluff speckled with flowers, and come to the hut with its glorious views. It certainly has a delectable setting.

To return to Lauenen by the same path will take two and a half hours. The way can be varied, though, by heading to the right at the southern end of the Lauenensee and taking a footpath and track back to the village. For an even better return, however, follow directions for Route 104 below. Added to the ascent route, this will give a very fine full day's circuit. As such it is certainly one of the classic walks in the Alps; but note that the grade is slightly higher than the approach route and there are some exposed sections to tackle.

Route 104:	Gelten Hut (2,008m) - Chüetungel (1,829m) - Lauenen (1,241m)

Grade:	3
Distance:	9 kilometres
Height loss:	767 metres
Time:	2¹/₂-3 hours

On the north-east side of the hut a steep grass-covered knoll has a narrow path snaking up to its crown. Clamber up this and follow the ridge heading north. The path is narrow in places but not difficult. There are grandstand views overlooking the Lauenental stretching ahead. Having gained the grassy ridge the path then crosses and descends its northern side, and traverses along the hillside to pass an isolated alp hut (Usseri Gelten). It now continues round the slopes of the Follhore where the trail descends steeply, once down a metal ladder, and comes to a neat scoop of pasture with the alp hamlet of Chüetungel (1,796m) nestling in it on the far side of a stream (about one hour from the hut).

At the stream there is a junction of paths and a signpost giving directions. Cross the stream by a footbridge and bear left on a narrow path. (**Note:** This follows the most potentially dangerous and exposed section of the circuit. Anyone nervous about taking it should follow the alternative signposted route down to Lauenen.) After wandering across rough pastures, the way then goes tightly against rocky crags with a steep and exposed drop to your left. For several minutes the exposure (and a very narrow section of trail) continues, but there are fixed cables in the worst places.

Eventually the path eases and goes through forest, then over pastures again, passing solitary alp huts and farms on a marked *Bergweg* path which eventually brings you down into the valley and onto a narrow road south of Lauenen. Wander along the road into the village.

Route 105:   Gelten Hut (2,008m) - Wildhorn Hut (2,301m)

Grade: 3
Distance: 7 kilometres
Height gain: 484 metres   Height loss: 191 metres
Time: 3¹/₂-4 hours

This hut to hut route gives a variety of scenery and could be very useful as part of a multi-day tour.

Take Route 104 as far as the alp hamlet of Chüetungel. Cross the stream at the junction of paths, go up to the cluster of buildings and follow the path that heads towards the obvious stony saddle above. The path is signposted to Tungelpass, Iffigenalp and the Wildhorn Hut. It is a well-used route and it eventually takes you up to a high bluff scantily covered with grass at 2,271 metres. Do not stray left to the Tungel Pass but go on, descending towards the east and the Iffigsee, but at a sign branch right on a narrow path that leads round a shoulder of the Niesenhorn and traverses steep grass slopes above the scree-cluttered hanging valley in which the Wildhorn Hut is found. Care should be taken on the final steep descent to the valley. The path brings you into the valley just below the hut.

The Wildhorn Hut can sleep one hundred in its dormitories. There is a guardian in residence in July and August when meals and drinks are available. The easiest way down from here is to follow the path down-valley to Iffigsee, and from there to Iffigenalp (one hour forty minutes) where you can take a bus to Lenk. (To complete the circuit, walk from Lenk to Lauenen via the Trüttlisberg Pass, described as Route 97.)

Route 106:   Lauenen (1,241m) - Krinnen Pass (1,659m) -
             Gsteig (1184m)

Grade: 1
Distance: 8 kilometres
Height gain: 418 metres   Height loss: 475 metres
Time: 2¹/₂-3 hours

The Krinnen (or Chrine) Pass is an easy wooded col at the southern end of the Höhi Wispile ridge, and it makes a convenient crossing to Gsteig, the most westerly of the villages in the Bernese Alps.

About 400 metres south of Lauenen, on the road to the Lauenensee, a signpost directs the start of the route to the pass. A somewhat meagre path drops on the right to cross a footbridge over a stream, and then wanders over meadows (boggy in places) rising past a farm or two and goes up to a broad spread of forest. Climbing through the forest the path is again very boggy here and there. At all junctions there are adequate markings to show the way to the pass and in a little under one and a half hours you come to a little gap in the wooded ridge. Ahead the massif of Les Diablerets is revealed.

On the western side you go down a meadow to a lone farm where the route divides. (See Route 106a for the alternative.) Bear left and soon come onto a farm road which you follow downhill. There are adequate short cuts on footpaths through woods and over more meadows. Just follow waymarks and arrows. It is an easy, pleasant descent and it takes not much more than an hour to reach Gsteig.

Route 106a: Krinnen Pass (1,659m) - Gsteig (1,184m)

Grade:	2
Distance:	5 kilometres
Height loss:	475 metres
Time:	1 hour 15 minutes

The right-hand path from the farm below the Krinnen Pass leads round among trees, rises at first, then comes to an open ridge. (By wandering uphill a few paces to the right there are expansive views north with the great slab of Gummfluh seen clearly to the north-west.)

Bear left and descend across a meadow, at the foot of which you come to a farm. Continue downhill half-left through the centre of a second meadow and steadily lose height among trees and more grass slopes, finally joining a narrow road. From here to Gsteig numerous short cuts, waymarked to excess so it is impossible to lose the way, lead to the village at the foot of the Col du Pillon.

Route 107:   Lauenen (1,241m) - Höhi Wispile - Gstaad (1,050m)

Grade: 2
Distance: 12 kilometres
Height gain: 666 metres   Height loss: 857 metres
Time: 4¹/₂-5 hours

An easy ridge-walk with long views north over a corrugated landscape, this makes a fine day out. There is the possibility of shortening it by descending from Stand by cableway, thus saving about one and a half hours of walking time if needed.

Take Route 106 as far as the Krinnen Pass and descend the meadow beyond as far as the farm. Now bear right, rising among trees, and when you emerge on an open ridge bear right once more to gain the crest of Höhi Wispile. Head to the left and take the path northwards. Follow this for about an hour to Stand (about two hours forty-five minutes from Lauenen) where you can take the cableway if required. The path continues to Obere Bodme, then to Under Bodme and the middle station of the cableway. A combination of service road, track and footpath leads all the way down to Gstaad. (Take Postbus from Gstaad back to Lauenen.)

Other Walks from Lauenen:
Numerous variations of walks, or combinations of routes, will extend the range of possibilities for a holiday based in Lauenen. The **WASSERNGRAT**, for example, is worth tackling from the **TRÜTTLISBERG PASS**, with a descent to **GSTAAD**; in fact a reversal of Route 100 already given. Also from the **TRÜTTLISBERG PASS** a route south to the **STUBLENI** and **TUNGEL PASS** would be worth considering for a long day, finishing with a descent through **CHÜETUNGEL** to **LAUENEN**.

On the other, western, side of the valley go up to the **KRINNEN PASS**, but instead of crossing over to Gsteig, bear left and follow the ridge to **HINDERI** or **WALLISER WISPILE** (superb views), then backtrack down the ridge a little to find an alternative path descending to the **LAUENENSEE**. Or continue from the alp down to **VORDERE WISPILE** and **BURG** for a novel approach to **GSTEIG** (see Route 108).

Gsteig

For advanced walkers with glacier experience (and equipment), there's a demanding route from the **GELTEN HUT** over the **COL DU BROCHET** (2,759m) just west of the Wildhorn, and down to **SION** in the Rhône Valley.

As for the ascent of peaks in the Wildhorn range, these lie outside the scope of this book. Walkers may be content simply to gaze on them from the flower-strewn footpaths.

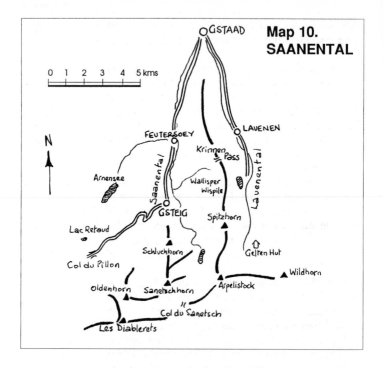

SAANENTAL

Position: Immediately to the west of the Lauenental, from
Col du Pillon to Gstaad.

Map: L.S. 5009 'Gstaad-Adelboden' 1:50,000

Bases: Gsteig (1,184m), Feutersoey (1,130m), Gstaad(1,050m)

Tourist Information:

Verkehrsbüro, 3785 Gsteig (Tel: 030 5 1231)

Verkehrsbüro, 3780 Gstaad (Tel: 030 4 1055)

The massif of Les Diablerets contains the most westerly summits of
the Bernese Alps, a great hulk of limestone with several peaks over

220

3,000 metres and with glaciers hanging on the north and east slopes where skiers gather even in summer, while elsewhere the landscape is abundantly green.

Les Diablerets is a watershed in several respects. Firstly, in the true sense, its streams flow south into the Rhône Valley, and also west by a devious route to join the Rhône farther down near the Lake of Geneva. But other streams drain from it too, to the east side of the Col du Pillon where they become the Saane and flow awkwardly through central Switzerland to join the Aare, which in turn feeds the Rhine. While the Rhône eventually spills into the Mediterranean, the Rhine empties into the North Sea.

Les Diablerets also marks the border, not only between the cantons of Bern and Vaud, but of Valais as well. And in addition it similarly signals the linguistic divide. East of the Col du Pillon, for example, all the Bernese Alps is German-speaking territory; to the west all villages and towns use French as their main language.

Below Les Diablerets the trim little village of Gsteig straddles the Col du Pillon road, and in the marshy meadows just outside it the Ruschbach and Saane streams converge. All is broad and gentle here; neatly shorn meadows sweep up to forest-clad hillsides. Set among the meadows are characteristic timber farmhouses, their roofs shallow-pitched, their eaves overhanging, their windows and balconies ablaze with petunias and geraniums. The valley flows gently northward with no great drop in altitude. Minor streams join the Saane from the eastern slopes, while two side valleys, the Tscharzistal and Meielstal, enter from the west. In the first of these there lies the attractive Arnensee, at the head of the second rises the majestic slab of the Gummfluh (2,458m). As you approach Gstaad some of the slopes have been laced with cableways, mainly for winter skiing, but also useful for summer walks.

If the lower hills are green and wooded, those at the head of the valley, forming a semi-circular basin, rise with a sense of drama. Oldenhorn and Sex Rouge, Mont Brun, the Schluchhorn and Mittaghorn come directly from Les Diablerets, while the conspicuous Spitzhorn sends its ridges south to the Schafhorn and Arpilhorn - the latter to act as the south-eastern bastion above the Col du Sanetsch, a traditional way from the Saanental to the Rhône Valley in Canton Valais.

Walking in and around the Saanental is as rich and varied as in most other areas visited within these pages. Some of the passes are surprisingly arduous to reach, their modest altitude distorting their true value. Certainly there are many surprises in store for those whose days have been largely spent in the heart of the Oberland and who suspect this western region of being rather tame by comparison. Those with an eye for the subtle shades and textures of the Alps, for the variations in form and substance, and for the soft brilliance of mountain light, will find many rewards here.

Valley Bases:

GSTAAD (1,050m) is dealt with fully under the previous section, the Lauenental, which should be consulted for details of facilities, accommodation etc.

FEUTERSOEY (1,130m) lies at the entrance to the Tscharzistal; a scattering of chalets and farms about six kilometres south of Gstaad. For accommodation and other general details this hamlet is linked with that of Gsteig, a further four kilometres up-valley. Between them they have only 900 inhabitants.

GSTEIG (1,184m) is also a tiny village, but somewhat more numerous in buildings than its neighbour to the north. The heart of the place is most photogenic, with the flower-bright Hotel Bären right on the road, the slender-spired church immediately behind it, and Mittaghorn, Schluchhorn and Les Diablerets seen as a backdrop. The Col du Pillon road begins its twisting ascent at this point, and a short distance up this road will be found the only campsite in the valley. Gsteig has limited shopping facilities, although as far as food for self-catering/backpacking is concerned, it is very good. Between them, Gsteig and Feutersoey have restaurants, PTT, a handful of shops and just three hotels with a total of sixty beds. But there are also 500 beds available for rent in holiday apartments and chalets. The valley is served by Postbus which travels between Gstaad and the village of Les Diablerets on the far side of the Col du Pillon.

Mountain Huts:

Below the north ridge of the Oldenhorn **CABANE DES DIABLERETS**

(2,486m) is accessible in about four hours from Gsteig (two and a half hours from Col du Pillon). It has spaces for one hundred and meals are available during the months of July and August when the guardian is in residence.

Route 108: Gsteig (1,184m) - Krinnen Pass (1,659m) - Hinderi Wispile (1,868m) - Gsteig

Grade:	2-3
Distance:	11 kilometres
Height gain/loss:	684 metres
Time:	4½ hours

This is a truly delightful walk, full of contrasts and with magnificent views. In places the path may be a little thin on the ground, in places the views shrouded by trees, but taken as a whole it makes a glorious day out. Choose a bright day of sunshine and wander slowly in order to absorb all the good things this corner of the Alps has on offer. There are no possibilities for refreshment along the way, so take a packed lunch and a drink and make a day of it.

The walk begins opposite Hotel Bären where a signpost gives directions to a number of destinations. Walk along a side street heading north-east; within a minute or two you will have passed several chalets and continue ahead through open meadows along the road still, but soon a sign directs you onto a footpath aiming straight ahead up a sloping meadow. Through meadow and forest for much of the way, the well-waymarked path leads up to the Krinnen Pass (using a narrow winding road in places). The pass is reached in a little over one and a half hours from Gsteig.

The Krinnen Pass has grass slopes on its western side, forest on the east. There are very fine views from here back towards Les Diablerets. Go through a fence and turn right to follow a narrow footpath among trees rising steadily along the ridge. Views are shielded for a while, but suddenly you come to a brief opening with a viewpoint overlooking the Lauenental to the left.

Continue up the ridge, finally leaving forest behind and crossing above meadows that are dense with alpine flowers early in the season. The path leads on and brings you directly to the alp hamlet of Hinderi Wispile with a magnificent panorama. There are two ways now to Gsteig; one continues up the ridge to Walliser Wispile, then cuts down to the alp of Vordere Wispile and rejoins our route. The other path (our route) swings off to the west.

Keeping to the left of a little pool pass a farm on your right and find the continuing path. It is likely to be confused by cattle tracks, but persist and you will find it. It skirts to the left of a deep limestone pit and occasional waymarks lead south-westwards sometimes through small boggy areas. Continue through a rather run-down alp (1,854m) and steadily descend beyond it across rough pasturelands, to come to a clear farm track that goes to Vordere Wispile (1,756m) - a busy alp whose buildings have a most unusual feature in that their roofs are of corrugated iron.

The track winds all the way down to Gsteig, and as you set off down it you will notice various alternative short cut footpaths to take. When you arrive at the alp of Burg, follow signs for Burgfälle and Gsteig. This path takes you down a tight wooded gorge with a series of waterfalls cascading into it. The trail itself is a delight, at times almost a catwalk of little bridges and balconies. Then through lovely woods and along a lane back to Gsteig.

Route 109:	Gsteig (1,184m) - Blattipass (1,900m) - Col du Pillon (1,546m)

Grade:	3		
Distance:	11 kilometres		
Height gain:	921 metres	Height loss:	559 metres
Time:	4 hours		

Blattipass is not marked on the 1:50,000 map. It's not a pass at all really, just one part of an easy green ridge separating the Tscharzistal from the main valley. But from it there is a surprisingly expansive view that includes many of the big Oberland summits stretching as far as the eye can see. The path to it is much steeper than appears at first glance. It leads through rampant vegetation with wild fruits in season tempting to all who struggle by. On the far side of the pass one looks down on the gleaming Arnensee, then the trail takes you round to a second pass, that of Voré (1,917m) with a grand prospect of Les Diablerets directly ahead. Lastly, there is an interesting descent to the Lac Retaud and through forest to Col du Pillon for the Postbus back to Gsteig. It's a grand walk, well worth tackling.

Leaving the centre of Gsteig wander along the road towards Feutersoey and Gstaad until just beyond Hotel Victoria where a signpost directs you left towards a farm. Behind it a footpath takes you up to a minor farm road where you turn right, and after one hundred metres cut off left over a meadow to rejoin the road once more. The road becomes a track and you follow it until a signpost by a barn points left to another path climbing steeply up a meadow bordered by trees. It's a demanding slope and it takes you through a jungle of wild raspberries, a grove of fir trees and up yet another meadow to the farm of Schöpfi (1,502m).

From the farm a vague grassy path climbs through steep pastures and eventually reaches a scattering of farms and barns at Vorder Walig (1,716m), reached after one and a half hours. The route continues uphill, and on gaining a shelf of hillside you join a track that contours comfortably round to the solitary alp of Topfelsberg (1,814m). The track leads south and becomes a narrow path and you then climb in long twistings to gain the panoramic Blattipass, about two to two and a half hours from Gsteig.

Descend leftwards on the western side of the ridge, passing Ober Stuedeli and continuing to the farm of Seeberg (1,712m) overlooking Arnensee. There is a junction of paths here. The way now climbs among alpenroses, juniper and bilberries in the direction of Col du Pillon. At the head of the slope go through a grass-carpeted col and enter a shallow basin of pasture. Pass a tarn on your right and gain the col of Voré marked by a dry stone wall on the very borders of Bern and Vaud. This is reached in three and a half hours. (Signpost)

Take the path on the south side descending steeply at first and veering right to reach a farm track where you head to the right. Very soon you come to the lovely Lac Retaud (refreshments). The track brings you to a road where you bear left and soon break away from this on a footpath that descends through forest and brings you to Col du Pillon (*refreshments*) with its large car park and cableway to Les Diablerets. From here you can catch a Postbus down to Gsteig.

Route 110: Gsteig (1,184m) - Blattipass (1,900m) - Arnensee (1,542m) - Feutersoey (1,130m)

Grade:	3		
Distance:	13 kilometres		
Height gain:	716 metres	Height loss:	770 metres
Time:	4½ hours		

This walk consists of two very distinct sections. The first entails a long and strenuous climb to the Blattipass, while the second is virtually all downhill, over shrub-bright hillsides, past several alp farms and alongside a lake. From the lake down to Feutersoey you will no doubt share the Tscharzistal with plenty of other walkers, while the uphill stretch will be much more quiet.

Follow route descriptions as far as the farm of Seeberg as for Route 109 above. This is reached after almost three hours from Gsteig. At the junction of paths take the trail leading down to the southern end of the Arnensee and walk along its left-hand (western) shore. There is a dam at the northern end and a road that leads from it down to Feutersoey. Either follow the road, or cross to the east side and take a footpath which makes a rising traverse of the hillside to Hinter Walig (1,723m) and on to Feutersoey. A third option is to continue through the valley as far as Linders Vorschess (1,392m), half an hour from the lake, and there branch away half-right on a direct footpath to Feutersoey.

Route 111: Col du Pillon (1,546m) - Lac Retaud (1,685m) - Col du Pillon

Grade:	1-2
Distance:	4 kilometres
Height gain/loss:	139 metres
Time:	1 hour

Lac Retaud and Les Diablerets Massif

A fine, short and easy walk, ideal if you've only half a day left before heading for home and wish to make the most of it. Lac Retaud is an idyllic little tarn set in a terrace of hillside with views across to Les Diablerets. It's accessible to motorists, but it's better by far to walk there. This route is a circular one, beginning and ending at the car park on the col.

Immediately behind the cable car station for Les Diablerets a track leads into woods. Walk along this and leave it at a *Wanderweg* footpath sign. A path now climbs steeply among trees and over rough pastures, then brings you onto a road by the Lac Retaud restaurant *(refreshments)*. Bear right and over a short rise you will come to the tarn (twenty-five minutes from the col). There are fine views from the northern shore looking across the water to Les Diablerets.

Turn right and follow a broad farm track heading along the hillside terrace and passing farm buildings. After one hundred metres you come to a solitary building where a path forks left to Voré, Arnensee and Feutersoey. Ignore this and continue along the track. It soon swings right and leads to an isolated farm. Pass to the right of the building and follow the right-hand fence, and you will come to a continuing path sloping down towards trees. The path takes you through forest (boggy in places), crosses two or three streams and eventually rejoins the original upward path. Bear left and a few minutes later you arrive at Col du Pillon.

Route 112:   Col du Pillon (1,546m) - Voré (1,919m) - Seeberg (1,712m) - Feutersoey (1,130m)

Grade:	2-3
Distance:	14 kilometres
Height gain:	373 metres **Height loss:** 789 metres
Time:	4 hours

This is one of the finest walks in the region, covering much lovely green countryside, visiting Lac Retaud and looking down on the larger Arnensee.

Follow Route 111 to the path junction beyond Lac Retaud. Leave the farm track here and branch away on the footpath slanting up the hillside. It makes steady height and reaches the dry stone wall marking the cantonal boundary at the pass of Voré (one hour from Col du Pillon). Cross over and descend the clear path to the right of a tarn seen in the level pastures below. Crossing the pastures go through a minor col and descend slopes carpeted with alpenrose, juniper, larch and rowan, with views ahead to the Arnensee. The path leads to the farm buildings of Seeberg and a junction of trails. Bear right on the path which leads to the Blattipass, but only take this as far as the alp of Ober Stuedeli. Instead of climbing to the pass continue round the hillside, in and out of trees, to Hinter Walig and Scheeweid (1,720m). From here the path begins its descent to Feutersoey.

Other Walks from the Saanental:

One of the longest routes attempted from Gsteig is the classic crossing of the **COL DU SANETSCH** (2,251m) to **SION** in the Rhône Valley. This nine and a half-hour walk follows a mule path nearly all the way. There's a hotel near the col at Tsanfleuron (four and a half hours) and a Postbus can actually be caught down to Sion from the lake before the col.

By direct contrast is the gentle valley walk from **GSTEIG** to **GSTAAD,** or up-valley to **REUSCH.** While in Reusch one could make the climb south into the corrie below the Oldenhorn and go up to **OLDENEGG** and the **GEMSKOPF** (2,525m) in about four hours from Reusch.

A walk over **COL DU PILLON** to the village of **LES DIABLERETS** can be achieved in three and a half hours from Gsteig, on pasture or woodland path nearly all the way. Or try a much more demanding walk (part of the Alpine Pass Route) from Gsteig to **COL DES MOSSES** in Canton Vaud for eight and a half hours of pleasure.

The tourist information office in Gsteig publishes a leaflet (in German) offering many more outline ideas of varying lengths.

MULTI-DAY TOURS

By far the majority of routes contained in this guide will be used as day walks beginning and ending at a recommended valley base. But it will be evident that numerous possibilities exist for linking given routes into multi-day journeys, circuits of mountain massifs, and the traverse of individual valleys or a number of valleys by the crossing of accessible passes. There are experienced and energetic mountain trekkers for whom this type of travel is the very essence of alpine wandering, the most rewarding of all: working through a challenging landscape day after day, either backpacking or travelling light, staying in mountain huts or cheap inns and *matratzenlagers* overnight. Such travel demands a high degree of fitness, an understanding of mountain terrain, a sure knowledge of map and compass work, and a certain amount of luck with regard to the weather - as a prolonged spell of storm can result in several days of frustration if marooned in an isolated hut or small tent.

For this class of wanderer the following suggested tours are recommended.

Route 113:	Oberland Passes

Maps:	L.S. 5004 'Berner Oberland' and 5009 'Gstaad-Adelboden' 1:50,000
Length:	7-8 days
Start:	Meiringen (Haslital)
Finish:	Gsteig (Saanental)

This superb trek forms the central (and in some ways, the most spectacular) part of the classic Alpine Pass Route (Sargans to Montreux). Every day there are high passes to cross, the highest being Hohtürli (2,778m) above Kandersteg. Every day there are magnificent mountain views, glaciers to pass beside, huge walls of rock, soft and gentle alpine meadows. It links most of the major resorts of the

Bernese Alps and looks on all the main peaks for which the area is justly famed. In short, it is one of the finest long walks it is possible to make in the Alps. The route is outlined as follows:

1: Meiringen-Grosse Scheidegg-Grindelwald (Route 10)
2: Grindelwald-Kleine Scheidegg-Wengen-Lauterbrunnen (Routes 29, and 37 in reverse)
3: Lauterbrunnen-Sefinenfurke-Griesalp (Routes 33, 34, 52)
4: Griesalp-Hohtürli-Kandersteg (Route 64)
5: Kandersteg-Bunderchrinde-Adelboden (Route 79)
6: Adelboden-Hahnenmoos-Lenk (Route 85)
7: Lenk-Trüttlisberg Pass-Lauenen-Krinnen Pass-Gsteig (Routes 97, 106)

For a full description of the complete Alpine Pass Route from Sargans to Montreux (325 kilometres, sixteen passes and a total of 18,000 metres of height gain) see the guidebook, *Alpine Pass Route* (Cicerone Press 1990).

Route 114: Grindelwald Circuit

Map:	**L.S. 5004 'Berner Oberland' 1:50,000**
Length:	**5 days**
Start:	**Schynige Platte (Wilderswil)**
Finish:	**Wilderswil**

A week's walking holiday could happily be spent in the Grindelwald/ Lauterbrunnen area tackling this route. It has so much to commend it; not least, some of the most spectacular views in all the Alps. It begins by taking the funicular to Schynige Platte (an alternative would be to walk from Wilderswil - about four and a half hours) and wandering the classic route to Grindelwald where the first night is spent. Then over Kleine Scheidegg to the Lauterbrunnental; walk via Stechelberg to Mürren; from there to Isenfluh and over the mountains to Saxeten before descending at last to Wilderswil.

1: Wilderswil/Schynige Platte-Grindelwald (Route 11)
2: Grindelwald-Kleine Scheidegg-Wengen-Lauterbrunnen (Routes 29, and 37 in reverse)

3: Lauterbrunnen-Stechelberg-Gimmelwald-Mürren
(Routes 36, and 47 in reverse)
4: Mürren-Grütschalp-Isenfluh (Routes 34 and 32 in reverse)
5: Isenfluh-Ballehochst-Saxeten-Wilderswil (Routes 31, and
12 in reverse)

Route 115:   Tour Wildstrubel

Maps: L.S. 5009 'Gstaad-Adelboden'
Length: 6-7 days
Start/Finish: Kandersteg

Tour Wildstrubel is being promoted as a week-long circuit of the
Wildstrubel massif by the tourist information offices of the various
villages the walk passes through, and a leaflet has been produced
giving brief outline details. As part of the promotion for the tour, a
certificate (a souvenir diploma) is awarded to those who complete it.
The leaflet needs to be stamped by either the local tourist office or
hotel on a minimium of five different stages to be eligible. (Enquire
in Kandersteg, Adelboden or Lenk for details and leaflet.)

But whether such certificates are aimed for or not, the tour in itself
makes a very fine week's walking. There are some high passes to
cross, and several of the stages are rather long. A *variante* is also
suggested whilst in the Kandersteg/Leukerbad region.
1: Kandersteg-Bunderchrinde-Adelboden (Route 79)
2: Adelboden-Hahnenmoos-Lenk (Route 85)
3: Lenk-Rawilpass-Anzere (not described)
4: Anzere-Tseuzier-Crans.Montana (not described)
5: Crans.Montana-Varneralp-Leukerbad (not described)
6: Leukerbad-Gemmipass-Kandersteg (Route 74 in reverse)
Variante 7:
Leukerbad-Restipass-Kummenalp (not described)
Variante 8:
Kummenalp-Lötschenpass-Kandersteg (72 in reverse)

APPENDIX A
Useful Addresses

1: Tourist Information Offices - other than those mentioned elsewhere with regard to specific bases.

Swiss National Tourist Office
Swiss Centre
New Coventry Street
London W1V 8EE

250 Stockton Street
San Francisco
CA 94108

104 South Michigan Avenue
Chicago
Il 60603

Commerce Court
Toronto
Ontario
M5L 1E8

608 Fifth Avenue
New York
NY 10020

Bernese Oberland Tourist Office
Jungfraustrasse 38
3800 Interlaken
Switzerland

2: Useful Addresses in Switzerland:

Schweizer Hotelier-Verein
 (Swiss Hotel Assoc.)
Monbijoustrasse 130
CH 3001 Bern

Schweizer Alpenclub
 (Swiss Alpine Club)
Helvetiaplatz 4
CH 3005 Bern

Schweizerischer Camping und
Caravanning-Verband
(Swiss Camping & Caravanning Assoc.)
Habsburgerstrasse 35
CH 6004 Lucerne

Verband Schweizer Campings
(Swiss Camping Assoc.)
Im Sydefädeli 40
CH 8037 Zurich

Schweizerischer Bund für Jugendherbergen *(Swiss Youth Hostels Assoc.)*
Postfach 3229
CH 3001 Bern 22

3: Map Suppliers:

Robertson McCarta Ltd
122 Kings Cross Road
London WC1X 9DX

The Map Shop
15 High Street
Upton-upon-Severn
Worcs WR8 0HJ

Edward Stanford Ltd
12-14 Long Acre
London WC2

Rand McNally Map Store
10 East 53rd Street
New York NY

APPENDIX B
Glossary

The following glossary lists a few words likely to be found on maps, in village streets or in foreign language tourist information leaflets. It is no substitute for a pocket dictionary, of course, but hopefully will be of some use.

German	English	German	English
Abhang	slope	Gasthaus or	
Alp	alp or high pasture	gasthof	inn or guest house
Alpenblume	alpine flower	Gaststube	common room
Alpenverein	alpine club	Gefärhlich	dangerous
Alphütte	mountain hut	Gemse	chamois
Auskunft	information	Geröllhalde	scree
Aussichtspunkt	viewpoint	Gipfel	summit, peak
		Gletscher	glacier
Bach	stream	Gletscherspalte	crevasse
Bäckerei	bakery	Gondelbahn	gondola lift
Bahnhof	railway station	Grat	ridge
Berg	mountain	Grüetzi	greetings
Bergführer	mountain guide		
Berggasthaus	mountain inn	Haltestelle	bus stop
Bergpass	pass	Heilbad	spa, hot springs
Bergschrund	crevasse between	Hirsch	red deer
	glacier & rock wall	Hoch	high
Bergsteiger	mountaineer	Höhe	height
Bergwanderer	mountain walker	Höhenweg	high route
Bergweg	mountain path	Horn	horn, peak
Blatt	map sheet	Hügel	hill
Brücke	bridge	Hütte	mountain hut
Dorf	village	Jugendherberge	youth hostel
Drahtseilbahn	cable-car		
		Kamm	crest or ridge
Ebene	plain	Kapelle	chapel
		Karte	map
Feldweg	meadowland path	Kirche	church
Fels	rock wall or slope	Klamm	gorge
Ferienwohnung	holiday apartment	Klumme	combe or small
Fussweg	footpath		valley
Garni	hotel with meals	Landschaft	landscape
	optional	Lawine	avalanche

German	English	German	English
Lebensmittel	grocery	Tal	valley
Leicht	easy	Tobel	wooded ravine
Links	left	Touristenlager	dormitory, tourist accommodation
Matratzenlager	dormitory		
Moräne	moraine	Über	via or over
Murmeltier	marmot	Unfall	accident
		Unterkunft	accommodation
Nebel	fog, low cloud, mist		
Nord	north	Verkehrsbüro/	
		Verkehrsverein	tourist office
Ober	upper		
Ost	east	Wald	forest
		Wanderweg	footpath
Pass	pass	Wasser	water
Pension	simple hotel	Weide	pasture
Pfad	path	West	west
Pickel	ice axe	Wildbach	torrent
Quelle	spring	Zeltplatz	campsite
		Zimmer	bedroom
Rechts	right	- frei	vacancies
Reh	roe deer		
Rucksack	rucksack		
Sattel	saddle, pass		
Schlafraum	bedroom		
Schloss	castle		
Schlucht	gorge		
Schnee	snow		
See	lake, tarn		
Seeli	small tarn		
Seil	rope		
Seilbahn	cable-car		
Sesselbahn	chair-lift		
Stausee	reservoir		
Steigeisen	crampons		
Steinmann	cairn		
Steinschlag	falling rock		
Stunde(n)	hour(s)		
Sud	south		

BIBLIOGRAPHY

1: General Tourist Guides:

There are many general touring guides to Switzerland on the market. The following will be found most useful:

Blue Guide to Switzerland by Ian Robertson (A&C Black, London. W.W.Norton, New York. Published in 1987 - 4th edition).

Off The Beaten Track - Switzerland (Moorland Publishing Co, Ashbourne. Published 1989)

2: Mountains and Mountaineering:

Countless volumes devoted to the Alps pack the bookshelves. Those containing references of particular interest to visitors to the Bernese Alps are listed below. The list is of necessity only a small selection, but there should be plenty of reading contained within it to provide a good background introduction and to whet the appetite for a forthcoming visit.

Wanderings Among the High Alps by Alfred Wills (Blackwell, London. Latest edition published 1939) - Wills' ascent of the Wetterhorn signalled the start of the Golden Age of Mountaineering.

The Playground of Europe by Leslie Stephen (Blackwell, London. Latest edition published 1936) - *Playground* ranks as one of the finest of all mountaineering books. Leslie Stephen was an eminent Victorian pioneer, some of whose adventures are recorded in this book. He made a number of first ascents in the Bernese Alps.

On High Hills by Geoffrey Winthrop Young (Methuen, London. Latest edition published 1947) - This book includes ascents in the Bernese Alps prior to 1914.

The White Spider by Heinrich Harrer (Granada, London. Latest edition published 1983) - Harrer was part of the rope that made the first ascent of the Eiger's North Face in 1938. This book is the history of attempts on the face up to and including that first ascent.

The Eiger by Dougal Haston (Cassell, London, 1974.) - Haston took part in the epic first direct ascent of the North Face in winter. This book records the history of 'modern' routes on the face.

The Mountains of Switzerland by Herbert Maeder (George Allen & Unwin, London, 1968) - Large format book with splendid illustrations, mostly in black and white.

3: Walking:

The Alps by R.L.G.Irving (Batsford, London, 1939) - Not strictly a 'walking' book, but it contains much of interest that will help fire enthusiasm for an active holiday in the Alps. As with several others in this list, *The Alps* has long been out of print, but should be available on order from public libraries.

Rambles in the Alps by Hugh Merrick (Country Life, London, 1951) - A large-format book which devotes considerable space to eulogising the Bernese Oberland as a walking area.

Backpacking in the Alps and Pyrenees by Showell Styles (Gollancz, London, 1976) - Contains an account of a backpacking journey across part of the Bernese Alps by some of the routes described in this guidebook.

Alpine Pass Route by Kev Reynolds (Cicerone Press, Milnthorpe, 1990) - A guidebook to this classic long-distance route which traverses the Bernese Alps on its journey from Sargans to Montreux.

Classic Walks in the Alps by Kev Reynolds (Oxford Illustrated Press, 1991) - Large format 'glossy' book which contains a number of routes in the Bernese Alps.

4: Climbing:

Bernese Alps East and *Bernese Alps Central* by R.G.Collomb (Alpine Club, London, 1979) both available from the Alpine Club, or from West Col Productions, Goring, Reading, Berks RG8 9AA, England.

5: Mountain Flowers:

The Alpine Flowers of Britain and Europe by Christopher Grey-Wilson and Marjorie Blamey (Collins, London, 1979) - A very useful pocket identification handbook.

Mountain Flowers by Anthony Huxley (Blandford Press, London, 1967) - Another fine book to help identify species found in the areas covered by the present book. Illustrations are by Daphne Barry and Mary Grierson.

Mountain Flower Holidays in Europe by Lionel Bacon (Alpine Garden Society, Woking, 1979) - This book tells you what to find and where. Although there are some good illustrations, it is best used in conjunction with one of the above-mentioned identification guides. Includes a section on the Bernese Alps.

ROUTE INDEX

Printed by Carnmor Print & Design, London Road, Preston. U.K.

THE BERNESE ALPS

KILOMETRES

0   5   10   15

N

THUN

THUNER-SEE

SPIEZ

NIEDER-SIMMENTAL

SIMME

DIEMTIGTAL

FRUTIGEN

KIENTAL

GRIESA

ZWEISIMMEN

OBER

ENGSTLIGENTAL

KANDER

SAANEN

GSTAAD

MATTEN

SIMMENTAL

ABELBODEN

KANDERSTEG

EGGESCHW

LENK

SAANE

REGENBOLDHORN

GASTERNTAL

FEUTERSOEY

LAUENEN

IFFIGENALP

WILDSTRUBEL

GSTEIG

LEUKERBAD

LES DIABLERETS

NILDHORN

LEUK

SIERRE

R

THE VAL

SION